GENERALIZATION
in the WRITING
of HISTORY

The Committee on Historical Analysis

WILLIAM O. AYDELOTTE
  State University of Iowa

THOMAS C. COCHRAN
  University of Pennsylvania

MERLE CURTI
  University of Wisconsin

ROY F. NICHOLS
  University of Pennsylvania

DAVID M. POTTER
  Stanford University

LOUIS GOTTSCHALK, *Chairman*
  University of Chicago

GENERALIZATION
in the WRITING
of HISTORY

A REPORT OF THE COMMITTEE ON HISTORICAL ANALYSIS
OF THE SOCIAL SCIENCE RESEARCH COUNCIL

Edited by LOUIS GOTTSCHALK

 THE UNIVERSITY OF CHICAGO PRESS
CHICAGO & LONDON

The University of Chicago Press, Chicago & London
The University of Toronto Press, Toronto 5, Canada

© *1963 by The University of Chicago. All rights reserved Published 1963. Second Impression 1964. Composed and printed by* THE UNIVERSITY OF CHICAGO PRESS, *Chicago, Illinois, U.S.A.*

Foreword

Historians (especially if the designation *historian* is broadened to include scholars in any field that uses the historical approach) commonly are said to fall into two groups. One may be called "descriptive historians"; they attempt to give an account of the event or situation under consideration in its own unique setting. The other may be called "theoretical historians"; they try to find in their subject matter a basis for comparison, classification, interpretation, or generalization. Every historian is likely to be in both groups at the same or different times even though he may emphasize his adherence to one rather than the other. In this report the Committee on Historical Analysis of the Social Science Research Council is concerned primarily with the theoretical historians.

Some misunderstanding may be avoided at the outset if a distinction is made between *history as the past of mankind* (called in the SSRC Bulletin 54 *history-as-actuality*) and *history as the study of the past of mankind* (called in that Bulletin *written or spoken history*).[1] In this report the Committee is concerned with history-as-actuality only insofar as the effort to recapture it is the objective of written or spoken history. We are concerned rather with history as a branch of learning, as a discipline. In that sense history displays some of the characteristics of science, some of art, and some of philosophy. Its character as science is based upon the fact that the immediate materials of the historian's study comprise extant objects that are capable of scrutiny, categorization, and generalization. These are the vestiges of the past (including literary texts and verbal testimony) which can be examined, authenticated, and classified by systematic methods.

Scrupulous weighing of extant evidence, however, is only a limited part of the historian's work, for his ultimate purpose is not alone the dispassionate study of historical vestiges but also a reconstruction of

[1] *Theory and Practice in Historical Study: A Report of the Committee on Historiography* (Social Science Research Council Bulletin 54 [New York, 1946]), p. 133. The problem of generalization and understanding in history is briefly discussed by Sidney Hook, *ibid.*, pp. 127–30. See also *The Social Sciences in Historical Study: A Report of the Committee on Historiography* (Social Science Research Council Bulletin 64 [New York, 1954]), esp. chap. 4, "Problems of Historical Analysis," pp. 86–105.

v

Foreword

mankind's past, of past beings and doings, of the course of human events. Perhaps the larger part of his subject matter for such a reconstruction can be studied only indirectly—that is, only through implications and inferences in the traces that a vanished past has left behind. A patent gap thus separates history-as-actuality from knowable history, and that gap can be filled only by an imaginative process, the reconstruction of events as they must have been or, at least, probably were from the inadequate clues still available in their vestiges. This is a creative (or better, re-creative or interpretative) act, and hence akin to art.

The historian ought not to be wholly artistic, of course, for then the boundary between history-as-knowledge and pure fiction would grow obscure or disappear entirely. Yet without some kind of imagination the opposite boundary, the one between history-as-interpretation-of-the-past and the mere compilation of verifiable historical data in a chronological order tends to disappear. The crucial question for the theoretical historian is: What kind of imagination is valid? The answer in part is obvious: The validation of any interpretation that the theoretical historian may advance requires that his imaginative filling-in of the gaps in his data at least conform to all the known facts so that if it does not present definitive truth it should at any rate constitute the least inconvenient form of tentative error. That means that it must be subject to certain general standards and tests—of human behavior, of logical antecedents and consequences, of statistical or mass trends. Here it becomes in large part dependent upon the findings of other disciplines. Hence the theoretical historian needs to have some knowledge of psychology, esthetics, ethics, social statistics, or other disciplines that deal with the interrelations of human beings with social events and natural forces. That is, he needs to have some conscious, if only *ad hoc*, philosophy or theory of purposes, causes, and ends.

The Committee on Historical Analysis never assumed that this problem was of equal interest to all historians or was of interest to historians alone; and that the theoretical historian's problem was not unique was made fully explicit by the Committee's philosopher-consultant, Hans Meyerhoff, professor of philosophy at the University of California at Los Angeles.[2] Nevertheless, the Committee chose de-

---

[2] Letter to the Committee, July 26, 1961: "There are some members of my profession who hold that there are *no* characteristically or specifically historical generalizations. According to this view, all generalizations employed by the historian are derived (or borrowed) from other, non-historical sources. In which case

Foreword

liberately not to engage in a formal philosophical consideration of the wider problem (for which perhaps it was dubiously equipped) but rather to direct its attention to the more concrete (or historical, if you will) subsidiary question of what the historian in fact has done when he has been concerned, knowingly or unknowingly, with data that are not particular, unique, or segregate. In fact, beyond the implication that a generalization is "a proposition asserting something to be true either of all members of a certain class or of an indefinite part of that class" (*American College Dictionary*) and therefore deals with data that are not particular, unique, or segregate, the Committee preferred, at least at the outset, not to define the word. Hence, stricter definition became one of the tasks of those whom the Committee selected to write the articles that make up this report. As will be seen, while they all discuss some kind or kinds of generalization, they do not all discuss the same kinds.

The history of the Committee has a distinct relevance to its problem. It was appointed in June, 1956, as an outcome of a preliminary meeting to which had been invited several scholars who had expressed some desire for a follow-up to the SSRC Bulletins 54 and 64. At that preliminary meeting the consensus seemed to be that since Bulletin 54 had, among other things, warned against the gratuitous assumptions and purposes that frequently underlie historical interpretations and since Bulletin 64 had emphasized the potential aids to historical accuracy in the interrelations of history and the social sciences, a new bulletin was needed that should address itself primarily to the question

---

there is, strictly speaking, no unique problem in history: the problem of 'generalizations in history' would coincide with the problem of 'generalizations in general'— or, at least, generalizations in other human and social disciplines. . . .

"Generalizations in any discipline raise the problem of explanation; for we appeal to generalizations 'proper' (i.e., hypotheses or general laws) as the grounds for explaining the phenomena we are studying. Thus, in the philosophical literature of our time the subject of generalizations in history is usually (and widely) discussed under the heading of 'historical explanation.' More specifically, the question is: How does a historian explain? Merely by telling a story . . . or by using 'pseudo-concepts' [e.g., periodization or the reificaton of abstract terms] . . . or by employing 'general laws' as we find them in other scientific disciplines . . . or by a combination of these methods? Explanation, needless to add, refers to causal conditions; i.e., the general law is believed to be a causal law. Hence the subsidiary problem of 'historical causation.' Generalization, explanation, and causation form a syndrome from a logical point of view."

In the same letter Meyerhoff indicated also that "descriptive (as distinguished from explanatory) concepts are characteristic of many scientific disciplines."

Foreword

whether the historian is at all competent from his own data and by his own methods to derive concepts that are neither so limited in scope as to be trivial nor so comprehensive as to be meaningless.

In the first two years of its existence the Committee went through three successive phases. At first, anxious to avoid any imputation that it was trying to oblige historians to become social scientists, it adopted the policy of merely keeping informed about and encouraging the efforts of other historians to examine the problem of generalization in history. During this phase the Committee was in minor part responsible for promoting a summer (1957) conference at Stanford University on generalizations regarding the history of large-scale communities and another at Rutgers University on generalizations regarding the history of American political behavior. Individual members of the Committee gave a helping hand to both these conferences as well as to a third at the 1957 convention of the American Historical Association on the causes of the American Civil War. It soon became clear that if this procedure were to have any results at all for the Committee's purpose, they would probably be in the form of a set of essays, but most likely a disjointed set, refighting the Civil War, the various presidential elections, the great revolutions, and similar debatable subjects. They would perhaps astutely indicate the use and abuse of generalizations in past debates about discrete historical episodes but might not lead to a general analysis of the process itself of historical generalization.

The Committee then decided that perhaps it ought to select for its own consideration a single historical development, with a view to examining the concepts, generalizations, and comparative propositions that had come out of the study of that development. It agreed upon the concept of national character as a good subject for such an examination. Moreover, for a time it contemplated asking interested specialists in the other social sciences to meet with it in order to widen and deepen the critique of the historians' generalizations about national character. Further reflection, however, brought apprehension that such a procedure might lead to a set of debates on national character or a set of essays by non-historians criticizing the historians' concept of national character, all of which might have intrinsic merit but might not deal directly and explicitly with the question whether the historian could make substantive generalizations that were more than truisms.

The Committee, therefore, embarked upon a third phase, which proved to be the definitive one. It selected mature historians who had worked intensively on some important aspects of history and who in the course of their study must have become familiar with the literature of their fields, and it asked them to write essays which, after sampling the concepts and generalizations in that literature, would undertake to indicate which in their judgment were wholly valid, partly valid, partly invalid, or wholly invalid, and in each case why. In this way the Committee hoped to get a set of essays dealing with the problem of generalization by the historian in several different contexts and from several varying points of view. From those essays as a point of departure it might then be in position to consult others about the problem as well as to discuss it among themselves. If nothing more, such a set of essays might at least present the variety of views among working historians on the use of generalization in historiography.

The articles that form this volume are the outcome of the Committee's canvass. As originally submitted, they became the focus of consideration in conferences of their authors with the Committee. In several instances a selected critic was asked to submit a supplementary article. Almost every article was modified to meet the criticisms brought forth by this process.

The circular letter of invitation to the prospective authors (dated on or about January 31, 1958) enclosed a tentative listing of some relevant topics which the Committee suggested for their consideration, leaving each author entirely free, however, to follow his own judgment. The suggested topics included "levels of generalization" (e.g., explicit or implicit), "kinds of generalization" (e.g., classification, interpretation, or universal law), "sources of generalization" (e.g., intuition, the sources, personal experience), and "subjects of generalization" (e.g., personality, communities, periods, change).

As was expected, the invited authors showed full awareness of the baffling nature of generalization in historiography; they did not always agree even upon how the word *generalization* is to be defined. Each, however, more or less explicitly subscribed to a set of obvious hypotheses implied in the headings of the tentative outline: (1) that historians use generalizations, however defined, with different levels of conscious intention to do so; (2) that historical generalizations range in kind from implicit comparisons or contrasts through studied classification or reasoned interpretations to universal laws; (3) that historians derive these generalizations by various means, only one of which consists of express conclusions from a systematic analysis of the sources they have studied; (4) that they generalize about a large number of subjects

Foreword

ranging from individual personality traits to complex changes in social aggregates; and (5) that though their generalizations are subject to question and criticism, the criticism need not always or necessarily be unfavorable. On these relatively simple matters the authors were more or less in accord; more complex issues raised some discrepancies, as we shall see.

The first papers came from Professors Robert R. Palmer (Princeton), Arthur F. Wright (then of Stanford, now of Yale), and Walter P. Metzger (Columbia). Palmer described his own experience with the problems of generalization in his study of the revolutionary movements at the close of the eighteenth century. Wright dealt tentatively with the complications that both Chinese and Western historians have to cope with in the generalizations already available about China's lengthy history. Metzger set for himself the problem whether a concept like *national character* has a verifiable validity. Further correspondence of the Committee with Palmer led to replies setting forth a more general statement of his view on historical generalizations, which is here appended to his article. Wright's paper was submitted to Professor Derk Bodde (Pennsylvania) for a critique, which in somewhat revised form here follows the reworked version of Wright's paper—reworked, it should be remarked, by the author's original design as much as or more than because of the comments upon it. Metzger's paper as here published is a considerably shorter version than the one originally submitted to the Committee. Professor Thomas C. Cochran (Pennsylvania), as a member of the Committee, undertook to expand upon Metzger's discussion of *social role* as a concept useful to historians, and his article follows immediately after Metzger's.

None of these papers examined generalizations concerned with the early history of Western culture. Hence, the Committee invited Professor Chester G. Starr (Illinois) to write an essay in his field—which he did, drawing his examples chiefly from studies of ancient Greek civilization. The Committee then asked Dr. M. I. Finley (Cambridge), with Starr's paper in mind, to give his views on the subject. Since the articles on particular fields of history are here arranged in a roughly chronological order, those of Starr and Finley are the first presented below.

Conferences and correspondence with the authors of all these papers had meanwhile encouraged several members of the Committee to ponder, more systematically than they otherwise might have done, the

Foreword

problem of generalization along less specialized lines. As a consequence, several of them prepared articles that, while naturally drawing upon their respective fields of specialization for illustration, were intended to delineate their view of the more general problem. Among these articles are those by the chairman on categories of historical generalizations; by Dean Roy F. Nichols (Pennsylvania) on the genealogy of historical generalizations as a criterion of their validity; by William O. Aydelotte (Iowa) on some questions of definition, inference, and theory involved in the problem of historical generalization; and by David M. Potter (Stanford) on some perplexities that the teaching of historical method frequently leaves unanswered or in need of further consideration. Each of these articles, too, underwent the close scrutiny of the Committee, and they now in revised form comprise Part II of the present report.[3] The last essay (also several times revised) is an attempt by the chairman to summarize and dovetail the component parts of the symposium. Part III is a bibliography by Mr. Martin Klein (Chicago) of recent works relevant to the problems of interpretation and generalization in history.[4]

Whatever the shortcomings of this report—and the Committee is perhaps more aware of them than any of its critics can be—it constitutes an exploratory work, useful perhaps for the very fact that seldom if ever have so many practicing historians pooled their talents and experience to air their views on the use of concepts and generalizations by historians. If it does no more than to prompt historians to be more conscious of the problem and its pitfalls, perhaps it will have justified itself. If it induces some of them to try their hands at modest and tentative generalizations, the members of the Committee at least, despite the inevitable risks, will have few regrets.[5]

[3] For several suggestions regarding the organization of this report, including a suggestion to divide it into two parts, giving the first to the essays concerned with the problem of generalization in particular fields or on comparable developments of history and the second to those concerned with the more general problem, the editor is indebted to Professor Meyerhoff.

[4] This bibliography is a rearrangement and supplementation of a tentative one submitted for the Committee's early consideration by Professor David S. Nivison (Stanford), whom the pressure of other work did not permit to draw up the final version. The Committee wishes to acknowledge its indebtedness to Professor Nivison.

[5] For the sake of clarity a word becomes necessary at the outset about a complication resulting from an unclear concept—what Wright calls (see below, p. 62 and n. 3) "that strange tripartite division of time." At times, words like *ancient*, *antiquity*, *classical*, *medieval*, and *modern* will be spelled below as indicated (i.e., with lower-case letters) and at other times with capital letters. The editor con-

Foreword

I am indebted to the Center for the Advanced Study of the Behavioral Sciences and to the Social Science Research Committee of the University of Chicago for their share in providing the free time and financial assistance required for my part in the preparation of this report. Pendleton Herring (SSRC) and C. Vann Woodward (Yale) participated in meetings of the Committee; Rowland L. Mitchell, Jr., served as SSRC staff representative on the Committee, 1960–62. Gail E. Kendrick was chiefly responsible for preparing the Index.

LOUIS GOTTSCHALK

sidered the distinction desirable for two reasons. The first was to avoid the application of a conventionalized Western terminology to non-Western areas: for example, *Antiquity* and *Classical* (with capital initials) will be used when referring to the period dominated by the ancient Greeks and Romans—while *antiquity* and *classical* (with lower-case initials) will be reserved for reference to ancients and classics elsewhere or in general. The second reason was to distinguish between persons and events contemporary to a given period and those at the same or other periods who were concerned with it: for example, "a modern [lower case *m*] historian" would be one who has lived in modern times even though he might write on Medieval history (i.e., in the West) or on antiquity (lower-case *a*) in China, but "an Ancient [capital *A*] historian" would be one who deals with the period of Western history called Ancient (and "a Medieval historian" one who deals with the period called Medieval and "a Modern historian" one who deals with the period called Modern) regardless of when or where he might have lived.

Contents

PART I

3   I. *Reflections upon the Problem of Generalization*
     CHESTER G. STARR

19   II. *Generalizations in Ancient History*
     M. I. FINLEY

36   III. *On the Uses of Generalization in the Study of Chinese History*
     ARTHUR F. WRIGHT

59   IV. *Comments on the Paper of Arthur F. Wright*
     DERK BODDE

66   V. *Generalizations about Revolution: A Case Study*
     ROBERT R. PALMER

77   VI. *Generalizations about National Character: An Analytical Essay*
     WALTER P. METZGER

103   VII. *The Historian's Use of Social Role*
     THOMAS C. COCHRAN

PART II

113   VIII. *Categories of Historiographical Generalization*
     LOUIS GOTTSCHALK

130   IX. *The Genealogy of Historical Generalizations*
     ROY F. NICHOLS

145   X. *Notes on the Problem of Historical Generalization*
     WILLIAM O. AYDELOTTE

178   XI. *Explicit Data and Implicit Assumptions in Historical Study*
     DAVID M. POTTER

195   XII. *Summary*
     LOUIS GOTTSCHALK

PART III

213   *Bibliography of Writings on Historiography and the Philosophy of History*
     MARTIN KLEIN

249   *Index*

PART I

I. Reflections upon the Problem of Generalization

BY CHESTER G. STARR

The establishment of generalizations on any historical topic seems usually to be a semiconscious process. This may be well for the peace of mind of practicing historians; when one begins to investigate the theoretical issues involved in this process, very disturbing difficulties quickly emerge.

Generalizations, for instance, are commonly the summation by the historian of those views of historical explanation and causation which he has exhibited less obviously in the selection and arrangement of his facts. When one links a mass of events in different places or times by a connective tissue of generalization, the uniqueness of such historical events is thereby limited, for generalization is possible only if we can establish the presence of valid similarity.

The manner, moreover, in which a writer places and phrases his general statements reflects major decisions on the best mode of communicating his thoughts to others. The problems which arise here are important, though they are often muffled nowadays in a widespread tendency to ignore literary style both in the theoretical discussions of historical criticism and in the practice of historical composition.

Finally, generalizations seem dangerously pliable to the subjective drive of the particular mind which produces them. Factual statements are commonly agreed to be true or not true. In making such assertions we are speaking in simple terms so as to pass over basic metaphysical problems of truth; in particular, whether specific statements may be called true, independently of their connections within general statements, is a serious issue.* Nevertheless, historians commonly concur in the belief that if our evidence is adequate we can assign a positive degree of validity to specific facts and can expect all men of sane mind to accept our demonstration. General statements are not so easily proved. Are they, indeed, provable at all? In view of the continuing popularity of the scientific approach, many historians would be un-

* [See the essays by Aydelotte (pp. 149–51 below) and Potter (pp. 183–87) for further discussion of the "truth" of factual statements.—EDITOR.]

happy if they were forced to give a negative answer to that question. I have been invited to survey the problem of generalization as it appears in the field of Ancient history. To avoid extensive detour into the issues which have just been sketched, I shall not give specific consideration to the content of generalizations in my field other than to comment that Ancient historians do formulate general statements on virtually every development for which any evidence at all exists (and at times where there is none). An investigation of two questions will be more useful: (1) To what extent can and do students in my field make general statements? (2) In what ways do they arrive at general statements? Thereafter will come brief comment on the validity of such statements. I shall also take up the practical limitations on generalization as a serious problem in graduate training.

At the beginning I should note that the Ancient phases of human history are now investigated by men living all about the globe—men whose ideological and physical backgrounds vary widely, as do also the areas of their principal interests and the intensity of their identification with Ancient problems. Bourgeois, totalitarian, and communist students, however, share to an amazing degree a common outlook on the problems which here concern us.

The Ancient historian, after all, is a modern citizen. He must exhibit the same general intellectual and other compulsions as an American student of the Truman administration or a Russian investigator of the NEP period. These common qualities may be assumed for the moment but will be dealt with more fully toward the close of my discussion. Yet in some respects the Ancient historian will necessarily follow a somewhat different path from students in other fields.

I

Certain peculiar qualities, that is to say, do mark Ancient history. These differences lie in the types of sources, the very extensive resources available in earlier studies, our inherited techniques of analysis, and the fields of interest for most Ancient historians.

The information available on virtually every aspect of Ancient development is extremely limited. Accidentally or intentionally destructive forces have had millenniums in which to wreak damage, and in any case the Ancient world was so much simpler than modern urban, industrial society that the initial store of evidence, written and physical, was not great. Today a historian is often forced to rely upon a single Ancient source—for example, mostly upon Thucydides for an

Reflections upon the Problem of Generalization

account of the Peloponnesian War. The mixture of specific and general statements by historians of such areas will reflect the pattern of the original account; independent generalization will be difficult. The modern student of Ancient history cannot extend his information by techniques available to Modern historians—the taking of polls, interviews, and so on.

Nor are truly usable statistics obtainable except within very limited ranges. From the several hundred surviving tombstones of sailors in the Roman imperial navy it is possible to generalize about the areas of their recruitment or the age of enlistment.[1] The results will be only as valid as the logic inherent in the sampling processes that were employed will allow (but we are not much worse off here than are many students of modern affairs). Wider statistical generalizations are impossible; despite the figures glibly presented in various accounts, we cannot estimate the population of the city of Rome or of the empire, complete ranges of prices, and the like.[2]

To construct a meaningful picture, the Ancient historian is forced to rely heavily upon arguments from parallel situations, whether in other early societies or in modern times.[3] He must also make use of what can only be called intuition. No less than the anatomic reconstruction of the ass from its jawbone, studies in Ancient history often illustrate Mark Twain's quip: "There is something fascinating about science. One gets such wholesale returns of conjecture out of such a trifling investment of fact." Where the factual elements are limited, the student is more likely to be driven to generalization. Uncontrolled general statements are accordingly somewhat more common in this field.[4]

Another characteristic of the evidence, however, restricts the practical effect of this lack of control. The Ancient historian, much more than the student of the modern world, must extend his gaze far beyond

[1] Cf. my *Roman Imperial Navy, 31 B.C.–A.D. 324* (2d ed.; New York: Barnes & Noble, 1960) and many other epigraphic studies by recent scholars.

[2] F. G. Maier, "Römische Bevölkerungsgeschichte und Inschriftenstatistik," *Historia*, II (1953–54), 318–51.

[3] And in turn the Ancient historian is inclined to apply concepts drawn from his field to other areas—e.g., Ronald Syme, *Colonial Elites: Rome, Spain, and the Americas* (New York: Oxford University Press, 1958).

[4] In defense of my colleagues, I may point out that their conjectures are sometimes borne out by the appearance of new evidence and that work in other fields of history is not lacking in the qualities noted in the text.

written materials and employ physical evidence of all types. Stones which have been worked into tools, skulls and graves, the remains of houses and settlements—all the physical equipment of life, works of art, and a host of other tangible objects are useful. This evidence is highly specific. A monograph based upon a mass of coins or inscriptions, reliefs and sculptures, or archeological sites is very likely to be factual; generalization here may be almost absent and when it occurs is often an unconscious process.

Besides the ambivalent effect of the nature of our evidence, equally divergent influences on generalization result from the facts that some of our information has long been known and that other parts are of recent discovery. In those areas which rest primarily upon written materials, the scholar of the twentieth century bases his own investigations upon a great mass of earlier work. The political history of the Roman world, insofar as it draws from Livy, Tacitus, and other Ancient accounts, has been repeatedly analyzed since the time of the Renaissance. The modern investigator of the Ciceronian age, for instance, has a wide store of inherited generalizations upon which to draw; within this store, almost all the possible conclusions have been examined. The weak and strong points of each have been analyzed, like those of chess gambits. A student of such matters will himself be led, almost forced, to generalize and will be able to do so more soundly.*

Nothing, however, is more fallacious than the idea that since Ancient history deals with ancient events it is all already known. In no field of history does new specific information appear more constantly, to upset old concepts and to enlarge our view of the area. Any work written twenty years ago is hopelessly out of date in its factual presentation of the earliest stages of man's development, down to 4000 B.C. Can the same be said of a survey of Jackson's administration or of the age of Louis XIV? Knowledge of Mesopotamian and Egyptian history has been much enlarged in recent decades; even for the better known areas of Greek and Roman history new epigraphic and archeological materials flow in steadily. On so important a subject as that of the origins of Greek civilization (1100–650 B.C.), the fountainhead of Western culture, generalization which rests upon sound evidence has become possible only in the past decade.

* [See the essay by Nichols (pp. 130–34 below) on the genealogy of generalizations as a test of validity.—EDITOR.]

Reflections upon the Problem of Generalization

The consequences of this flux must always lurk in the back of an Ancient historian's mind. What he writes today will not be the whole story ten years from now and may even need drastic alteration purely on the factual level. Generalization in such cases is likely to be tentative, and the timid may eschew it altogether in those areas where additional information may confidently be expected to appear.

Not all practitioners in the field of Ancient history follow the same techniques of analysis. Some men have been reared in the pure light of historical method as canonized in the pages of Bernheim and others and essay to confine their thought within the channels of objectivity there prescribed. Many teachers and scholars, however, are located in departments of Classical languages and literature. These men have been trained in one of the oldest continuous traditions of scholarship in Western civilization, which runs back through the Renaissance and the Middle Ages to the founders of Alexandrian literary criticism.[5] The products of men so trained are not necessarily less valuable than the monographs of historians, but one can often sense a genuine difference in their approach. Generalization seems to me more common here and is achieved within a frame of aesthetic standards. At the opposite pole are the archeologists, whose discipline is relatively new and becomes ever more scientific. In their work generalization is less common and, as I shall show later, is almost frowned upon.

All the factors identified thus far lead the Ancient historian to accept generalization. They also, interestingly enough, help to broaden his gaze—a factor which in turn encourages generalization. German historiography of the nineteenth century, which reached its zenith in the lofty figure of Theodor Mommsen, shared the common tendency of the era to emphasize institutional history; there are Ancient historians today who concentrate their gaze on purely political developments;[6] and the blinders of economic materialism, which have seriously affected the vision of bourgeois and socialist historians alike, are worn by some students in the Ancient field. But, on the whole, scholars in this area have remained interested in the cultural as well as the political and the economic aspects of human history. The nature of the

[5] See J. E. Sandys, *A History of Classical Scholarship* (3 vols.; Cambridge: At the University Press, 1903–8) or the articles on "Scholarship" in *Oxford Classical Dictionary* (New York: Oxford University Press, 1949).

[6] E.g., Ernst Stein, *Geschichte des spätrömischen Reiches*, Vol. I: *284–476 n. Chr.* (Vienna: L. W. Seidel, 1928).

evidence drives them in this direction; so too does the inherited humanistic tradition of Classical studies.[7]

Ancient historians, I believe, are more inclined to draw universal laws of human nature from their detailed discussions than are students of more modern eras, to observe mankind *sub specie aeternitatis*. Arnold Toynbee, for instance, began his reflections as a student of ancient Greece. Problems of periodization affect all fields but are perhaps more consciously attacked in the Ancient field.[8] Let me note, however, that there are Ancient historians who dissent strongly from any but the most limited generalization, on the grounds that historical development is a series of unique events which can be only chronicled.[9]

II

Lest this essay remain itself a mass of generalizations, I shall now consider two specific examples of the methods by which students of Ancient history create general statements. One of these illustrates the use of modern scientific techniques; the other is a more conventional historical approach.

A well-known psychologist, D. C. McClelland, has recently investigated the Achievement Motive (*n* Achievement) in various historical epochs as a primary factor in the growth and achievement of those epochs. Persons possessing this motive, that is to say, are energetic risk-takers who are likely to stimulate society if they are present in large numbers as an entrepreneurial class. McClelland found that a suitable method for measuring the degree to which men of this stamp were present in a specific culture lay in scoring achievement imagery found in its imaginative stories.

This approach was then applied by one of his students, David E. Berlew, to Greek literature in a paper entitled "The Achievement Motive and the Growth of Greek Civilization."[10] The hypothesis for

[7] On this matter, see my essay "The History of the Roman Empire, 1911–1960," *Journal of Roman Studies*, L (1960), 149–60.

[8] E.g., Hans E. Stier, *Grundlagen und Sinn der griechischen Geschichte* (Stuttgart: Cotta, 1945); Alfred Heuss, "Die archaische Zeit Griechenlands als geschichtliche Epoche," *Antike und Abendland*, II (1946), 26–62.

[9] See J. A. O. Larsen's comments on the laws adduced by Fritz M. Heichelheim, *Ancient Economic History*, Vol. I (Leyden: Brill, 1958), in *Classical Philology*, LIV (1959), 280–81.

[10] I am indebted to Professor Fred E. Fiedler, Department of Psychology, University of Illinois, for drawing my attention to this material and providing a copy of Berlew's paper; and also to Professor McClelland, Department of Social Rela-

which Berlew sought proof was: "*n* Achievement is the key factor in the genesis and growth of a civilization. To establish *n* Achievement as a cause, rather than a result, of progress, it was hypothesized that the *n* Achievement level would be highest *before* the civilization had fully developed (during its growth), that it would have dropped sharply by the time the climax had been reached, and would have reached a low point during the subsequent decline of the civilization."

Toward this end selected authors from the periods of (1) Growth (900–475 B.C.), (2) Climax (475–362 B.C.), and (3) Decline (362–100 B.C.) were scored for (*a*) the amount in each of achievement imagery on six subjects—man and his gods, farm and estate management, public funeral celebrations, poetry, epigrams, and war speeches of encouragement—and (*b*) the presence of achievement-related "values" such as future orientation, impulse control, and dominance of man over nature. The three periods were determined ostensibly on the basis of economic prosperity.[11] Considerable difficulties were encountered in applying to Greek authors tests of achievement imagery which had been developed in connection with modern psychological tests, but the difficulties were met by various modifications in the details of the tests.

The results were expressed in mathematical tables, which I shall not reproduce. These figures, in Berlew's judgment, proved his thesis: the level of *n* Achievement was "highest during the birth and growth of the civilization, lower during the climax and lowest during the period of decline." Changes in *n* Achievement preceded and presumably caused economic progress rather than the reverse.

In his concluding pages, Berlew discusses possible factors responsible for this observed change. First, he notes the hypothesis that a high level of *n* Achievement was a racial characteristic of the northern invaders into Greece but observes that, while plausible, it is "diffi-

---

tions, Harvard University, for lending me a preliminary draft of his further reflections on the use of measures of social motivation in Spanish, English, and Peruvian history. Berlew's findings are available in *Motives in Fantasy, Action, and Society*, ed. John W. Atkinson (Princeton, N.J.: Van Nostrand, 1958), chap. 37; I have quoted from the text of the original paper. See also D. C. McClelland, J. W. Atkinson, R. A. Clark, and E. L. Lowell, *The Achievement Motive* (New York: Appleton-Century-Crofts, 1953).

[11] As based on Sorokin, Heichelheim, Gomme, and Michell. But cultural considerations played a greater part in their periodizations than Berlew fully recognized. McClelland's chapter in *Motives in Fantasy, Action, and Society* also reports that the scoring of "doodling," etc., on Greek vases produced similar results.

cult to follow up." Much more attention is devoted to a discovery of modern psychological analysis that children taught to be independent at an early age tend to have high n Achievement and to the argument that children are weaned later in societies of low protein diet. "We may speculate, then, that the early Greeks subsisted on a high protein diet and weaned their children very early (evidence from Homer indicates that they did like roast meat)," whereas later the Greek diet shifted from roast meat toward cereals. More demonstrable in Berlew's view is the increasing use of slaves as nurses and tutors in Greek society, a factor which would decrease the n Achievement of the children so reared. With this increase of slavery would go an increasingly capitalistic economy in which the poor became dependent upon state support.

My other example, likewise in the field of earlier Greek history, is an essay by Hermann Strasburger, "Der Einzelne und die Gemeinschaft im Denken der Griechen."[12] This study proceeds along the main line of conventional historical analysis. Its principal thesis is the proposition that the Greek felt no strong sense of political unity in an ideal community; on the contrary, he considered himself an individual in a rural, personal environment.

In proving this hypothesis, which stands in direct opposition to most generalizations on the subject, Strasburger first limits his area of investigation to the archaic and classical eras, to the concept of the city-state, and to male citizens therein. The last limitation he justifies on the grounds that the upper classes alone make history.[13] He then rejects that abstract scheme of thought which first presumes the existence of an ideal collective spirit in the early Greek people and argues that this spirit was corrupted in the passage of time by the growth of individual consciousness. Instead, he turns to the facts of the situation.

The oldest and most abundant evidence on the relations of the individual to the community is afforded by the Homeric epics. Since later literary views accord remarkably with this picture and since, moreover, the epics became a common source of ideals for all Greeks, Strasburger feels justified in drawing the main proof for his hypothesis from Homeric lines. In the *Iliad*, *fatherland* is not an abstract term but

[12] *Historische Zeitschrift*, CLXXVII (1954), 227–48.
[13] *Ibid.*, p. 220

a shorthand symbol for one's family and property; loyalties are of rural type. For further proof, the author investigates the meaning of two concepts from Homer onward—*aristie*, individual greatness expressed in a competitive spirit, and *eleutheria*, "freedom."

Beside this positive line of approach Strasburger places a negative proof by investigating the real absence of a conscious concept of community. Here he notes the distorting effect of modern idealizations of ancient Greece. Since a search through all Greek literature on the topic at hand would lead the student into a host of special problems, he proceeds on the assumption that "one will most easily gain a clear picture if one bases one's views on a comparison of outstanding witnesses."[14] The term *community* in the modern sense of *Gemeinschaft* he does not find in Greek literature, and bonds appear in a negative sense as a necessary evil. As a final example (which he probably intended as a clinching argument) he adduces Alcibiades, the unscrupulous, self-directed Athenian leader during the later stages of the Peloponnesian War.

While basing his main line of thought upon the continued existence of a common Greek outlook, Strasburger observes an evolution in consciousness of individuality. In his opening paragraph he comments that his subject has a bearing not only on early Greek but also on general Ancient views, especially those of the nobility in the Roman Republic; indeed, light can perhaps be thrown on the attitudes of humanity as a whole. But he specifically refuses to engage in sweeping conclusions on this matter. Not all Ancient historians, as I have already observed, would be equally circumspect.

III

These two studies are more than adequate food for reflection on the problems of generalization in Ancient history. I only regret that I cannot here furnish a full commentary upon their treatments paragraph by paragraph.

Between the two, the average Ancient historian would surely prefer the second approach. Berlew's essay he would read with interest but probably without much stimulation. The main conclusion is, in simple English, that Greek civilization was more dynamic in its earlier than its later stages, or had more energetic people at the outset. Insofar

---

[14] *Ibid.*, p. 246.

as this conclusion is correct, it is already known through other, more subjective, means.[15]

Is such a generalization better proved by mathematical tables? The scientist will feel so, for the generalization about the quantity of n Achievement present in each author can be tested independently by other students who apply the same tests to the same material. In Berlew's study another scorer is reported to have come to much the same results as did the author himself. This fact lends a pleasant air of certitude to generalizations so achieved; but is not the apparent validity as much due to their quality as logical inferences from presuppositions as to the mechanical measurement which was carried out? Whenever I have analyzed scientific efforts to reduce historical phenomena to measurable quantities, I have found that the basic periodizations and hidden values which determine the grouping and selection of statistical data have been those already given by the historical discipline itself.*

Whatever conclusions one may reach on this matter, there is another important aspect of generalization which must be considered. General statements are useful to the historian not only as valid inferences and summations of specific historical facts but also as stimuli for further thought; the most desirable generalizations are those which place the facts in a new light and lead to further generalizations based upon these facts. "Statistical research is for the historian a good servant but a bad master. It profits him nothing to make statistical generalizations, unless he can thereby detect the thought behind the facts about which he is generalizing."[16]

Berlew does try to explain changes in the amount of n Achievement. When he does so, his statistical approach quietly disappears. The first suggestion, that of a racial inheritance, he properly rejects in essence; this is in root nothing more than the Nordic myth, an enduring curse of Greek scholarship. The second, based on weaning and protein diet, strikes me as no more valid, an effort to support mathematical treatment of human development by mechanistic interpretations of human

[15] McClelland (in *Motives in Fantasy, Action, and Society*, pp. 522–25) essays to defend his approach against such charges and also against the kind of criticism given below that it does not consider all factors; as is evident from my text I do not consider this defense convincing.

[16] R. G. Collingwood, *The Idea of History* (Oxford: Clarendon Press, 1946), p. 228.

* [See the essay by Aydelotte below, especially pp. 172–77, for a fuller discussion of quantitative procedures in historical research.—EDITOR.]

beings. And the last two, the growth of slavery and of a state-supported proletariat, are very insecure on the factual level; they also rest on questionable hypotheses about the evil effects of slavery and capitalism (hypotheses, incidentally, reflecting *modern* states of mind which are far from scientific).[17]

The Ancient historian, moreover, will feel that the scope of Berlew's treatment is at once too broad and too simplified to result in sound generalizations. Like many scientific studies in the field of history, his essay seeks to cope with an extremely broad range of time and requires such diverse chains of development as the Ionian, Attic, and Alexandrian to become bed-partners in the same Procrustean couch. The concept of *n* Achievement is defined in economic terms alone.

We may be grateful for the insistence that the historian treat the great problems of his subject as well as study *in parvo*, but we may also feel that analysis in terms of such an abstract universal as *n* Achievement does great violence to the wide web of interlaced aspects of human life with which the historian must always deal. In the laboratory the nature of scientific experiment restricts the range of variable factors so as to achieve useful theoretical results. The historian too may restrict his gaze but only with an awareness that a tremendous host of other elements lie about and beneath his specific subject. The opening lines of Strasburger's essay, which is itself restricted, deserve quotation:

Wer je die Erfahrung gemacht hat, wie schwer es ist, sich über ein bedeutenderes geistesgeschichtliches Thema kurz zu fassen, ohne vollkommen an der Oberfläche zu bleiben, der wird es verstehen, wenn ich meine heutige Aufgabe verengere und die Auswahl des Einzelnen subjektiv treffe, um nur überhaupt etwas Persönliches geben zu können.

While the scientist's inclination is toward the general, the historian can win through to this level only after long concentration upon the specific.

The generalizations which Strasburger has reached will strike the average historian as more soundly based than Berlew's. They are stimulating for further thought, particularly inasmuch as they are in opposition to the *communis opinio*. Strasburger's proof rests upon de-

---

[17] See, e.g., my essay "An Overdose of Slavery," *Journal of Economic History*, XVIII (1958), 17–32; and A. H. M. Jones, *Athenian Democracy* (New York: Praeger, 1957).

tailed investigation of the meaning of various Homeric and other passages and upon analysis of the changing implications of important terms and is illuminated, even buttressed, by the citation of specific examples such as Alcibiades. The complications of the subject are set forth in some detail, and several lines of attack, both positive and negative, are employed. Major and minor aspects are distinguished to a greater extent than was apparent in the lists of subjects scored by Berlew. No less than in Berlew's study, underlying assumptions are essential to Strasburger's argument—for example, the opinion that the *Iliad* represents also the views of men of later centuries or the assertion that we need consider only the attitudes of the upper classes. These assumptions are perhaps more fully stated by Strasburger than by Berlew, and they are of the type which historians are predisposed to accept—though that fact does not necessarily make them more valid.

The results of Strasburger's essay are not expressible in the precise terms of mathematics, and he even admits that one Platonic dialogue (*Crito* 49d–54) contains a concept of the community as a unifying force far beyond that to be found anywhere else in the literature he surveys. Whereas Berlew could check his results by having an independent scorer, no other historian will necessarily draw the same generalizations from Strasburger's factual material. Indeed, I for one feel that he has overstressed the naïve enthusiasm of the Greek aristocracy in an era when *n* Achievement was strong, and I hold that the resulting expression of individualistic views—important as they are in setting a current in Western civilization—must be taken against a background of traditional (and so less expressed) communal loyalty.[18] Alcibiades was not the only man active in Athens during the late fifth century; its other citizens fought desperately for their state and yielded to Sparta only when they were starved into submission.

My disagreement with Strasburger may suggest the enduring problem the historian faces in generalizations based upon conventional historical methods. By what methods can we test general statements in the field of Ancient history and so create generalizations which will

---

[18] The same problem appears in Berlew's paper, which postulates that authors "reflect the same drives, the same goals, as the general population." This is true, but the extent to which upper-class attitudes affect the surface of literature can never be overlooked; cf. my *Civilization and the Caesars* (Ithaca, N.Y.: Cornell University Press, 1954), pp. 207–11.

be universally acceptable? At the present time, however a conclusion is arrived at in a specific work, other Ancient historians may not accept it and may create other generalizations of their own.

In recent decades students of history have been much concerned over cognate problems, such as the nature of historical causation, the subjective quality of the historians' product, or the underlying element of faith implicit in inductions from limited, specific facts. The general spirit in most treatments has been one of horror at the discovery that historians do differ. Then come feverish efforts to secure a method of agreement or, among more realistic investigators, a desperate resignation to a totally unsatisfactory situation.

This horror is entirely unnecessary, and I have observed that historians who yield to it have tended to become paralyzed. The followers of Clio do not now have methods by which they can reach agreement on the generalizations obtainable from a given mass of facts. (Agreement on the truth of the facts themselves, let it be noted, is commonly considered a rather different matter.) Nor, so long as history is an honorable subject, will they ever so agree. Historical generalizations cannot be "tested" in a scientific sense.

This situation, as *1066 and All That* would put it, is a good thing. History is not a science, and one of my objectives in citing Berlew's study has been to suggest the dangers of impoverishment and ill-founded assumption which would result if we tried to convert history into another discipline. Generalization is not to be condemned if it is personally based. As inheritors of the rational tradition of Western civilization we need to apply firmly logical principles to our specific facts (which we have tested properly), to eliminate the subjectivity of open prejudice, and to exhibit some humility in our conclusions. The interpretations thus achieved by a sound scholar conversant with the facts will persuade some of his confreres and will stimulate those who disagree into a deeper, wider investigation of the subject.

IV

The immediately preceding observations lead to the last aspect of generalization in Ancient history which I wish to consider; this is also the aspect on which I think attention should be focused with a view to possible improvement.

Many students are aware, if only unconsciously, that their generalizations do not now command universal assent and that this situation does not seem to prevail so widely in the sciences. They also sense that historians have not found a method of analysis which can properly produce universally acceptable generalizations. The process of generalization, moreover, requires the use of judgment, logical inference, and synthesis, and the expression of results so achieved leads to problems of literary style which do not arise in purely factual discussion. The effect of these factors, far too often, is a refusal to generalize at all.

This tendency is markedly prominent in the training of graduate students. The manuals which treat of historical method concentrate upon the problems of the validity of facts, though the humanistic traditions of the historical profession usually lead the authors of such manuals to survey the problems of synthesis. This matter, nevertheless, often seems a vestigial appendix, and students certainly treat it in this light. Anyone who has read doctoral dissertations over the years will be aware that students rarely dare to generalize.

Nor are they encouraged to do so when they turn to the collective wisdom of the historical profession, as exhibited in the review pages of our journals. I have recently gone through a number of current issues of scholarly periodicals, both of a general nature and of specialized interest in Ancient history, and have found almost no criticism of a book as engaging in *too little* generalization. The current is strongly in the other direction.

A volume which does little more than pile up masses of facts in orderly heaps will commonly get good marks. In contrast, any author who generalizes extensively will undergo heavy attack, which much too frequently will take the form not of debate on his generalizations themselves but of triumphant citation of specific exceptions. A fledgling historian, in particular, may expect a sharp rap and advice that greater value would have resulted "from a more limited application of his interpretive devices to the material and region with which he was thoroughly familiar."[19]

In the present connection there is much food for thought in Oscar Broneer's praise of a study by R. H. Howland on Greek lamps found in the Agora excavations:

He has refrained from drawing far-reaching conclusions regarding the historical or economic implications of his study. He has made the data for such

[19] James B. Griffin, reviewing *Trend and Tradition in the Prehistory of the Eastern United States*, by Joseph R. Caldwell (Menasha, Wis.: American Anthropological Association, 1958), in *American Journal of Archaeology*, LXIII (1959), 414. Here and below I have chosen reviews of archeological works because they express most clearly the attitudes under consideration, but the same spirit is widely spread in review pages.

use of the material available to historians and others who wish to build further upon them. Had the author succumbed to the temptation of synthesizing, he might have made his book more readable and his own task more enjoyable, but the value of such deviation from his appointed task might be questionable.[20]

I do not urge that either young students or their elders should rush into wide-scale generalization. We all know sad examples of this tendency. Yet in spite of the indiscretions involved, the perversity of human nature is such that we do generalize; when we do so, our training and conventions prepare us inadequately for skillful, conscious elevation above the level of the specific. Howland, the author of the study on Greek lamps, provides a striking example of this human perversity. To quote Broneer further, Howland has occasionally "permitted his imagination to roam briefly, as when he suggests that certain 'behemoths' of the first century B.C. 'may have been commissioned by arrogant Roman conquerors who felt no compunctions about squandering captured Athenian oil reserves.' " A student, in other words, who has deliberately refused to generalize on subjects about which he could make useful remarks has casually engaged in a completely unwarranted observation. Do we know the Roman conquerors were wasteful? Were there any oil reserves in Athens when it was conquered by Sulla? Experience induces me to suspect that this casual remark about "arrogant Roman conquerors," singled out as it has been in a review, is likely to creep into the thinking of future historians of Athens and Rome. On the other hand, the "far-reaching conclusions regarding the historical or economic implications" of this material which might more justly have been advanced have not been made.

Taken as a whole, the peculiar qualities of Ancient history which have been sketched above probably lead scholars in that field to generalize more often than would be required in fields where factual evidence is more abundant and less digested. The methods employed to arrive at general statements have been suggested in the case of one article (Strasburger's). I see no reason to pile up other examples, because these methods are essentially the same in all historical areas—a combination of positive and negative chains of argument, an appeal to specific cases as embodying general principles, and so on. The resulting generalizations cannot hope to command universal support, but this is no ground for despondency or, worse yet, refusal to generalize.

[20] *American Journal of Archaeology*, LXIII (1959), 402.

On the contrary, my conclusion must be that in far too many essays and volumes on Ancient history the process of generalization is unduly limited. An underlying difficulty, which I have not thus far mentioned and do not wish to investigate further here, is the possibility that we live in an age of transition when the standards of the past are being severely shaken (though historians will be aware that all ages are transitional); men, accordingly, may seek security of mind by working on the level of the specific. But if my suspicion is correct that even students of the particular will generalize unconsciously, then it would be far better for them to admit the necessity for generalization.

One result would be greater attention in the training of graduate students to the problems of logic and literary style which are inherent in generalization,* as well as a commonly applied requirement that they not stop short on the factual level in their papers and dissertations. Another eminently desirable consequence would be a broadening of the standards of historical criticism.

* [See the essay by Potter (pp. 192-94 below) for a similar recommendation.—EDITOR.]

II. *Generalizations in Ancient History*

BY M. I. FINLEY

I

This essay has a pervasively critical tone, which is neither accidental nor "unconscious." Its subject is methodological—the nature and problem of generalizations—not historical. It is not concerned with the content, the truth or falsity, of any particular generalization in Ancient history; it is concerned with the way Ancient historians go about their work, what they say or do not say, what they assume or overlook. I have deliberately adopted the expository device of the polemic, but I have not sought out atypical, heterodox studies, nor have I looked for Aunt Sallys and easy targets. Silly generalizations can be found; Ancient history is no more immune from bad work than is any other discipline. I have tried to choose my few examples from typical and responsible writing by well-known historians. The choices are arbitrary, but only in the sense that the illustrations are those which happen to be more familiar to me because of my special interests. It is not suggested that the particular subjects and areas selected for illustration are better (or worse) instances of what is being done than any others or that the examples cannot be readily countered by others with different tendencies and approaches. I do believe, however, that the problem of generalization is not often studied with sufficient rigor by Ancient historians and that loose, inadequate, and even erroneous conceptions are common enough to warrant a polemical discussion.

It is generally agreed that Ancient historians rarely discuss questions of method (other than questions of technique in ancillary disciplines such as archeology or textual criticism). It would be difficult, for example, and perhaps impossible to compile even a short anthology in the field comparable to Pieter Geyl's *Debates with Historians*.[1] Max Weber and Eduard Meyer once debated problems of method and Mommsen's centenary has recently stimulated some analysis, but who has studied the underlying assumptions and methods of Rostovtzeff or

[1] London: Batsford, 1955; N.Y.: Meridian Books, 1958.

Glotz, of Tenney Frank or Beloch or Bury?[2] Admittedly many historians think the subject is better off without such discussion. Historians, one hears all the time, should get on with their proper business, the investigation of the concrete experiences of the past, and leave the "philosophy of history" (which is a barren, abstract, and pretty useless activity anyway) to the philosophers. Unfortunately the historian is no mere chronicler, and he cannot do his work at all without assumptions and judgments—without generalizations, in other words. Insofar as he is unwilling to discuss generalizations explicitly—which means that he does not reflect on them—he runs grave risks.

In the present context, the weakness which results at once is a misconception of the nature and extent of the problem of generalization. "The perversity of human nature is such that we do generalize," says Professor Chester G. Starr in the foregoing article (p. 17). How much *should* the historian generalize? How little? That is the question he poses, and "perversity" suggests, as does much of his discussion, that the issue is a moral one or, at least, that there is a free, personal choice: to generalize or not to generalize. "Generalizations," he writes (p. 3) more or less as a definition, "... are commonly the summation by the historian of those views of historical explanation and causation which he has exhibited less obviously in the selection and arrangement of his facts." Unlike "factual statements," "generalizations seem dangerously pliable to the subjective drive of the particular mind which produces them" (p. 3).

No doubt there is an element of truth in these remarks. And no doubt they would receive widespread assent—they are familiar enough to everyone who has read anything on the subject. But they start the discussion at the wrong end. Some generalizations are the *summation* after long study of a historian's views about historical explanation and causation. But those are not the only generalizations, nor the most common, nor (perhaps) the most important. It is the others which tend to escape consideration, and they, at least, cannot be usefully analyzed in terms of "shall" and "ought," of human frailty, subjectivity, and "perversity." The first question is not how much or how little generalization but what kinds and levels of generalization. That

---

[2] The obvious answer to my rhetorical question is: Professor Arnaldo Momigliano, most of whose articles relevant to this question are now collected in two volumes, *Contributo alla storia degli studi classici* and *Secondo contributo* ... (Rome: Edizioni di Storia e Letteratura, 1955 and 1960). The magnitude, however, of the task he has undertaken merely highlights the paucity of other writing of the kind.

use of the material available to historians and others who wish to build further upon them. Had the author succumbed to the temptation of synthesizing, he might have made his book more readable and his own task more enjoyable, but the value of such deviation from his appointed task might be questionable.[20]

I do not urge that either young students or their elders should rush into wide-scale generalization. We all know sad examples of this tendency. Yet in spite of the indiscretions involved, the perversity of human nature is such that we do generalize; when we do so, our training and conventions prepare us inadequately for skillful, conscious elevation above the level of the specific. Howland, the author of the study on Greek lamps, provides a striking example of this human perversity. To quote Broneer further, Howland has occasionally "permitted his imagination to roam briefly, as when he suggests that certain 'behemoths' of the first century B.C. 'may have been commissioned by arrogant Roman conquerors who felt no compunctions about squandering captured Athenian oil reserves.'" A student, in other words, who has deliberately refused to generalize on subjects about which he could make useful remarks has casually engaged in a completely unwarranted observation. Do we know the Roman conquerors were wasteful? Were there any oil reserves in Athens when it was conquered by Sulla? Experience induces me to suspect that this casual remark about "arrogant Roman conquerors," singled out as it has been in a review, is likely to creep into the thinking of future historians of Athens and Rome. On the other hand, the "far-reaching conclusions regarding the historical or economic implications" of this material which might more justly have been advanced have not been made.

Taken as a whole, the peculiar qualities of Ancient history which have been sketched above probably lead scholars in that field to generalize more often than would be required in fields where factual evidence is more abundant and less digested. The methods employed to arrive at general statements have been suggested in the case of one article (Strasburger's). I see no reason to pile up other examples, because these methods are essentially the same in all historical areas—a combination of positive and negative chains of argument, an appeal to specific cases as embodying general principles, and so on. The resulting generalizations cannot hope to command universal support, but this is no ground for despondency or, worse yet, refusal to generalize.

[20] *American Journal of Archaeology*, LXIII (1959), 402.

On the contrary, my conclusion must be that in far too many essays and volumes on Ancient history the process of generalization is unduly limited. An underlying difficulty, which I have not thus far mentioned and do not wish to investigate further here, is the possibility that we live in an age of transition when the standards of the past are being severely shaken (though historians will be aware that all ages are transitional); men, accordingly, may seek security of mind by working on the level of the specific. But if my suspicion is correct that even students of the particular will generalize unconsciously, then it would be far better for them to admit the necessity for generalization.

One result would be greater attention in the training of graduate students to the problems of logic and literary style which are inherent in generalization,* as well as a commonly applied requirement that they not stop short on the factual level in their papers and dissertations. Another eminently desirable consequence would be a broadening of the standards of historical criticism.

* [See the essay by Potter (pp. 192–94 below) for a similar recommendation.—EDITOR.]

is a commonplace, so obvious that it is easily forgotten. I believe we must first concentrate on the obvious—on the generalizations with which a historian begins his work, so to speak—*must begin it*—long before he is ready to sum up his conclusions (which, in practice, he may or may not do).

II

For convenience of discussion, I shall set out (and comment on) a rough typology of generalizations, for which I make no claim other than that it may help to clarify the issues.

1. The most rudimentary and indispensable generalizations are *classificatory*. Consider the word *Greek*, whether as noun or as adjective. It is literally impossible to make any statement including *Greek* which is not a generalization. Furthermore, it is impossible to make such a statement which would be true without greater or lesser qualification (of course excepting such truisms as "All Greeks must eat"). In the first place, there is no meaningful definition of *Greek* which does not differentiate in time—between a Homeric Greek and a contemporary Greek, to give the most extreme example. Second, applied to the Ancient world any definition must face the fact of mixed populations, part Greek, part something else. Third, any meaningful statement, even when restricted to "pure" Greeks at a fixed moment in time, must allow for variations in ideas or practices, whether by region or by class or for some other reason.

No one will suggest that, because of such difficulties, the word *Greek* had better be dropped from historical writing. Exactly the same situation prevails with such specifically Greek institutional terms as *polis* ("city-state") or *assembly*, which I shall not discuss. The case is different, however, with a special category of classificatory generalizations—namely, those which transcend Ancient history altogether: trade, agriculture, peasantry, empire, democracy, slavery, and so on.*

* [Meyerhoff in his letter to the Committee, cited above (see pp. vi–vii, n. 2), underlines Finley's point, questioning whether classificatory generalizations, or "labeling generalizations," are, strictly speaking, generalizations at all. "They are classifications or abstract concepts or 'ideal types' as they may be found in the taxonomic, descriptive phase of any science. More simply, they are abbreviations or short-hand descriptions. Such descriptive concepts do cause trouble in history and elsewhere. In history, for example, they raise the problem of reifying abstract terms or the problem of periodization. More serious, perhaps, is the fact that we also use these terms for the purpose of *explanation* in history. Thus we say, 'owing to the rapid growth of a capitalist economy . . . ' or 'because of the revolution . . .' and we may fail to see that these concepts are descriptive only, not explanatory in the strict sense. At any rate they are defective; some radical empiricists

Here there is much room for analysis, much need for clarification. One example will serve as a pointer.

In a paper on slavery in the Greco-Roman world, Professor S. Lauffer wrote as follows:

> The word *Sklave, esclave, schiavo*, which stems from the Middle Ages and originally marked Slavic war captives from eastern Europe, can be transferred to Antiquity only in an anachronistic way, and that means with misunderstanding. Furthermore, the word brings to mind the Negro slavery of North America and the colonial areas in the most recent centuries, which makes its transfer to the relationships of Antiquity even more difficult. The Ancient "slave" is an entirely different social type.[3]

Few (if any) of the Ancient historians present at the discussion of Lauffer's paper looked with favor on this radical suggestion to abandon the word *slave*, and, in fact, it is an evasion of the difficulties, not a solution. The historian seeks to describe Ancient slavery concretely, and it can be argued that the label does not matter; that, furthermore, if it is misleading in part, it should be replaced by a neutral one. The obvious choice for the Greek historian is the Greek word *doulos*, which can have no non-Greek associations. But this is pretense, a pure fiction. All words have associations, and they cannot be removed by fiat. Even nonsense syllables or algebraic symbols, which can be presumed to start life without associations, necessarily acquire them if they are used in a substantive context. *Doulos* as an isolated word has no meaning to a modern historian, but as soon as he reads and thinks about *douloi* in Athens he cannot, being human, avoid making connections with servitude, and hence with slaves. He may persist with absolute rigor in calling them *douloi*, never slaves, but all that he will accomplish by this artificial procedure will be to prevent his generalizations from being made explicit, from being examined systematically (by himself or his readers). Lauffer has suggested a sweeping conclusion about Ancient slavery, not, as he seems to think, a safer working method. Out of a desire to escape the evils of a false generalization he has produced another generalization. He may or may not be right in

---

(not myself) would say they are 'pseudo-concepts,' because the abstraction is only an abbreviation for the sequence of events which it is called upon to explain." See also Wright's essay, below, esp. pp. 36–37.—EDITOR.]

[3] "Die Sklaverei in der griechisch-römischen Welt" in the *Rapports* of the Eleventh International Congress of Historical Sciences (Uppsala: Almqvist & Wiksell, 1960), II, 81.

his conclusion—that is not the point at issue—but he (and we) must be quite clear about what he has done.

And where does this process logically end? "The Ancient 'slave' is an entirely different social type" implies that the Ancient slave *is* a social type. Is it? The Greeks regularly used the word *doulos* (and the abstract noun *douleia*) to cover a range of statuses. Even if we ignore the more metaphorical uses—"the allies became *douloi* of the Athenians"—there remains the famous crux of the Spartan helots. Contemporary Greeks had no qualms about calling them *douloi*. Most historians today object: they will not allow the translation *slaves* for the helots while employing it for the *douloi* of Athens and, curiously and most inconsistently, for the debt-bondsmen of pre-Solonic Attica or early Rome. Essential differences among these Ancient status categories are undeniable. Therefore, one should argue on the Lauffer line of reasoning, the Ancient *slave* is not a social type at all, any more than *slave* in general. One should insist on breaking the concept down still further, on using different words for helot, debt-bondsman, and so on.

This process, carried far enough, would make all historical discourse impossible: even the sparest annalist would find himself in trouble, for he could safely say no more than that individual X performed action Y in a given place on a given day. At least that would be a consistent procedure. What often happens in current practice has neither that virtue nor any other. Instead of grappling with the difficulties which Lauffer noticed—and they are serious ones—students of Antiquity often run from them to the illusory safety of the term *serf*, which they apply most commonly to Spartan helots but sometimes even to the pre-Solonic debt-bondsmen in Attica and to other groups that seem not to be chattels in a strict sense. It should be immediately evident that this procedure merely transfers the problem *in toto* from one rubric to another, from *slave* to *serf*. It solves nothing. The conclusion is demonstrable that at present, on this particular topic, the use of classificatory generalizations is in an unsatisfactory state, in which the inconsistent terminology reflects a deeper confusion in the interpretation of the institutions themselves.[4]

2. A comparable kind of generalization is *classification by period*. Current practice is not altogether uniform. *Classical* and *Hellenistic* are standard terms in Greek history (though there is no agreement where to end the latter), but there is less unanimity for the earlier periods,

[4] See M. I. Finley, "The Servile Statuses of Ancient Greece," *Revue internationale des droits de l'antiquité*, 3d ser., VII (1960), 165–89.

for which various labels are used, drawn almost entirely from art and archeology, such as *archaic, Geometric,* even *sub-Geometric* and *proto-Geometric.* Roman history, on the other hand, is traditionally divided according to political systems—kingdom, Republic, Empire (with subdivisions: early and late, Principate and Dominate). There are obvious reasons why the practice differs between Greek and Roman history. There are equally obvious difficulties with, and justifications for, the practice of periodization, but they are substantially the same in Medieval and Modern history. I can do no more here than exemplify the prevailing situation in Ancient history.

The validity of the scheme of periods (or their essentials, which is the same thing) is rarely discussed.[5] The traditional Roman scheme, in particular, is customarily accepted without examination, as if it were self-evident. I do not wish to challenge it here, but I must point out that it presumes a very big generalization—namely, that the form of political organization is the pivotal institution; the form, furthermore, in its crudest sense of monarchy or not-monarchy. As soon as one concerns oneself with other aspects of Roman history, this generalization is put to the test and difficulties arise. In Roman law, for example, there is still no agreement among the experts on the right way to divide the subject into periods, apart from the break between classical and post-classical law, which is said to have occurred in the third century of our era. Insofar as this lack of agreement is but another instance of the usual difficulties with all periodization in history, it requires no comment in the present context. But there is also a difficulty peculiar to this situation, and that is the apparent lack of synchronization between legal history and political history. What does one do?

As a test case, I choose H. F. Jolowicz's excellent *Historical Introduction to the Study of Roman Law,*[6] a standard work. In the opening chapter, entitled "Periods in the History of Rome and in the History of Her Law," Jolowicz sketches and characterizes the periods in six pages, first "in history" (a rubric that should be pondered) and then "in the history of the law." The latter he divides in this way: (1) the period of conjecture (to the XII Tables), (2) from the XII Tables to the end of the Republic, (3) the first century of the Empire, (4) the

---

[5] An important exception is Alfred Heuss, "Die archaische Zeit Griechenlands als geschichtliche Epoche," *Antike und Abendland,* II (1946), 26–62. It is worth noting that such a work as H. E. Stier, *Grundlagen und Sinn der griechischen Geschichte* (Stuttgart: Cotta, 1945) has been almost completely ignored.

[6] 2d ed.; Cambridge: At the University Press, 1952.

classical period (from Hadrian to the Severi), (5) the post-classical period down to the reign of Justinian, and (6) the reign of Justinian. In principle this is a very poor classification, since the basis oscillates between the state of our knowledge and the state of the law. It is also very poor in substance, precisely because it tries to combine two developments by the Procrustean device of forcing legal history into political periods. Despite Jolowicz' statement regarding period 2 that "it is impossible to find any obvious break in this long stretch of some four hundred years," his book leaves no doubt that a break must be found and made (this is most obvious from his chapters on the sources of law and on legal procedure). As for periods 3 and 4, he himself destroys them as soon as he creates them. "The change from republic to empire," he writes, "did not make any immediate difference to private law"—so much for one end; as for the other, "this period [3] indeed merges into" period 4. And all that is claimed to have happened in the course of period 3 is this:

Bringing peace after about a century of turmoil, the new order was favorable to legal development. It is also perhaps true to say that now, opportunities for political distinction being necessarily few, the law remained the chief avenue for men who aspired to a public career.

There is the usual caution:

If it is difficult to divide general history into periods without introducing a false idea that a people develops by starts rather than continuously, it is still more difficult with legal history, for there are seldom any violent breaks.

Nevertheless, not only does Jolowicz make the attempt in the introductory chapter but he then organizes his entire book accordingly. To do otherwise would be impossible. That is why it is important to stress (*a*) that the organization is set down in the most casual way, without any significant explanation or justification, without serious presentation of the criteria or implications; (*b*) that two possibly distinct developments are merged arbitrarily, with the political one in the prior position, again without any attempt at justification; and (*c*) that in the course of these six pages a number of sweeping generalizations are introduced, which are not essential to the periodization, which embrace law in general, not merely Roman law, and which are stated *ex cathedra*. Among these *ex cathedra* generalizations are: (1) It is "a false idea that a people develops by starts rather than continuously"; (2) peace, not "turmoil," is "favorable to legal development"; (3) because there were few "opportunities for political distinction"—"necessarily" so because the Republic had been replaced by the Empire—"the law remained [why "remained"?] the chief avenue for men who aspired to a public career." None of these propositions is self-evident. Indeed, the one about peace is thrown into doubt on the following page when Jolowicz notes that the next time there was a "restoration of order" following an "era of confusion"—that is to say, with the accession of Diocletian—it "did not revive legal literature." No explanation is suggested.[7] There is one, however (again a great generalization laid down *ex cathedra*), in Fritz Schulz's *History of Roman Legal Science*[8]—namely, the complete "victory of bureaucracy." Schulz thinks it important to give some bibliography to justify the label "classical" but gives none to justify his substantive proposition about the effect of bureaucracy on classical (which he also calls "aristocratic") jurisprudence.[9]

3. These considerations at last bring me to the kind of generalization on which attention is usually concentrated—to *interrelations* of events and, beyond that, to *causes*, to answers to the question Why?

If the historian does nothing else, he arranges events in a temporal sequence. If he did no more, if he were a chronicler in the narrowest sense, there would be no problem other than getting the dates right. But he always does much more, even when he is working within a very restricted field. When Thucydides selected the incidents at Corcyra and Potidaea for a detailed narrative rather than any of the other events which occurred in the years 433–432 B.C., his choice was dictated by a decision he had made about causes. He said so explicitly, and he underscored his decision by dismissing the Megarian decrees in a few words and by refusing even to mention a contemporary belief that Pericles deliberately provoked the Peloponnesian War in order to distract attention from his personal peculations. Thucydides need not have talked about the problem of causes at all; the excision of a very few sentences and phrases in his text would have converted his account into a strict narrative, leaving the question of causation, in any explicit formula-

---

[7] The problem is touched on in the final section of the book, but even there one cannot find a clear explanation, and surely none which throws light on the apparent contradiction within the opening chapter itself.

[8] (New York: Oxford University Press, 1946), p. 101.

[9] In this discussion I have not been at all concerned with the labels. The implications of a word like *classical* are interesting, but what I have written would not be affected in the least if the word were replaced by something else, by dates for example (fifth and fourth centuries B.C. in Greek history).

tion, to the reader. That is what historians frequently do. Yet there is no fundamental difference in the two procedures, however different they may appear in the end-product, aesthetically or psychologically. The choice of events which are to be arranged in a temporal sequence, which are to be interrelated, necessarily rests on a judgment of an inherent connection among them, whether that judgment is or is not expressed in so many words.

The next step in the argument carries us to a point which has usually escaped notice in the relevant discussions. War has always been a central theme in Western historiography—its causes, main events, and results. The Peloponnesian War alone has been the subject of more books and articles than perhaps any other single topic in Ancient history. What Thucydides began has never ended. It is therefore a startling paradox to be reminded, as Professor Arnaldo Momigliano tried to remind us a few years ago, that there is "a great deal of truth" in F. M. Cornford's old, neglected thesis that Thucydides was "not interested in causes":

> The Greeks came to accept war as a natural fact like birth and death about which nothing could be done. They were interested in causes of *wars*, not in causes of *war* as such. Yes, the golden age had been free from wars, but then that was the golden age. In ordinary life you could postpone *a* war, but you could not avoid *war*. . . .
>
> . . . I think there would be some truth in saying that historical writing from the Renaissance to the beginnings of this century has been much more successful in dealing with causes of political revolutions than with causes of external wars, just because it has been so largely under the influence of Greek and Roman historiography.[10]

The heritage of Greek historiography was a sharp distinction between causes and pretexts, between remote and immediate causes—between *"isolated episodes of past history"* (my italics) and other episodes which were nearer at hand and therefore more obviously linked with a particular war. The twentieth century, Momigliano continues, has finally broken with the "classical interpretation of war" in order to seek "all-pervading economic, social, religious and psychological factors." Yet, with the century more than half over, he is compelled to close his article by enumerating ten major topics, connected with Ancient warfare, which have not been systematically investigated: the idea of a just war, "the propensity to attribute strictly personal reasons—some-

---

[10] Momigliano, "Some Observations on Causes of War in Ancient Historiography," *Secondo contributo*, pp. 13, 27.

times silly ones—to declarations of war," the role of public opinion, the idea of war guilt, and so on.

Even if Momigliano is right in his cautiously stated view that the inadequacy of Western historiography in this field can be explained by the influence of Greek and Roman historiography—I do not discuss that—a crucial point emerges. Hardly a month goes by without another article on the causes of this or that Ancient war, and still no one (or scarcely anyone) turns to the "all-pervading factors." The matter of generalization lies at the root of this neglect. A thorough study of, say, the role of public opinion must end with conclusions, big generalizations, and it may even begin with them. The causes of a single war, on the other hand, customarily are studied in isolated episodes, and it is assumed that therefore the subject is a concrete study of particular events, the historian's proper business, because it is essentially free from generalizations, given the usual warnings about prejudice, about every man's being a product of his own time, and the like. I suggest that there is a fundamental fallacy here, that behind the carefully "objective" correlating of events, in which no connections are made other than those dictated by "common sense," there lurk generalizations as sweeping as those which are sedulously avoided, usually the biggest of them all, that war is "a natural fact like birth and death." These generalizations are no less sweeping or "perverse" for being unexpressed and undiscussed; they are merely less defensible, less likely to rest on Greek or Roman economic, social, religious, and psychological factors, more likely to rest on contemporary factors as the individual historian accepts them (by habit, not by reflection) in his role as an individual in his own society (not in his role as a reflecting historian); and, therefore, they are less objective than the avowed generalizations which he dismisses as subjective and unverifiable.

In sum, in this third type of generalization, precisely the same situation prevails as in the other two. The alternative which is presented, usually by implication but often enough (especially in book reviews) by sharp assertion, between generalization and no-generalization (or "little generalization") turns out not to be that at all. Every attempt, no matter how cautious, to order the unique events of history in some fashion—by classification or by interrelation—entails as much generalization as any attempt frankly to state general propositions about public opinion and war or the effects of slavery or the decline of the Roman Empire. Epistemological and metaphysical considerations apart, every historian is plunged into all-pervading causes the moment he goes beyond mere naming or counting or dating. The illusion that he can draw essential distinctions of the kind I have been trying to examine serves merely to stultify him. It does not make him more objective, more circumspect, more of a historian (and surely not a better historian).

III

Nothing I have said so far bears specifically on *Ancient* history, as distinct from any other history, Medieval or Modern, Eastern or Western. Does the study of Ancient history have special qualities or characteristics which give some kind of twist to the problem of generalization or require special approaches?

Starr (p. 17) says that "the peculiar qualities of Ancient history . . . probably lead scholars in that field to generalize more often than would be required in fields where factual evidence is more abundant and less digested." This belief would undoubtedly receive wide assent. Neither Starr nor anyone else has assembled any statistical evidence on the point, and it would therefore be futile to try to defend or challenge the statement on the question whether it is a fact that Ancient historians "generalize more often" than Modern historians. But I believe it needs to be challenged on its reasoning. That Ancient historians have a smaller body of source material than most historians and that they must rely much more on belles lettres and archeological finds and proportionately less on documents cannot be denied. It follows that they are more concerned with textual criticism and with material objects, that they often have less control over the reliability of a source, that they must often depend on a single statement by a single author, that there are greater gaps in the chain of data—in short, that they must more often guess and hesitate and qualify and end with a *non liquet*. But what have any of these things to do with the *frequency* of generalizations as distinct from their greater or lesser probability? Do Ancient historians draw more generalizations about slavery, for example, than do historians of the American South? On the contrary, I think they tend to draw fewer (and, sometimes, worse ones) precisely because of the limitations imposed by the evidence.

One should not confuse extrapolation and inference with generalization. In dealing with such factors as population or prices, the Ancient historian lacks the material for a series. Therefore he extrapolates more freely—but that does not mean that he generalizes more freely. On the contrary—again, as with slavery—the tendency is to throw up one's hands in despair at the lack of evidence. Or consider this example of inference: We know that in Attica at the beginning of the sixth century B.C. there was a deep agrarian crisis, which Solon failed to solve, whereas in the fifth century the small-farmer class was numerous and, if not prosperous, at least relatively secure; some historians, therefore, infer that the tyrant Peisistratus redistributed a fair amount of land, although not a single existing source says so. Whether right or wrong, this inference is no more than a kind of extrapolation, working from one isolated episode to another* (much like a discussion of the causes of the Peloponnesian War). Probably Ancient historians are forced to this kind of reasoning oftener than others. But such an inference is not a generalization; insofar as it rests on generalizations, the situation is no different from what I have discussed in the previous section of this paper. There is nothing peculiar to Ancient history in the reasoning process.

Only in one respect, perhaps, does the Ancient historian face a rather special (though not unique) problem. Gaps in the evidence send him (should send him more often than they do, I may say) to other societies and periods for help. This is a legitimate procedure even for historians with much more abundant material, and it raises the familiar problems inherent in all comparative social analysis. Those I shall not discuss, but I think there is something rather special in the field of Ancient history, namely, that the classificatory generalizations and the underlying assumptions are derived in very large part from more or less recent experience. How much writing about Ancient economics, for example, assumes without discussion that trade and money have characteristics and impacts which are universally the same, except for differences in quantity or scale? The answer will be obvious to anyone who has read the modern literature on, say, Aristotle's brief discussion of exchange in the fifth book of the *Nicomachean Ethics*.

A generation ago Johannes Hasebroek, influenced by Max Weber, urged a reconsideration of the accepted assumptions about Ancient economics. His work had serious defects, but he was neither corrected nor answered on the central issues; he was crushed and dismissed, sunk without a trace. The remarks by the late A. W. Gomme are typical:

* [See the article by Gottschalk (pp. 117–18) for another example of "working from one isolated episode to another."—EDITOR.]

Hasebroek has to admit of course that Athens imported most of the corn and almost all her timber. He often makes a point that these were necessities; and somehow or other persuades himself that there is some essential difference between trade in necessities, in articles of primary consumption, and other trade. . . . We might go indeed further: one of Hasebroek's main arguments is that the policy of ancient states was never determined by commercial considerations—neither foreign nor internal policy; yet a country dependent on supplies of *necessities* from abroad would, one might suppose, be more likely to take trade into consideration than one which traded in non-essential goods. . . . The Greeks were well aware that imports and exports must in the long run, somehow, balance.[11]

Gomme's rejoinder is usually cited as sufficient dismissal of Hasebroek's work. If there is any doubt about the source of Gomme's economic ideas, it is removed a few pages later when he offers a longish argument, obviously derived from Adam Smith, to support the certainly erroneous contention that the Greeks "were perfectly familiar with the principle of sub-division of labor." Gomme's argument is exactly the kind of modern argument his one source, Xenophon, *was not making*. The very few Ancient writers who mention division of labor at all do so in a context and from a point of view which are essentially different from Adam Smith's. They were interested in the quality of manufacture, not in quantity or efficiency. Indeed, the very notion of "efficiency" is one of the best examples of a modern concept which, though taken as self-evident, turns out to be missing (in such contexts) throughout Antiquity.

If I am right, if it is the case that much of the subsurface generalization in Ancient history comes from outside, so to speak, then the Ancient historian is placed under a particular burden, one which is made still heavier by a contingent factor. Ancient history is unique in Western history (but has parallels in Middle and Far Eastern history) in that its professional practitioners are by long tradition often men who are not in the first instance historians at all but men trained in language and literature who call themselves Classicists (or Hellenists) and Classical philologists, epigraphists, and papyrologists. In raising this point, I make no suggestion that there is something arcane about history or even that it requires technical training in the same sense in which the natural sciences do. The implications lie in two other directions.

[11] "Traders and Manufacturers in Greece," in *Essays in Greek History and Literature* (Oxford: Blackwell, 1937), pp. 42–66.

First, there is an unmistakable tendency for Classicists, steeped as they are in the literature of Greece and Rome, to follow the lead of Ancient writers, and particularly of Ancient historical writers. The example of the causes of wars has already been given. Another is the characteristic remark that since one must "rely . . . mostly upon Thucydides for an account of the Peloponnesian War . . . independent generalization will be difficult" (see pp. 4–5 above). I agree that Classicists find it difficult, but I believe that the reason is not the one given but rather a mind-set, a deeply rooted value-judgment which, consciously or not, inhibits and even prohibits "independent generalization" (that is, a different explanation). When Cornford argued that the Peloponnesian War was primarily due to economic causes, the immediate reply was that Thucydides was unaware of such causes. Cornford was probably wrong in this particular argument, but the silence of Thucydides is no proof against him. Hindsight is more than a subject for bad jokes; it is shorthand for the truth that further experience may, and often does, provide understanding which contemporaries missed—in other words, for new and better generalizations.

Second, Classicists by definition do not have the habit of thinking about history and historical problems other than those on which they happen to be working, do not, by and large, even read history (in a serious way) outside the Ancient field. Their general historical views, in a sense, are fixed in their schooldays (like their economic ideas), and those make up their basic assumptions, their subsurface generalizations, from which they proceed to classify and order events and institutions of the Ancient world. Their independent study is restricted to the superstructure and is not often checked by re-examination of the substructure which came from the outside. It was not without justification that Professor E. R. Dodds wrote in the preface to *The Greeks and the Irrational*:

> To my fellow-professionals I perhaps owe some defense of the use which I have made in several places of recent anthropological and psychological observations and theories. In a world of specialists, such borrowings from unfamiliar disciplines are, I know, generally received by the learned with apprehension, and often with active distaste. . . . I see here good reason to be cautious in applying to the Greeks generalizations based on non-Greek evidence, but none for the withdrawal of Greek scholarship into a self-imposed isolation. Still less are classical scholars justified in continuing to operate—as many of them do—with obsolete anthropological concepts.[12]

---

[12] (Berkeley and Los Angeles: University of California Press, 1951), p. viii.

To the objection that Dodds is talking about something else, about the relationship between history and *other* disciplines, I reply that for many Classicists history is in effect another discipline. No doubt few will go so far as to offer an apologia like this:

> I realize that the subject matter of this book belongs to a field of research more appropriate for a trained jurist than for a general student of Hellenic antiquity. . . . Nevertheless, in studying Athenian private law the novice has one advantage which is denied to the professional. He can approach the subject free from all preconceived notions derived from other legal systems.[13]

But, apart from the astonishing conception of human knowledge which is implied (things learned are condemned as misleading preconceptions), this statement does reflect much actual practice. What is "a general student of Hellenic antiquities"? No historian of France (or Germany) is likely to dismiss his professional qualifications and call himself "a general student of French (or German) antiquities." The difference expresses the peculiar situation in Ancient history.

Common sense is no substitute for professionalism. Let me explain what I mean by *professionalism*. When the late Professor W. L. Westermann wrote, "Serious revolts of slaves did not occur during the period 500–320 B.C., which is a significant commentary upon the generally mild treatment of slaves during that time," he implied a common-sense generalization—that slaves revolt when they are treated harshly, not when they are treated mildly.[14] It happens to be, almost certainly, a false generalization, as a study of slavery in other societies reveals. As before, however, the substance of the generalization is not what concerns me but the manner of reaching it. Of course, I cannot pretend to be able to recapitulate Westermann's mental processes when he wrote that sentence, but the practice is common enough. We all do it. Given fact A—in this instance the almost total absence of slave revolts for two centuries—fact B is at once linked with it as an obvious explanation. What I mean by *professionalism* is, among other things, the habit of mind, which comes from experience with historical

---

[13] John V. A. Fine, *Horoi, Studies in Mortgage, Real Security and Land Tenure in Ancient Athens* (*Hesperia*, Supp. IX, 1951), pp. v–vi.

[14] *The Slave Systems of Greek and Roman Antiquity* ("Memoirs of the American Philosophical Society," Vol. XL [Philadelphia, 1955]), p. 18. In a clever tour de force, Paul F. Lazarsfeld said all that needs to be said about common sense in the opening pages of his "The American Soldier—an Expository Review," *Public Opinion Quarterly*, XIII (1949), 377–404. See p. 120, n. 4 below.

study and reflection, that sends up a warning light every time one makes such a connection. Professionalism tells a historian what questions to ask, not what answers to give.

IV

Obviously no historian can be asked to make a systematic personal study of every term, concept, assumption, and interrelation he employs. If he were, he could never accomplish anything. The conclusions I draw from what I have said are merely: (1) historians generalize all the time at the beginning and in the course of every study they make, and the more conscious they are of this, the more control they will have over their generalizations; (2) since generalization is inherent in the work of the historian, it is absurd for him suddenly to become "cautious" and to refuse to generalize at the end of a study.

Ultimately the question at issue is the nature of the historian's function. Is it only to recapture the individual, concrete events of a past age, as in a mirror, so that the progress of history is merely one of rediscovering lost data and of building bigger and better reflectors? If so, then the chronicle is the only correct form for his work. But if it is to understand—however one chooses to define the word—then it is to generalize, for every explanation is or implies one or more generalizations. There is a curious fallacy in many minds that the whole issue is a product of the late nineteenth century, stimulated simultaneously by modern physical science on the one hand and by Marxism on the other. Let us grant the impact of both—on history as on other disciplines. But even the most casual acquaintance with pre-nineteenth-century historians, from Herodotus to Vico or Herder, ought to leave no doubt that, each in his own way, the important historians, the ones we still read as historians (and not merely as possible sources of factual information), were deeply concerned with general truths and with the difficulties in both establishing them and communicating them, often explicitly so (in the case of Thucydides, at least, obsessively so).

What modern science and Marxism between them have accomplished is to inject unnecessary fears into the situation. The arguments go: Human behavior does not lend itself to quantitative analysis and to repeated re-examination under identical conditions, and therefore all generalizations are unreliable; Marxism distorts human behavior by reducing it to a monistic theory; worse still, like all varieties of "historicism" (in Karl Popper's sense) it is morally noxious. The reply to such arguments is too easy. Must every discipline either be physics or be abandoned? Must all generalizations be dropped because some are demonstrably untrue or even dangerous? Is a limited reliability no better than useless? Verification of historical generalizations is extremely difficult and apparently cannot be achieved, at best, beyond the establishment of a greater or lesser probability. The historian (of the nineteenth century as well as of Antiquity) can only within baffling limits employ the research techniques and the quantitative analyses available to the student of the current social scene. These are aspects of the problem of historical generalizations which require careful, detailed consideration. But such an analysis need not be made—and probably can be made least effectively—in the field of Ancient history. The issues in one historical period are not essentially different from those in another.

III. *On the Uses of Generalization in the Study of Chinese History*

BY ARTHUR F. WRIGHT

Hegel once passed this judgment upon Chinese historiography: "History among the Chinese comprehends the bare and definite facts, without any opinion or reasoning upon them."[1] If this were true, we could begin this paper with the introduction of "opinion or reasoning" about historical fact that came with the Western invasion of China; in other words, generalization in Chinese history would begin with the nineteenth century. That such is not the case I shall hope to demonstrate in Part I of this paper, where I shall discuss the origins and uses of certain generalizations that are as old as the Chinese histories themselves. In Part II, I shall turn to certain generalizations of Western provenance which came in the twentieth century to be applied to the study of Chinese history; there I shall deal also with the continuing authority of traditional generalizations in the works of twentieth-century historians, both Chinese and Western.

In speaking of *generalization in history* I shall use the term in two distinct senses. The first refers to what we do when we pick a subject matter to talk about, forming categories, selecting or constructing general terms. Examples of this mode of generalization are: "the literati," "the Chinese Empire," "time of troubles." These I shall call "labeling generalizations." The second sense in which *generalization* is here used is to refer to statements which take the form of laws. Thus, for example: "As a dynasty ages, the land tax rises"; "invasions of settled empires are preceded by periods of desiccation of the steppe"; "ideas generally proceed along trade routes." These I shall call "regularity generalizations." The two types are often interrelated in complex ways. For example, the labeling generalization "time of troubles" is a shorthand reference to Arnold Toynbee's theory regarding the decline of civilizations, and this theory is but one component of a larger system of ideas. Again, as we shall see below, a labeling generalization may be based on a complex of assumptions that a people

[1] G. W. F. Hegel, *Lectures on the Philosophy of History*, trans. J. Sibree (New York: Dover Publications, 1956), p. 135.

make about themselves and on notions of causation that are embedded in their particular world view. The distinction just made between types of generalization is rough and tentative;* it leaves out of account many of the critical problems which are of interest to philosophers of history, but it has seemed to me useful in organizing the discussion which follows.

I

It is well known that no people on earth possesses so voluminous a record of their past as the Chinese. The sum of recorded particulars for the two and a half millenniums of "formal" history writing is incalculable. To translate the twenty-five standard histories would require forty-five million English words, and this would represent only a minute fraction of the total record.[2] It is not surprising that a scholar-statesman of the thirteenth century remarked with a sigh that when he contemplated the (then) seventeen dynastic histories, he hardly knew where to begin.[3]

The careful record-keeping, the work of editing, re-editing, compilation, and annotation absorbed the energies of innumerable scholars in every generation. We may ask why the study of the past was so esteemed and what sorts of value were ascribed to it. Chinese thinkers offer many answers to these questions, but a few of these echo and re-echo down the centuries, apparently commanding widespread assent. One is that the successes and failures of the past provide sure guidance for one's own time. In a passage which may date from the beginning of the first millennium B.C., one of the founding statesmen of the new dynasty of Chou says to his prince: "We should by all means survey the [preceding] dynasties of Hsia and Yin."[4] Half a millennium later, Confucius was enjoining his disciples to follow his example and seek guidance from the ways of the ancients. The Confucian tradition, as it developed, perpetuated the injunction to study the past as a repository of relevant experience.

[2] Homer H. Dubs, "The Reliability of Chinese Histories," *Far Eastern Quarterly*, VI (1946), 23–43.

[3] A remark attributed to the Sung statesman Wen T'ien-hsiang (1236–83). See *Hsü Tzu-chih t'ung-chien* (Ssu-pu pei-yao edition), chap. 184, p. 16b.

[4] *The Book of History*, "The Announcement of the Duke of Shao" as translated by James Legge, *The Chinese Classics*, III, part 2 (Hong Kong and London: Trübner & Co., 1865), 429.

* [See the essays by Gottschalk (pp. 113–29 below) and Potter (pp. 183–92) for further discussion of types of generalization.—EDITOR.]

A second justification for history was elaborated as Confucianism evolved over the centuries into a full-blown orthodoxy sustained and reiterated by social and political institutions. This was that, whereas the Classics—the corpus of traditional wisdom—provided the guiding principles, history provided the instances and the proofs of the working of those principles in the affairs of men.[5] To add to the historical record was to participate in the great work the sages had begun, and to study history was to understand in clusters of concrete instances how men had fared when they lived in accord with or in defiance of the moral injunctions of the Classics.

Such a rationale of historical study had several corollaries. First, the historian, who was almost invariably both a scholar and a man of action, enjoyed an authority and prestige unknown in the West; it would have been inconceivable for a Chinese prince to greet a historian as the Duke of Cumberland greeted Edward Gibbon: "So, I suppose you are at the old trade again—scribble scribble scribble."[6] Second, history was an integral part of the formal education of the elite, of the state-examination curriculum, and of the formulas for self-cultivation developed by later Confucian teachers. Third, the historical mode of argumentation came to play a dominant role in all serious discussions—whether of aesthetics, military strategy, fiscal policy, or law. In the voluminous state documents of imperial China almost every memorial and every edict makes an appeal to history and tends to argue not from general principles but from precedents.

When history was given such weight in education and the conduct of public affairs and when the record grew in voluminous detail from generation to generation, the relevant lessons, the recurrent patterns, had to be isolated for use. Indeed, this process was begun by the historians' own selection of particulars and grouping of events; it was carried further by statesmen and educators who used certain configurations of events or recurrent behavior patterns in policy argument and didactic writings. This rendering-down of record into pattern is the process by which generalizations of both types specified above were formed.

[5] Chao I (1727–1814), in the preface to his famous *Notes on the Twenty-two Histories*, gives a typical statement of this view in aphoristic form: "The Classics are the principles of government; the histories are the evidences (lit., traces) of government." "Government" (*chih*) in China's holistic culture encompassed far more than political machinery and political behavior.

[6] D. M. Low, *Edward Gibbon* (London: Chatto & Windus, 1937), p. 315. There are other versions of the encounter.

But what governed the search for patterns? What defined the scope of generalizing activity and in turn the content of the generalizations? In the broadest terms the determinant was the world view of the historians as members of the Chinese educated elite. It was what I have elsewhere called the "self-image of Chinese civilization"—a self-image that was the property of the literati. This was not a timeless or unchanging mental set, nor was it unaffected by varieties of temperament and intellectual interests. But it contained certain radical continuities and uniformities, and we must refer briefly to some of them since they are the source of the generalizations in traditional historiography.[7]

By reason of its relative isolation China developed a high degree of self-sufficiency in technology, institutions, language, and ideas. And for long ages the Chinese elite knew of no other "civilization" in any way comparable to their own. Looking landward toward the steppe and aboriginal peoples of eastern Asia or looking across the seas to less favored island cultures, the Chinese were sustained in two views that are basic to the literati self-image. One was that China was the physical center of civilized life; the other was that China was superior to all other cultures in all spheres—manners and morals, the organization of state and society, technology and the arts, the cultivation of character and intellect; a corollary of the latter view was that China had a "civilizing mission" in eastern Asia, and this was translated into colonial and foreign policies that ranked all China's neighbors in degrees of subservience and dependence. The first of these views is crystallized in the most used term for China—*Chung-kuo* ("The Central Kingdom"). The second is reflected in an alternate term—*Chung-hua* ("Central Cultural Florescence").[8] We shall consider the connotations of these terms in our discussion below of labeling generalizations.

A second element of the self-image is the view that China enjoyed its pre-eminence because of its moral superiority. The sage rulers of

[7] For a fuller analysis of this self-image and its effects on the study of China in Asia and the West, see Arthur F. Wright, "The Study of Chinese Civilization," *Journal of the History of Ideas*, XXI (1960), 233–55.

[8] A Yüan dynasty definition puts the difference succinctly: "*Central Cultural Florescence* is another term for *Central Kingdom*. When a people subjects itself to the Kingly Teachings and subordinates itself to the Central Kingdom; when, in its clothing it is dignified and decorous, and when its customs are marked by filial respect and brotherly submission, when conduct follows the accepted norms and the principle of righteousness, then one may call it [a part of the] Central Cultural Florescence." Cf. the fourteenth-century comment by Wang Yüan-liang on a passage of the *T'ang-lü shu-i*, as quoted in Morohashi, *Daikanwajiten*, p. 293.

remote antiquity had not only tamed the land and the waters; they had set up principles for the conduct of life that had a timeless and universal validity. And interpreters of those principles, from Confucius on down, had taught men how to live by them, to perfect themselves, and to build the good society. The history of the past, properly written and properly studied, would validate those principles; great works of art and literature would directly or indirectly reveal their truth. Educated men, in their lives as statesmen or writers, were to provide living examples of these moral principles, so that lesser folk, Chinese or foreign, might be inspired to do likewise. When men deviated from the moral standards, then all manner of social discord and political chaos would follow. Eternal moral values expressed in enduring social norms were therefore believed to lie at the heart of China's greatness.

A third key element of the self-image is holism—the belief that all strains of thought, all institutions, all forms of behavior should embody and express a common set of values. Ideally the emperor, guided by the teachings of the sages, should preside over an indoctrinated officialdom who were his agents for the maintenance of harmony and uniformity throughout state and society. Artisans and peasants should be taught their place and provided with instruction in proper conduct and with minimum conditions for productive life in the shops and fields. Each subject of the emperor would know his place and his role, and the result would be a frictionless order; there would be no dissenting opinions, divisive groups, heterodox beliefs, or mass rebellions.[9]

It need hardly be said that these elements of a self-image suffered rude shocks from reality: China was often overrun by barbarians, and for half a millennium (*ca.* A.D. 300–800) innumerable Chinese embraced the values of Indian Buddhism. Men would not or could not live according to the great principles of the Chinese sages, rulers were corrupt or incompetent, society was disturbed by the strivings of power-hungry men and rent apart by mass rebellions. Yet the elements we have mentioned—along with many others—survived as part of the persisting self-image, the body of myth to which the Chinese elite returned again and again to find their way out of chaos into a new period of prosperity and peace. Let us see how they shaped some of the generalizations of traditional historiography.

[9] For an important discussion of the holistic ideal and its implications, see David S. Nivison's introduction to D. S. Nivison and A. F. Wright (eds.), *Confucianism in Action* (Stanford, Calif.: Stanford University Press, 1959), pp. 3–24.

One of the most important of the regularity generalizations in traditional historiography is the dynastic cycle. On the surface this is a life-cycle analogy: polities, like men, have their periods of birth, growth, maturity, senescence, and death. Yet these successive phases were never seen as the product of natural law or blind fate. The dynamic behind them was moral, and the lessons to be drawn from the study of dynastic rise and fall were moral lessons. In its genesis a dynasty received the mandate to rule from Heaven, which recognized the justice and promise of the new regime. And at its end a dynasty lost the mandate when its performance had flouted the moral norms and destroyed the moral basis of a good society.

If we recall what was said earlier about the rationale of history and historical study, we will not be surprised to find that historians reflected long and hard on the causes of dynastic prosperity and failure. Ssu-ma Kuang (1019–86), memorializing the throne in regard to his great comprehensive history of China, said:

Disregarding my inadequacy I have constantly wished to write a chronological history . . . taking in all that a prince ought to know—everything pertaining to the rise and fall of dynasties and the good and ill fortune of the common people, all good and bad examples that can furnish models and warning.[10]

The great historian views the rise and fall of dynasties as an established rhythm, but he implies that a wise prince can learn from past cycles to make the moral choices that will protract the prosperity of his house.

The notion of the dynastic cycle gave rise in turn to a host of related regularity generalizations.[11] For example, it was often argued that the phase of prosperity was correlated with the length of individual reigns,[12] that the influence of women at court was both a symptom and a cause of dynastic decline, that "when officials are oppressive, the people rebel"—a syndrome of decline. The "bad-last ruler" of a dynasty became a stock figure who played out his role in a recurrent pat-

[10] Translated by Edwin Pulleyblank, in "Chinese Historical Criticism" in W. G. Beasley and Edwin Pulleyblank (eds.), *Historians of China and Japan* (New York: Oxford University Press, 1961), pp. 153–54. Pulleyblank's introduction to this important symposium (pp. 1–9) is a valuable survey of Chinese historiographical traditions.

[11] For a discussion of these, see Lien-sheng Yang, "Toward a Study of Dynastic Configurations in Chinese History," *Harvard Journal of Asiatic Studies*, XVII (1954), 329–45 (reprinted in L. S. Yang, *Studies in Chinese Institutional History* [Cambridge, Mass.: Harvard University Press, 1961], pp. 1–17).

[12] *Ibid.*, pp. 339–40 and 342. A long discourse on this subject by Chao I (1727–1814) is translated.

tern of amoral behavior—thus demonstrating the justness of Heaven in conferring the mandate on the challenger, the "good" founder of a new dynasty.[13]

The dynastic cycle and its related regularity generalizations were not hypotheses for the detached interpretation of historical events. Rather they comprised a symptomatology of political life which provided rulers and statesmen with material for political diagnosis and prescription. Moreover, when the symptomatology became the basis of behavior for those in power, their actions tended to sustain the regularity. For example, when Chinese statesmen thought they discerned the classic symptoms of dynastic decline, they began to qualify the support they gave to the ruling house and thus contributed to its ultimate collapse.

"Dynastic cycle" implies for the Westerner sequences of political events, but the persistent holism that was part of the self-image of Chinese civilization meant that the phases of the cycle were thought to be reflected in all areas of culture—creativity in poetry and painting, the ethos of the peasant villages, the morals and mores of the elite, the tone and tenor of popular songs and drama, the rise and fall of the price level. It is not surprising, therefore, to find regularity generalizations that correlate effete or overornamented literary styles with dynastic decline. Vapid philosophizing ("empty words"), obscene or subversive popular songs, moral slackness, and greed among the elite were similarly correlated.[14]

In the major regularity generalization that is the dynastic cycle and

[13] See Arthur F. Wright, "Sui Yang-ti: Personality and Stereotype" in Arthur F. Wright (ed.), *The Confucian Persuasion* (Stanford, Calif.: Stanford University Press, 1960), pp. 47–76. A characterology of the "bad-last ruler" is presented on p. 62.

[14] There were noted historians who felt that the emphasis on dynastic history distorted the record of China's past. One of the greatest of these was the thirteenth-century scholar Ma Tuan-lin, who wrote in the preface to his institutional history of China:

"Thus from the Ch'in and Han down to the T'ang and Sung, the regulations concerning rites, music, warfare, and punishments, the system for taxation and selection of officials, even the changes and elaborations in bureaucratic titles or the developments and alternations in geography, although in the end not necessarily the same for all dynasties, yet did not suddenly spring into being as something unique for each period.... Therefore to understand the reasons for the gradual growth and relative importance of institutions in each period, you must make a comprehensive and comparative study of them from their beginnings to their ends and in this way try to grasp their development." Translation in Wm. T. deBary (ed.) *Sources of Chinese Tradition* (New York: Columbia University Press, 1960), p. 501.

in all its corollaries we see the formative influence of the self-image, notably the holistic ideal, the belief in moral dynamics and a pronounced Sinocentrism; as Professor Lien-sheng Yang points out, traditional discussions of the cycle focused on factors at work in the "Central Kingdom" and ignored or underrated alien influences.[15]

The labeling generalizations are similarly related to the traditional self-image. Here we can discuss only a few examples. The two words for *China* mentioned earlier are among the most potent and persistent generalizations of this type. "Central Kingdom" (*Chung-kuo*) and "Central Cultural Florescence" (*Chung-hua*) are old and persisting generalizations about China's place in the physical and cultural universe. In the beginning *Chung-kuo* was probably conceived as an embattled island of high culture amid the surrounding barbarians, but as that culture spread and the Chinese empire took shape, the term implied more—the physical center and pivot of the cosmos; the radiating center of all the arts of civilized life; the rightful center of power legitimately used to chastise peripheral peoples who posed a threat, were restive in their proper subservience or resistant to China's efforts to civilize them; the center to which less fortunate people came to learn and from which they returned to improve their own backward states. The term thus implied a galaxy of generalizations regarding China's centrality—ideas that shaped the understanding and writing of history. Evidence of the influence of such ideas is to be found on every hand—in the organization of historical works which give little attention to "barbarians" and then only in minor sections toward the end of the work, in the kinds of arguments statesmen make in time of military or cultural threat from without, in modes of address to foreigners, in cartography, and in symbolic representations of the Chinese universe. As we shall see in Part II of this article, this generalization continues to have great influence on recent historical writings.

A second variety of labeling generalization may be illustrated by the term *feng-chien*, by which the Chinese historian meant a division of political power over land and people between an overlord on the one hand and local lords on the other. The set of institutions which embodied this division of power was sometimes accorded a more ancient pedigree, but it was given its "classic" form—later much idealized—in the Chou Dynasty, whose traditional dates are 1122–221 B.C.[16] In the

[15] Yang, p. 333.
[16] See Derk Bodde, "Feudalism in China" in Rushton Coulborn (ed.), *Feudalism in History* (Princeton: Princeton University Press, 1955), pp. 49–92.

latter year the system—by then long decayed—was swept away and unified empire began. Thereafter historians and statesmen when they contemplated, whether with alarm, nostalgia, or hope, the resurgence of local hereditary power, often identified it as a variety of the classic *feng-chien* system.[17] By some it was looked back to as an ideal hierarchy—an expression, we would say, of the holistic ideal. By others, in later times, signs of its resurgence were regarded as retrogressive, a threat to the power and stability of the Central Kingdom. Yet for all who used it, it was a labeling generalization identifying an institutional complex or fragments thereof as conforming to a known pattern. We shall refer to the strange later history of this generalization in Part II.

A third variety of labeling generalization in traditional historiography is closely related to a fundamental characteristic of Chinese thinking and literary expression. This is the tendency to deal in paired opposites or paired complements, to speak of "successes-and-failures" instead of "vicissitudes," of "Heaven-and-earth" instead of "the universe." There are many theories concerning the origin of this proclivity, but evidence of it is to be seen in almost every Chinese utterance.[18] In the writings of historians and statesmen such terms imply a recurrence of like phenomena, place an event in a class of events occurring repeatedly through time past. For example, the term *chih-luan* ("government and disorder") subsumes most of political history and carries the implication that the one phenomenon alternates with the other. *Hsing-shuai* ("prosperity and disaster") is parallel in its meaning and implications. Of a slightly different order are such pairs as *hun-chün* and *pao-chün*, terms for bad rulers of two different classes: the muddleheaded and the tyrannical. To use one of these terms is to place the named ruler in a specific class, of which there are other examples in other historical settings, and at the same time to assert that he does not belong to the alternate class.

Some of the labeling generalizations applied to specific historical situations are terse, apodictic statements which imply a regularity, a fixed linkage between two orders of events. An example of this is *kuan pi min pien* ("officials oppress, the people rebel"). The word order suggests that the first is the cause of the second. Another example is

[17] See Edwin Pulleyblank, "Neo-Confucianism and Neo-Legalism in T'ang Intellectual Life," in Wright (ed.), *The Confucian Persuasion*, pp. 99 and 102–3.

[18] See, for example, Marcel Granet, *La pensée chinoise* (Paris: La Renaissance du Livre, 1934), pp. 56–82, 115–48, and *passim*; Nakamura Hajime, *The Ways of Thinking of Eastern Peoples* (Tokyo: Japanese Commission for UNESCO, 1960), pp. 166–297 *passim*.

nei-luan wai huan ("internal disorder, external disaster"), which suggests, though it does not specify, that disorder within the Central Kingdom is often (if not invariably) followed by invasion or pressure from beyond the frontiers. In both these cases, the phrases are used to identify recurrent situations. They are thus labeling generalizations with implications of regularity.

Perhaps enough has been said to suggest the range and some of the types of generalization employed in traditional Chinese historiography and to show that it was not limited, as Hegel believed, to "bare and definite facts." In some of the examples we have pointed out specific linkages to elements of the literati self-image, but in all we have said it should be obvious that these generalizations are bound tightly to a single culture. There is no comparative reference of the type which we find in Ibn Khaldun or among eighteenth-century European historians before "progress" focused their attention inward upon Europe itself. The Sinocentric view of history and its regularities was not to change until, in recent decades, Chinese culture itself was riven by the expanding West.

II

The generalizations we have thus far discussed found their claims to validity and persuasiveness in the institutions of a great civilization and in the ideas which sustained and rationalized them. By the early twentieth century the institutional structure was disintegrating under the impact of internal decay and assaults from the West. And as crisis deepened, there began a fevered search for new values, for ideas that would help men understand their desperate plight and point the way to a better future.

Historians shared with other self-conscious Chinese the emotional and intellectual need to find new ways to locate themselves in time, space, and culture. The Confucian tradition had once provided a total view, and this was now discredited. Traditional historiography, for all its limitations, had provided methods of sorting, labeling, and interpreting the mass of particulars about China's past. Most of these methods came now to be regarded as anachronistic—as outmoded as the Confucian world view itself.

For another modernizing people such as the Turks, whose historical records covered a shorter span and whose devotion to the historical mode of explanation was less strong, the need for a new historiography was much less acutely felt. In twentieth-century China the historian retained something of the prestige and the authority he had enjoyed in the long centuries of empire. There was pressure on him to provide a new past for a new future, to draw new lessons from the long record of history—lessons that would give the Chinese their bearings and a sense of direction in a vastly changed world. And historians were to do this not in the quiet of well-run universities but in a maelstrom of crisis and war. As one would expect, traditional interpretations of man and society were rejected outright by the bold, modified by the less venturesome, and clung to with desperate nostalgia by a diminishing few.

In the early borrowings of Western historical methods and theories it was the more limited techniques which could be most readily adopted. For example, Western methods of textual criticism could be easily grafted onto a mature Chinese philology. But the Chinese discovery of comparative history and comparative sociology was revolutionary in its effects on historical studies. As one of the great modern historians said: "Our eyes have been opened to a new world of hitherto uninvestigated and unorganized materials; questions which once were believed to have no significance now take on an entirely new meaning."[19]

The discovery of new ways to understand China's past was but one aspect of the great period of intellectual ferment and experimentation that began in 1919. Concepts and systems of ideas from Montesquieu to Marx to Dewey were eagerly studied and debated among the intelligentsia. Historians were caught up in this "tide of new thought" and adapted a wide variety of Western ideas to the study of China's past. The mere translation of these ideas into Chinese had far-reaching effects on how they were understood and how they were used. Sir Charles Eliot once remarked: "The most imposing definitions of Herbert Spencer seemed naked, shivering and unfledged when rendered in the austere monosyllables of Cathay."[20] This effect, which

[19] Ku Chieh-kang, preface to the *Ku-shih pien* ("Symposium on Ancient Chinese History"), Vol. I (Peking: P'u-she, 1926), trans. Arthur W. Hummel, *The Autobiography of a Chinese Historian* (Leyden: Brill, 1931), p. 161. For a useful survey of trends in modern Chinese historiography see J. Gray, "Historical Writing in Twentieth Century China: Notes on Its Background and Development," in Beasley and Pulleyblank (eds.), *Historians of China and Japan*, pp. 186–212.

[20] Quoted by Sir George Sansom in his address at the Annual Ceremony of the School of Oriental and African Studies, the University of London, 1956; see the *Report of the Governing Body* . . . (London: The University, 1956), p. 81. I have touched on this general problem in "The Chinese Language and Foreign Ideas," in Arthur F. Wright (ed.), *Studies in Chinese Thought* (Chicago: University of Chicago Press, 1953), pp. 286–303.

one can see in the first Chinese efforts to use Western historical terms and theories, was not simply the result of translation into a strange language. It came, perhaps more importantly, from the fact that these ideas were discussed without their contexts, their intellectual antecedents, and the implicit qualifications that accompanied their use in the culture that had produced them. Neologisms were created or borrowed from the earlier modernizing Japanese, and suddenly there were Chinese words—labeling generalizations—for a variety of phenomena first isolated in Western history. They were pressed into service immediately for the urgent task of reinterpreting China's past. But, for the reasons just suggested, they were used falteringly, and Chinese history was strained and warped by being suddenly forced into categories developed to explain a very different history. Modern Chinese historians were sensitive to the defects and distortions that resulted from many of the experiments with Western categories but continued to be inspired by the possibility of perfecting them through trial and error. The most courageous and persistent historical scholars have succeeded in refining and adapting these categories, and the future of indigenous historiography seems to lie with this small embattled group. For the majority, a slow, stumbling advance that at best made sense only of limited data on limited topics was too arduous a course, especially under all the pressures these men were subject to. What they wanted was a total theory or scheme that would equal in comprehensiveness the Confucian system of an earlier day. The case of Fan Wen-lan, recently the high panjandrum of the historical sciences in Peking, illustrates the progress of a timid mind from one closed and total system to another. As late as 1933 Fan, in contrast to his innovating colleagues, was comfortably writing within the conventions and categories of traditional historiography. In 1941, a few years after his flight to Yenan, he published *A Short General History of China* that reveals his complete acceptance of Marxist theory as authoritatively interpreted by Mao Tse-tung.[21]

Thus twentieth-century Chinese historians borrowed methods, then concepts, and finally systems from the West. Yet the hidden power of tradition was strong. It was present on every page of the documents they used; it was embedded in the terminology of historical discourse; certain of its values were subtly reinforced by the sentiments of modern nationalism. When we come, later in this section, to

[21] I am here indebted to Dr. Kai Yu Hsü's excellent paper, "The Historiography of Fan Wen-lan," presented to my graduate seminar in Chinese history in 1958.

illustrate the types of generalization which emerged in modern Chinese historiography, we shall find in every case a complex blending of Chinese tradition and borrowings from the West.

The handful of Western scholars who began in the twentieth century to concern themselves with Chinese history naturally came to their subject from a different vantage point; yet in many ways their approaches were remarkably close to those of their Chinese colleagues. There are many reasons for this, but we shall mention only a few of the most important. First, Sinology as a Western discipline had been remarkably subject to the literati self-image of Chinese civilization, and Western historians, schooled in Sinology, were only slowly able to free themselves from its influence.[22] Second, the Western historian developed empathy for China, its past and its modern problems—an empathy which drew him close to his Chinese colleagues. Third, the Westerner, with his limited control of sources, was bound to depend in large measure on the choice of problems and the interpretations of leading Chinese historians, especially since many of these problems and interpretations were derived from Western traditions. Finally, many historians, both Chinese and Westerners, were drawn into ideological conflicts and were led to make more or less qualified commitments to one of the competing systems of ideas—systems that were not simply analytic but also prescriptive.

But, having specified these similarities, we should note a striking difference. The Westerner was even more appalled at the complexity of China's past and at the mountains of accumulated documentation than was his Chinese counterpart. He was a stranger in a strange land. Professor David S. Nivison has described some of the Westerner's special problems:

To the extent that many European historians have been satisfied with an ideal of writing history "as it actually happened," this ideal was probably sustained more than was realized by the Western historian's familiarity with his milieu. He was able to coast along on countless small-scale generalizations, intuitions, human insights, which were sufficiently reliable in *his* form of society, without being aware that he was using them. In other words he is constantly in minute ways connecting and explaining in terms of each other facts, events, actions, circumstances, from a tacit assumption that the people he studies are being reasonable in his sense of reasonable or unreasonable in comprehensible and

---

[22] For a fuller account of this phenomenon, see my article "The Study of Chinese Civilization," cited in note 7 above. [Cf. Finley's remarks above (pp. 31–33) on the Classicist and the Ancient historian.—EDITOR.]

familiar ways. In China, to a disturbing extent, this subconscious stratum of historical reasoning failed to work. The historian of European or American background and training approaching China has therefore tended to grasp at or throw together theories, often distorted projections of broad situations occurring in the European or American historical picture, which would fill the gap by enabling him in at least a loose, informal way to explain human behavior and utterance which tend to be opaque to intuition.[23]

Thus the Western historian of China was tempted to work his concepts and his theories to the limit—first, to relate those widely separated phenomena of which he might have detailed knowledge and, second, to "make sense" of Chinese history in a Western language for a Western readership. It is from these two groups of historians, those in China and those in the West—with their many common preoccupations and significant differences—that the generalizations of modern Chinese historiography have come. It should be noted that in both groups there is a range from the bold theorizers to those who make cautious and selective use of a few interpretative concepts. Let us turn now to some illustrative generalizations that are the product of both Western and Chinese efforts to understand Chinese history in new ways.

In discussing illustrative generalizations we shall first consider the dynastic cycle in its modern forms, then certain labeling generalizations of both Western and Chinese provenance and finally regularity generalizations that are derived from broad general theories of history and society.

The dynastic-cycle generalization and its corollaries in their traditional form have not disappeared from historical writing. Here, as in other examples we shall introduce, the break with tradition has not been sharp, complete, or uniform. In historical writings we still find elements of the traditional symptomatology of rise and decline; textbooks and institutes for historical research still retain the division of history by dynasties. But two developments have had far-reaching effects on this generalization. One is, broadly speaking, an interest in historical process, an interest that stresses continuous and cumulative change in such newly defined fields as social history, economic history, and intellectual history. Dynastic periodization was often retained, and a typical monograph title would be *T'ang-tai she-hui shih* ("A

[23] Unpublished memorandum, "Some Preliminary Reflections on Generalization in History" (Stanford, Calif., 1958).

Social History of the T'ang Period")—the period a labeling generalization from the older historiography, the subject matter newly identified and labeled with a new concept introduced from the West. The effect of this change was to de-emphasize political-dynastic events and to work toward continuous histories of one or another nexus in the historical process.

While this trend developed, historians—both Chinese and Western—turned to the dynastic cycle with fresh perspectives. It was no longer of interest as a guide to the making of choices by those in power or as exemplary instances of the working of the principles of the sages. But dynastic transitions remain as problems in the study of Chinese history, and modern historians have used dynastic-cycle generalizations as working hypotheses for the analysis of those transitions. The result has been a steady flow of new studies—most of them focused on a particular dynasty—which add new dimensions to our understanding of dynastic rise and fall.[24] The recording of portents of doom has been critically examined and correlated with political and social events; the relation between the rise of land tax and the fall of dynasties has been critically examined; so also the incidence of floods and drought in relation to dynastic strength and weakness. Peasant revolts, traditionally viewed as symptoms of dynastic decline, have been intensively studied, and variety in leadership, social base, and ideology has been revealed. Dynastic change is no longer viewed solely in terms of Chinese events but is related to the influences and invasions of alien peoples.[25] Today the dynastic cycle is viewed as a cluster of regularity generalizations, many of them limited to specific periods. It has a far

[24] For English digests of samples of these new works, see John de Francis and E-tu Zen Sun, *Chinese Social History* (Washington: American Council of Learned Societies, 1956).

[25] The following are samples of the newer writings referred to in this paragraph: Hans Bielenstein, "An Interpretation of the Portents in the Ts'ien Han shu," *Bulletin of the Museum of Far Eastern Antiquities*, XXVI (1954); Wolfram Eberhard, "The Political Function of Astronomy and Astronomers in Han China" in John K. Fairbank (ed.), *Chinese Thought and Institutions* (Chicago: University of Chicago Press, 1957); Wang Yü-ch'üan, "The Rise of Land Tax and the Fall of Dynasties," *Pacific Affairs*, IX (1936); articles on the chronological and geographical distribution of droughts and floods by Yao Shan-yu in *Harvard Journal of Asiatic Studies*, VI (1942) and VIII (1944), and in *Far Eastern Quarterly*, II (1943); Vincent Y. C. Shih, "Notes on Some Chinese Rebel Ideologies," in *T'oung Pao*, XLIV (1956); Franz Michael, *The Origin of Manchu Rule in China* (Baltimore: Johns Hopkins Press, 1942); K. A. Wittfogel and Feng Chia-sheng, *History of Chinese Society: Liao (907–1125)* (Philadelphia: American Philosophical Society, 1949); Owen Lattimore, *Inner Asian Frontiers of China* (New York: American Geographical Society, 1940).

less symmetrical appearance than the classic formulations, and historians who speak of regularities in dynastic rise and decline generally use terms and concepts derived from Western thought and make due allowance for secular and cumulative changes that were as characteristic of Chinese as of any other history.

At the same time the influence of the classic dynastic-cycle formulation is discernible in a variety of historical works. The following passage from a widely used survey of Chinese history describes the later years of the great T'ang Dynasty (618–906):

> However, while outwardly the T'ang was still imposing and Ch'ang-an ... was impressive and fairly prosperous, the family of Li [the T'ang ruling house] was declining. In the luxurious life of the court, eunuchs were acquiring the control which so often presaged the end of a dynasty and spasmodic attempts at reform brought no lasting improvement. Toward the end of the ninth century ineptitude and luxury at the capital and misgovernment in the provinces led to widespread discontent and revolt.[26]

Here, among other elements, the notion of court "luxury" as a sign of impending doom is straight from the symptomatology of the classic dynastic cycle. So, too, is the rising power of eunuchs, whose role in this particular debacle was in fact less decisive than that of the regional warlords. And modern research has isolated social and economic forces that greatly modify and qualify the late ninth-century sequence of events here summarized as "ineptitude and luxury ... misgovernment ... discontent ... revolt." Again, the use of non-official sources has made us wonder whether decline was as palpable or universal as the dynastic history, written by the T'ang's successors, would have us believe.[27]

Some of the corollary generalizations from the traditional formulation continue to appear in historical writings, and the effect is sometimes incongruous. Here is a characterization of the "bad-last ruler" of the Sui Dynasty (581–618) which retains the moral judgments of the traditional characterology but introduces new evaluations derived from Western thought (I italicize the latter):

> Yang-ti had the animal courage and the ambition of Ch'in Shih-huang-ti and Han Wu-ti, but his abilities were not the equal of theirs; he was as cruelly

[26] K. S. Latourette, *The Chinese, Their History and Culture* (3d rev. ed.; New York: Macmillan Co., 1946), p. 192.

[27] For example, the accounts of the Japanese traveler Ennin as translated and interpreted by E. O. Reischauer in *Ennin's Diary* and *Ennin's Travels in T'ang China* (New York: Ronald Press, 1955).

tyrannical as Chieh [the last ruler] of Hsia and Chou [the last ruler] of Shang, but in treachery and cold-bloodedness he exceeded them. He had all the extravagance and fantastic licentiousness of [two other last rulers], but their extravagant palaces . . . did not approach the grand scale of Yang-ti's Western Plaisance and Maze Pavilion. Yang-ti was truly a *grand composite of ancient Chinese rulers*. But he had few of their good points, while their treachery and cruelty, their licentiousness and extravagance, were all embodied in him. Therefore we say that his achievement was slight and his guilt was heavy; his goodness little, his evil great. He *constituted a barrier to social development*. He was the tyrannical ruler [*pao-chün*] of Chinese history, the *criminal oppressor of the people*.[28]

The labeling generalizations from traditional historiography have also undergone drastic modification. The revolution in the Chinese written language—the shift to discursive writing in a vernacular—has greatly weakened the force of the old apodictic statements of complementary or alternating phenomena. These now appear only as clichés embedded in attenuated analytic or descriptive sentences that translate all too readily into "social scientific" English. The context of thought and discourse that gave them their force is gone forever.

A century of weakness and humiliation, 1850–1950, inspired many historians to study past periods of invasion and disunity and to reassess the influence of alien peoples on China's development. Yet there lingers a strong residue of the Sinocentric view of history derived from the literati self-image and symbolized in the words used for China. For example, in a Chinese history textbook for colleges that was first published in 1926, one finds this interpretation:

The Chinese people conquered by culture, other people by the use of military force. When other peoples overcame the Chinese by military force, the Chinese subdued them with culture. Therefore through every conflict Chinese power expanded. And, in the end, other peoples lost their identities and all were amalgamated with the Chinese. Thus, through the coalescence of numerous peoples, there has been moulded the great China ("Central Kingdom") of the present day.[29]

Echoes of the generalizations associated with centrality are to be detected also in the excellent general history of China by C. P. Fitzgerald

[28] Han Kuo-ch'ing, *Sui Yang-ti* (Changsha, 1957), p. 92. The author is unhappily caught in a web, some strands of which are stereotypes from traditional historiography and others the clichés of a vulgar Marxism.

[29] Wang Tung-ling, *Chung-kuo shih* ("A History of China") (Peking: various printings, 1926–34), p. 19.

when he speaks of "this self-contained culture" and when he states: "No territory once fully subjected to this civilisation has ever been wholly lost, and no territory permanently incorporated in the Chinese area has withstood the penetration of Chinese culture."[30]

On a more sophisticated level one finds the eminent philosopher-historian Hu Shih, in his interpretation of Buddhism in Chinese history, making the assumptions, perhaps unconsciously, that Chinese civilization is central, self-perpetuating, and self-sufficient and that foreign influences are unwonted and baneful intrusions that somehow deflect the "normal" course of development. Thus he remarks of the thinkers who worked at the reformulation of Confucianism from the eleventh century onward:

They were quite honest in their attempt to revive a secular [Chinese] thought and to build up a secular society to take the place of the other-worldly religions of Medieval China. They failed because they were powerless against the accumulated dead weight of over a thousand years of Indianization.[31]

Yet such terms as "Indianization" and "Medieval China" represent new concepts derived from the West—concepts that have no analogues in traditional historiography. Thus, generalizations of centrality, when they appear in modern writings, are modified by a new view of the world and new, largely Western, concepts of history.

The effect of Western ideas and theories of history on the traditional labeling generalization *feng-chien* has been dramatic and far-reaching. It will be recalled that *feng-chien* had been used by statesmen and institutional historians of the old order to refer, first, to the system of regionally delegated political power instituted by the Chou Dynasty and, second, to analogous systems, actual or ideal, when these were discussed in later centuries. When Chinese translators, in the early part of this century, were casting about for familiar terms in which to communicate Western history, they hit upon (or borrowed from the Japanese) *feng-chien* as a translation of "feudal." The noted contemporary historian Ch'ien Mu remarks: "To take the two characters *feng-chien* from Chinese history to translate the 'feudalism' of Western

[30] C. P. Fitzgerald, *China: A Short Cultural History* (rev. ed.; New York: Praeger, 1954), p. 2.

[31] Hu Shih, "The Indianization of China: A Case Study in Cultural Borrowing" in *Independence, Convergence and Borrowing* (Cambridge, Mass.: Harvard University Press, 1937), p. 247. For a different interpretation see chapters 4 and 5 of my *Buddhism in Chinese History* (Stanford, Calif.: Stanford University Press, 1959).

history is to fall into a serious terminological tangle."[32] He goes on to point out what many historians would now agree on—that the differences in genesis and structure between Chou Dynasty *feng-chien* and Western feudalism, however defined, are so great that they quite outweigh the similarities and make the terminological equivalence more misleading than otherwise. But the difficulties raised by the equivalence have wider ramifications.

In the historical discussions and polemics of modern China *feng-chien* was despoiled of its Chinese specificity and was loaded instead with the ideological overtones which *feudal* and *feudalism* had accumulated in the West. The tendency in recent years has been for Chinese historians to use the term in a Marxist context and to characterize one or another period of Chinese history as "feudal" in order to get China on the allegedly universal Marxist escalator of progress. This is not the decision of a historian who has somehow satisfied himself that a given period or institution is closely analogous to something in the West that has, on specified criteria, been termed feudal. It is, rather, an act of ideological commitment. The effects of this have been grotesque because it has involved historians and ideologues alike in the tortured effort to explain how great centralized bureaucratic empires can be "feudal." Such usage of the term has been sanctioned by the unimpeachable authority of Mao Tse-tung: "Chinese feudal society lasted for about 3000 years. It was not until the middle of the nineteenth century that great internal changes took place in China as a result of the penetration of foreign capitalism."[33] What has happened in the case of *feng-chien* is that it has been appropriated by a Western theory of history with claims to universal validity, and it is therefore no longer useful as a working hypothesis for the study of the institutions of the Chou period—the classical age of *feng-chien*—nor of the period *ca.* A.D. 220–589, when there was a resurgence of some of the features of the first age of *feng-chien*.

[32] Ch'ien Mu, *Kuo-shih hsin-lun* ("New Discourses on Chinese History"), (Hong Kong, 1956), p. 1. For the ramifications of the *feng-chien*–feudalism equivalence, see Bodde, "Feudalism in China," cited in note 16 above.

[33] Mao Tse-tung, *Selected Works*, III, 77, as quoted by Albert Feuerwerker in "China's History in Marxian Dress," *American Historical Review*, LXVI (1961), 329. This excellent analysis of developments in Chinese historiography since 1949 also presents observations on recent efforts to modify the crude Marxist historiography of the early years of the Communist regime. For critical summaries of the writings of important mainland historians, see Albert Feuerwerker and S. Cheng, *Chinese Communist Studies of Modern Chinese History* (Cambridge, Mass.: Harvard University Press, 1961).

When we turn to our final group of generalizations—those newly and directly taken from Western history and usually expressed in Western terms or Chinese neologisms—we come face to face with the appallingly primitive state of the modern study of Chinese history. Among the labeling generalizations used by Westerners—and by some Chinese—are those that characterize the figures of Chinese history by reference to well-known persons in Western history. The late René Grousset was one among many who made free use of this device. He referred to the first unifying emperor, Ch'in Shih-huang-ti, as "le César chinois," to Kublai Khan as "le Grand Sire," and to the emperor Yang of the Sui as "le Xerxès chinois" because his attempts at foreign conquest brought his downfall.[34] Such labels suggest that there is a class, say, of "Caesars" and that Julius Caesar and Ch'in Shih-huang-ti are members of that class. The disciplined comparative study of the traits of *homo politicus* or some other universal and definable human type may one day yield rich returns, but the practice just described is both undisciplined and misleading. What happens is that each label conjures up for the reader a stereotype in which the historical personality has disappeared behind a cliché made up of a few traits, in which one is usually dominant. To the degree that the Western figure has further dimensions for the reader these tend to pull the Chinese figure out of context and to set in motion thinking and associations the net effect of which is distortion.

A similar type of labeling generalizations is one to which Western historians of Chinese art have long been addicted. This is transfer of Western stylistic terminology to periods and genres of Chinese art. Thus Ludwig Bachhofer writes: "As a painter he was also the exponent of a neoclassicism in which many artists saw salvation from the utter destruction of form wrought by a baroque style."[35] The two terms for style in this sentence are familiar to Western readers. They are at once evocative and ambiguous when used of Western art, and whatever they may lead the reader to associate with the Chinese styles in question will be sure to mislead for the same reasons that "the Chinese Caesar" misleads.

The greatest difficulties are brought on by the use of Western theoretical terms for social classes or types of society to label Chinese phenomena. It is characteristic of such usages that they survive and

---

[34] René Grousset, *Histoire de la Chine* (Paris: A. Fayard, 1943) and *The Rise and Splendour of the Chinese Empire* (London: Routledge, 1952).

[35] *A Short History of Chinese Art* (New York: Pantheon, 1946), p. 119.

command wide assent with only limited empirical tests that might result in their proof, disproof, or modification. Furthermore, as Nivison remarks: "Historians of China lean on theoretical constructs of this kind much more heavily in getting from place to place. They tend to be constitutive in the historical exposition rather than functioning as intellectual apéritifs or concluding flourishes."[36] For example, the Chinese upper class of imperial China has been labeled a "gentry" for at least two decades, yet precise empirical studies to determine its genesis, characteristics, and composition through two millenniums are few indeed. The contrast between the situation of the Chinese historian and the historian of the West in respect to theory and proof may be dramatically seen in J. H. Hexter's review of the controversy over the nature of the sixteenth- and seventeenth-century English gentry.[37] Though sharp interpretative differences remain, all parties to that controversy are building on generations of archival, statistical, and demographic studies. Only an infinitesimal fraction of the relevant Chinese data has been analyzed, and the whole question whether the Chinese elite at any particular time can justifiably be called a "gentry" is debated on fragmentary data, hunches, and dogmatic commitments.

For similar reasons regularity generalizations concerning Chinese history that derive from the theory of "Oriental Society" or "Oriental Despotism" are hotly debated and widely challenged. This theory is far too elaborate to be summarized here, for it contains, in its latest formulation, a welter of terminology and statements of alleged regularities that can only with difficulty be reduced to a paradigm.[38] But it should be noted first of all that the regularity generalizations associated with "Oriental Society" are derived from a body of doctrine which, for its leading advocate, Dr. Karl A. Wittfogel, has great emotional and ideological authority. They are not developed out of the study of Chinese history itself; rather Chinese history—along with other histories—is used to *illustrate* the truth of the generalization. We noted earlier that China—with its old historiography in ruins and with a new historiography struggling to be born—fell an easy prey to theories with universal pretensions. The lack of a formidable body of

[36] Memorandum of 1958, cited in note 23 above.

[37] J. H. Hexter, "Storm over the Gentry: The Tawney–Trevor-Roper Controversy," *Encounter*, No. 56 (May, 1958), pp. 23–34.

[38] See Karl A. Wittfogel, *Oriental Despotism: A Comparative Study of Total Power* (New Haven: Yale University Press, 1957).

monographic studies, of intensive studies of the social and economic history of specific periods, meant that a universalistic theory rushed into an interpretative vacuum. Something of this kind occurred in the case of the Wittfogel theses.

The central thesis of this body of theory is that in China—as in other "oriental" or "hydraulic" societies—the structure of social, political, and economic institutions derives from the need for control of large-scale waterworks. This need leads to the growth of a managerial bureaucracy which is the servant of a despotic ruler. Such a society cannot change "basically," though small-scale mutations are possible. The regularities stated here have never been proved, and in the thirty years since the theory was first stated there has been only one intensive study of a delimited range of data on the nature and distribution of waterworks in China.[39] Recent studies of early Chinese agriculture suggest that it was upland farming, and it is difficult to see how this would call for large-scale waterworks and all that is alleged to follow from such a need.[40] Again, as we learn more, in the ever shifting and tentative categories of modern research—for example, the varieties of institutional growth, the secular shifts in the distribution of power—it becomes ever more difficult to reconcile them with generalizations about "Oriental Societies."[41] Meanwhile these generalizations command a considerable following and have spawned a variety of grotesque popular summaries of Chinese history and society.

Despite their defects, generalizations of the type just discussed have been constructive as catalysts. They have helped to free the historian from the weight of the literati self-image and from the historical stereo-

[39] Chao-ting Chi, *Key Economic Areas in Chinese History* (London: Allen & Unwin, 1936).

[40] Ch'ien Mu, "Chung-kuo ku-tai pei-fang nung-tso-wu k'ao" ("A Study of Northern Agricultural Products in Ancient China"), *Hsin-ya hsüeh-pao* ("The New Asia Journal"), I, No. 2 (1956), 1–27.

[41] See, for example, Frederick W. Mote, "The Growth of Chinese Despotism: A Critique of Wittfogel's Theory of Oriental Despotism as Applied to China," *Oriens Extremus*, VIII (1961), 1–41 and Denis Twitchett, "Some Remarks on Irrigation under the T'ang," *T'oung Pao*, XLVIII (1961), 175–94. Twitchett concludes his article with this statement: "Unless the investigation of the position under other dynasties shows a radically different situation, it seems to me that 'Hydraulic Despotism' in the terms in which it is conceived by Wittfogel should be consigned to oblivion, together with the equally misleading facile generalisations such as Slave Society and Feudal Society, until such time as historians have collected sufficient factual material for it to be possible to begin to draw such general conclusions. These hypotheses seem more likely to inhibit rather than to assist us in attaining a deeper understanding of Chinese social structure."

types that were its by-products. They have tended to discourage antiquarianism and to focus scholarly attention on basic problems of the nature and growth of Chinese civilization. But when such generalizations become the objects of ideological commitment, as they are in mainland China and elsewhere today, the effect is not liberating but constricting—as destructive of creativity in historical thought as orthodox Confucianism at its worst. Generalizations used as hypotheses—not asserted as dogmas—offer the best hope for the eventual development of a mature Chinese historiography that will slowly order and illuminate the millennial history of a great civilization.

IV. *Comments on the Paper of Arthur F. Wright*

BY DERK BODDE

Generalizations are man's attempts to find uniformities and regularities in his own life and in the natural world around him. Without the formulation and acceptance of countless generalizations, man could not create a stable society nor could he communicate ideas on more than a very rudimentary level.* Obviously, therefore, there is a vital need for generalization. At the same time such generalization always carries with it a grave inherent danger—the possibility that, as a brief formulaic summary of what in reality is often a complex and changing body of fact, it will only distort or oversimplify what it purports to clarify.

In such an inexact field of study as history this danger is, of course, particularly apparent. How it manifests itself in the specific field of Chinese history and what are the main sources of generalizations in this field are discussed with admirable lucidity and insight in Professor Wright's paper. In what follows we shall adopt his excellent classification of such generalizations, as based upon their derivation, into two main categories—those deriving from the self-image of Chinese civilization traditionally held by the Chinese literati themselves and those which, though initially derived from Western thought, are today often applied to Chinese history by Chinese and Westerners alike.

1. *Generalizations Derived from Chinese Thought*

The generalizations based on elements of the literati self-image discussed by Wright belong in general to four main groups—those deriving from the concept of China's central position in the world (political and cultural as well as geographical), those deriving from the concept of the dynastic cycle as the basic unit of Chinese history, those associated with the ancient Chinese political system known as *feng-chien*, and those expressed in the form of rubrics consisting of opposing or

---

* [See also the essay by Finley (pp. 21–23 and 28–29 above) for the application of this view to the historian in particular.—EDITOR.]

complementary paired verbal terms. These several kinds of generalization by no means exhaust, of course, all facets of the Chinese traditional self-image. The following are three important further examples.

The first is the concept of political legitimacy as epitomized in the labeling generalization *T'ien Ming* or "Mandate of Heaven." According to a widely held Chinese political theory, the Mandate of Heaven could and did pass repeatedly from one ruling house to another, but never, even for a moment, could it be interrupted. Nor at any one time could it be simultaneously held by more than one house or ruler. This explains the unbroken sequence of "legitimate" dynasties parading across the pages of traditional Chinese history, neatly dovetailed into one another so that not even a single year of interregnum separates them. It is also why during periods of political disunion only one of several co-existing states could be regarded as legitimate, even though, once it was destroyed, its Mandate of Heaven necessarily had to pass to a rival. In this way it was possible for even a "barbarian" dynasty like that of the Mongols to acquire eventual legitimacy by destroying all its predecessors and thus becoming sole possessor of the Mandate. In traditional Chinese historiography a rebel who succeeds in founding a new dynasty is *ipso facto* a great man, whereas one who fails to do so is portrayed as a mere "bandit." Differing but parallel sets of words are often used to differentiate the actions of the legitimate ruler from those of the "bandit" rebel, but the final rulers of dynasties, because they are responsible for loss of the Mandate, therefore tend to appear either as villains or weaklings. The distortions resulting from this concept of legitimacy, particularly in the handling of the crucial transition periods from one dynasty to another, may readily be imagined.

Another concept belonging to the traditional Chinese self-image is the overriding importance of personal morality as the deciding factor of history. The quality of a government depends in this view above all on the morals of the men who operate it, and so great is the psychic power of the ruler and his ministers that it even influences the movements of nature: a deteriorating government is marked by floods, droughts, and the like, a rising one by bountiful crops and other signs of cosmic harmony. This moralistic interpretation naturally reinforces the idea, mentioned by Wright, that "luxury" and similar evils in the court invariably accompany (and bring about) dynastic decay. The figures of history tend, consequently, to be polarized by the historian into "virtuous" and "evil" characters, and history itself becomes a "mirror" wherein men of today may see reflected moral lessons from the past.

The facts of geography, economics, and institutions, on the other hand, are not adequately evaluated even though they are recorded.

A third cause of misleading generalization lies in the traditional Chinese view of the origin of civilization. The major artifacts and institutions of civilized man, according to this view, were all created within a relatively short time and in finished form by the sages of antiquity. Before the golden age in which these sages lived there was no preparatory period of growth, and after them there has been only a gradual decline. This concept, accepted consciously or unconsciously by many Chinese and Western writers on China, has led to serious distortion in the study of early Chinese civilization. More than this, it has confirmed the view of later history as a relatively unchanging entity, punctuated only by the repetitive cycles of successive dynasties.

While recognizing the weaknesses of these and other such generalizations stemming from the Chinese self-image, we should also recognize that, like generalizations elsewhere, they often contain a modicum of truth. The concept of the centrality of China, for example, despite Wright's telling criticism, *does* rest on the historical fact that China developed in greater isolation than any other major Eurasian civilization of antiquity. The dynastic cycle, despite all strictures, *does* constitute a convenient and in many ways meaningful unit of time and should not be given up until we are reasonably certain that whatever system of periodization takes its place is really more meaningful. Likewise, court "luxury" and similar evils *do* often seem to appear—together with many other phenomena that are probably more significant —when a dynasty is going downhill. (Wright's contrary evidence [see his note 27] cited from the testimony of a ninth-century Japanese visitor is not really conclusive. The English emissary Lord Macartney, for example, was also considerably impressed with what he saw in China in 1793; yet dynastic decay, as we know, had then already begun, with the government being dominated by the notorious court favorite Ho-shen, a man responsible for enormous corruption.)[1]

A final comment before passing to the next topic is the reminder that in China, as elsewhere, generalizations derived from the self-image often exist on more than one level. Some, especially those having chauvinistic appeal, may achieve wide currency, whereas others, of a

---

[1] See David S. Nivison, "Ho-shen and His Accusers: Ideology and Political Behavior in the Eighteenth Century," in D. S. Nivison and A. F. Wright (eds.), *Confucianism in Action* (Stanford, Calif.: Stanford University Press, 1959), pp. 209–43.

more sophisticated sort, may be restricted to a much smaller group. It would probably not be difficult, for example, to match the crude generalizations quoted by Wright (p. 52) from the 1926 Chinese textbook on Chinese history with equally crude generalizations found in American textbooks on American history of the same decade. It by no means necessarily follows, however, that generalizations of this kind would in either country find acceptance among top historians.

2. *Generalizations Derived from Western Thought*

To the many excellent examples cited by Wright from Western historians—among others the application to Chinese history of labeling generalizations like "feudalism," descriptive epithets like "the Chinese Caesar," and all-inclusive socio-political theories like that of "Oriental Society"—it is again possible to add further instances. For example, as Wright himself has elsewhere remarked,[2] more than one modern scholar has subjected Chinese history to "that strange tripartite division of time which Westerners had stumbled into: ancient, medieval, and modern." Chinese philosophy has likewise been subjected to the categories and terminology of Western philosophy, and Chinese society has been variously interpreted according to the theories of Durkheim (as applied by Granet), Weber, Toynbee, Northrop, and others.

Indiscriminate transfer to China of generalizations based on Western history is clearly dangerous. Does this mean, however, that we are to avoid such generalizations simply because of their Western origin? Obviously not, for if done consistently, this avoidance would virtually eliminate the possibility of fruitful comparison between Western history and that of China or, for that matter, of any other country; each would have to be studied by itself *in vacuo*. And this vacuum would give added impetus to yet another distorting generalization long current among certain Sinologists—the idea that Chinese civilization is unique, *sui generis*, and that its norms do not agree with those of any other civilization.

What is needed, therefore, is not the wholesale rejection of Western-derived generalizations as such but rather their testing and refinement in the light of what we actually know about China itself. And this leads us to one of Wright's most important observations—the fact that modern historians, faced by the enormous time span and the

[2] "The Study of Chinese Civilization," *Journal of the History of Ideas*, XXI (1960), 233–55, esp. 248.

many poorly explored reaches of Chinese history, often seem ready to accept grandiose theory as a substitute for concrete fact. Such acceptance, of course, is especially likely to occur if the theory is one that can satisfy certain ideological or emotional needs on the part of the historian. A notable example is the practice, common in China today, of loosely labeling long periods of Chinese history as "feudal," not on the basis of careful analytical study but simply in order thereby to fit China into the all-embracing framework of a preconceived political theory. The present writer quite agrees with Wright's strictures on this practice.

On the other hand, this writer is not among the purists who would allow a correlation to be made between a term or theory of Western origin and a corresponding aspect of Chinese civilization only when a total or nearly total congruence between the two can be established. He would not, for example, agree with the opinion occasionally voiced by Western philosophers that there was no "philosophy" in pre-modern China simply because among the writings of pre-modern China what is today commonly classified under the Western-derived label of "philosophy" differs widely in content, aims, and organization from philosophy as known in the West. By the same token, he would not deny the validity of correlating the Western term *feudalism* with the Chinese *feng-chien* system of the Chou Dynasty, provided such correlation can be demonstrated through serious scholarly analysis to extend to a series of significant facts and provided likewise that not only the similarities but also the undoubted differences between the two are taken into account. Here the writer must disagree with Wright's assertion (p. 54) that "the differences in genesis and structure between Chou Dynasty *feng-chien* and Western feudalism . . . are so great that they quite outweigh the similarities and make the terminological equivalence more misleading than otherwise."[3]

It is noteworthy that when speaking of Western-derived generalizations, Wright never uses the term *self-image* as he does when referring to the generalizations indigenous to China. Why this should be so is unclear, since *feudalism* seems on the face of it to be just as much the product of a Western self-image as is the "centrality of China" that of a Chinese self-image. Perhaps, to be sure, no significant distinction is intended. And yet, to this commentator at least, use of the term *self-image* for China only, and not for the West, carries a derogatory implication. For in this context the term seems to suggest as peculiar to

[3] See Derk Bodde, "Feudalism in China," cited by Wright, p. 43, n. 16.

China various traditional attitudes, feelings, and values that are vaguely sensed rather than consciously formulated and that thus stand in unfavorable contrast to *feudalism* and other Western generalizations of the sort discussed by Wright, which are clearly the products of conscious theorizing.

Leaving aside the question whether generalizations like *feudalism* may properly be said to derive from a Western self-image, this writer would like to remind readers of the obvious fact that many other generalizations also exist in the West which unquestionably do derive from such a self-image—or rather a series of such self-images. These generalizations are less specific, less tangible, and less intellectual in formulation than those described by Wright; at first sight they may seem to have no direct bearing on the study of Chinese history itself. Nevertheless, they can in many subtle ways often significantly influence the manner in which a Westerner approaches this as well as other subjects.

It is well known, for example, that nineteenth-century Western writers on China were usually very much less favorable in their attitudes than those of the eighteenth century. What had been regarded by the Enlightenment as a land of mandarins and sages had degenerated in Western eyes by the nineteenth century into a land of coolies. No doubt this intellectual shift reflects changes occurring within China during this time, but, more importantly, it also reflects the much more profound changes simultaneously occurring in Western society itself. These changes naturally produced changes in Western man's image of himself and, by the same token, in his attitude toward the non-Western world. "The white man's burden," for example, is a late nineteenth-century Western generalization such as would have been inconceivable during the Age of Enlightenment. Inevitably it colored what many Westerners of its time had to say about the non-white world.

Self-images differ, however, not only from epoch to epoch but also between nationalities or professional groups. A British diplomat, an American Protestant missionary, and a French Sinologue might all live in the same nineteenth-century Chinese city and there write about the same Chinese subject, yet their underlying attitudes might differ profoundly. This would be not merely because of differences in their knowledge and training but also because of the differing self-images from which they started. More often perhaps than is commonly realized, modern Western writers on China continue to be influenced by these accumulated self-images from the past—in addition to which, of course, each has his own contemporary self-image. Not surprisingly,

Comments on the Paper of A. F. Wright

therefore, the generalizations of a present-day American writing on Communist China will not only differ from those of a Soviet writer but also, quite possibly, from those of a British or a Canadian writer as well.

These remarks are perhaps somewhat tangential to the main subject. Yet it may be useful to keep them in mind while examining the kinds of generalization more directly relevant to China that have been discussed by Wright. While few of us can hope to remain wholly free from distortions caused by one or another of such generalizations,* we can at least make ourselves more keenly aware of their existence, and for this Wright's paper provides a splendid introduction.

One final comment brings us back to Wright's insistence on the need for more abundant facts to balance the plethora of theories. In "The Study of Chinese Civilization," already mentioned, Wright remarks that Western Sinology has in the past expended no little effort on the accumulation of concrete facts. Too often, however, they have been facts of a scattered and incidental nature, failing to add up to anything of over-all significance. What is needed, therefore, is the channeling of future research into topics that are concrete and manageable in scope, yet that have a bearing on problems of broad general interest. From the resulting monographs it may eventually become possible to formulate generalizations that are factually secure as well as intellectually alluring.

* [For consideration of similar distortions in Western history see the essays by Starr (pp. 12–13 above) and Finley (pp. 30–31) and by Aydelotte (pp. 157–58 below) and Potter (190–91).—EDITOR.]

V. *Generalizations about Revolution: A Case Study*

BY ROBERT R. PALMER

The SSRC Committee on Historical Analysis, as I understand it, wishes to have some remarks made on the use of concepts in history, perhaps of the sort that may be made by one who has given little systematic attention to the problem but has been aware of it in the process of working on a particular piece of historical writing. For this purpose it may be that the work I am engaged in may serve as a case study. It is entitled *The Age of the Democratic Revolution*, with a subtitle, *A Political History of Europe and America, 1760–1800*, and is planned in two volumes, of which the first, on the years 1760–91, was published by the Princeton University Press in 1959. The following is drawn from experience in preparing this book and is offered with the apologies necessary in talking so much about myself but in the hope that it will at least provisionally serve a useful purpose.

I doubt that history is a social science but do believe that it should make use of concepts drawn from social science or any other useful source. In most histories, however, these general ideas will appear unobtrusively, to give meaning and relevancy to the particular. The *particular* is here taken to mean either single small items or the subject as a whole, such as the whole era 1760–1800 considered as one particular phenomenon or bit of human experience. I am here deliberately avoiding the often used term *unique*.

The original conception for a historical book, I suspect, does and should come from two altogether different kinds of sources—(1) the knowledge that workable bodies of information exist and (2) some general idea. In the present case it was known, or discovered, that a great deal existed in print, both of source collections and of historical treatments, pertaining to a dozen or more countries, which, however, no single person had ever tried to bring together. The general idea, held in advance, was that there had been a "revolutionary era" in all these countries, not adequately perceived as a "culture-wide" phenomenon in the various nationally oriented histories of the American and French Revolutions and other movements of the time. (I should perhaps make clear that terms like *culture-wide* do not appear in the book; whether or not such terms have any utility in social science, history in my opinion should be written in the ordinary language.)

There were therefore certain general ideas that antedate the composition of the book now being considered and that recur throughout it. Their role seems to have been at least threefold: (1) to provide a thesis or argument, of which the contents of the book are offered as empirical justification or evidence, (2) to give a basis for structure, or arrangement and interdependence of parts, and (3) to suggest relevancy and significance, which seems in the end to mean a relationship between these eighteenth-century events and persons now living.

The first of these antecedent ideas is that of Western Civilization as a unit. The term *Atlantic Civilization* is used at the outset but thereafter very sparingly, since it may arouse opposition or raise problems not essential for the purpose of the book. In 1955 Professor Jacques Godechot of Toulouse and I examined "Le problème de l'Atlantique du 18e au 20e siècle" at the Tenth International Congress of Historical Sciences, meeting at Rome; and some of our conclusions are taken over, but not argued, in the present book, notably the idea that the concept of an Atlantic Civilization had probably more validity in the period 1775–1825 than at any other time. The point is to maintain the existence of a certain culture area, "Western Civilization," as a zone having certain ideas and problems in common and a degree of mutuality of communications and influence. The book treats in some detail Anglo-America, Great Britain, Ireland, France, Belgium, Holland, Switzerland, Sweden, Poland, and the Hapsburg Empire including Belgium and Milan. Prussia and Russia figure less prominently. There is no explicit discussion of whether Russia belongs to "Western Civilization," but the account of the growth of aristocratic institutions under Catherine II points out European analogies. In the second volume events will be followed in the same countries, and more will be said on Germany and Italy as a whole, and on Canada, Latin America, and perhaps the Cape Colony. The attempt to use Western Civilization as the meaningful unit of inquiry is thought to have these advantages: (1) to be probably near to the truth, (2) to illuminate national histories by comparison and contrast, and (3) to have present-day relevancy in view of contemporary interest in the nature, character, and identity of Western Civilization itself.

A second general idea that antedates the book and recurs in it is that of revolution. Nowhere do I offer or commit myself to an explicit definition of this term. Its use is in part justified empirically; the American, French, Genevese, Belgian, and Polish "revolutions" form a large part of the content. Revolution is said also to be essentially a conflict or disagreement on fundamental interests and principles not reconcilable without struggle. Both or all sides in the conflict are regarded as equally real—that is, conservatism is not represented as the mere target of innovators. It is held that certain objectives, or views of society and of justice, which in some countries reached the point of outright revolution were present in other countries in a subrevolutionary way, yet recognizably in the same family of ideas, notably in the British and Irish movements for parliamentary reform and in the reforms of Joseph II of the Hapsburg empire.

Use of the concept *revolution* induced the author to face the question of the relationship between the revolutions of the eighteenth century and those of the twentieth. This question was essentially whether the eighteenth-century revolution, and the French Revolution in particular, were to be thought of as (1) a point in the genesis and growth of a continuing or "perpetual" revolution, "leading" to Marxism, communism, "totalitarian democracy," etc., or (2) a passing phase of crisis, conflict, excitement, and violence "leading" to what we understand by Western democracy. This problem is discussed briefly at the opening of the book, without claim to systematic rigor. The second alternative is favored. It is admitted, however, that there is a degree of truth in the first, the idea that the eighteenth-century revolution prefigured and in a way "caused" the twentieth-century revolution; this view is identified both with Marxist and with conservative treatments of the era of the French Revolution. It is insisted that late-eighteenth-century events were a true "revolution," that the term and concept of *revolution* has changed since then, that there are resemblances and differences between the eighteenth-century and twentieth-century revolutions, that one's attitude toward twentieth-century revolution (i.e., communism) should not affect one's attitude toward eighteenth-century revolution, etc.

A third recurring idea is that the eighteenth-century revolution was, or may be thought of as, democratic. Expecting this to be somewhat more contested, I justify it at some length at the outset, though the whole book is designed to persuade to this belief. The justification is, again, in part purely empirical: it is shown that people at the time used the word *democratic* for the new movement, in a meaningful and reasonable way, whether to favor it or to oppose it. It is shown that this was precisely the period when the nouns *democrat* and *aristocrat* were coined in the various European languages. It emerges, in the first chapter and throughout the book, that the democratic movement was primarily anti-aristocratic. The term *democratic*, I think, is by no means forced upon the reader. He may call the movement whatever he likes. He is, however, asked to believe that there was a movement, in many countries and however named, against the monopolizing of public authority by certain in-groups; against the principle that some men are called upon to rule, others to be ruled; against inheritance of position, hereditary orders and estates, legal hierarchy, family self-perpetuation, property in office, co-opting governing bodies, etc. All the ideas thus contested are referred to as *aristocracy*. With *democracy* are associated the ideas that all authority is delegated, that public officers are responsible and removable, that persons should qualify for office without regard to family, rank, or church affiliation, that no person may govern by his own right or by right of status, leadership, or "history"—with an occasional hint that communist elitism or revolutionary vanguardism are if anything "aristocratic" (i.e., modern manifestations of what the eighteenth-century revolution was against). These hints remain implicit, and many readers may miss them; there is no attempt to engage in current debate. They suggest, however, how eighteenth-century matters may be made relevant to twentieth-century matters at a level of generalization that comprises both.

"Aristocracy" is discussed in the second and third chapters of the book as characteristic about 1760 of the society established in all countries, including the Anglo-American colonies. It is described in institutional terms, partly to give concreteness, partly because it was against certain definite institutions that the revolutionary and quasi-revolutionary movements were directed. Family self-perpetuation, intermarriage, inheritance of position, and privileged or special access to government and to its emoluments or profits are found to have been common phenomena over a wide range of institutions—the governors' councils in the British American colonies, the two houses of the parliaments of Great Britain and Ireland, the parlements and provincial estates of France, the town councils and estates of Belgium, Holland, Switzerland, Italy, and Germany, the diets of Hungary, Bohemia, Poland, and Sweden. For all these the term "constituted bodies" was invented. This term became one of the principal generalizations in the whole structure of the book.*

The movement of ideas is discussed in the context of defense of and opposition to these "constituted bodies." Ideas of Montesquieu, Delolme, Rousseau, Burke, John Adams, Turgot, Sieyès, and various others are treated in this way. It is argued that ideas like the "sovereignty of the people" arose not as intellectual abstractions but as practical replies to claims of sovereignty, or at least of non-removability and non-responsibility, made by the constituted bodies. Ideas of "equality" are likewise represented as arising from the actual existing forms of inequality and in answer to the theoretical justifications of inequality and of special rights that were currently made. It is also maintained that if radical thought became unhistorical, abstract, and rationalistic, it was for the very good reason that historical argument was pre-empted and emphasized by exclusive, closed, hereditary, or co-optative constituted bodies. By this interpretation the history of ideas is, in short, woven closely into the history of real events and real conditions. The ground is thus removed from under the ancient historiographical dispute over whether the French Revolution arose from "ideas" or "circumstances"; or, in the terms of this dispute, the thesis of "circumstances" is favored, by showing that "ideas" had a constructive relevancy to real problems. I am aware that my whole book, though I hope not in an obvious or naïve way, is pro-revolutionary (and say as much, through a literary device, on the first page).

The concept of an "aristocratic resurgence" in the eighteenth century, long familiar to students of French history, is applied to Europe and America as a whole. Evidence is offered, that is, to show that the world was not only "aristocratic" but in some important ways becoming more so. The famous generalizations of Tocqueville—that history shows a long process toward equality of social conditions and that the Revolution only brought on violently what would have happened more slowly in any case—are viewed with a certain reservation. It is argued that exclusivism, aristocratic class-consciousness and emphasis on inheritance were increasing and that it was from these facts that bourgeois class-consciousness, frustrations, and social maladjustments were derived. Acute class-consciousness, along with ineffectual fiscal policies and awkward administrative and personnel recruitment systems, is represented as one of the social evils resulting from these ten-

---

* [This would be, in Finley's nomenclature, a "classificatory" generalization or, in Wright's, a "labeling" generalization: see pp. 21 and 36 above.—EDITOR.]

sions. Social mobility and legal equality are represented as desirable not only ethically or to prevent personal frustration but to make a complex society operate more effectively. The terms *integration, assimilation, segregation* are used occasionally and discreetly but purposely in the belief that these abstractions will suggest relevancy to our own time.

Around the concept of the constituted bodies and their "official" philosophers (Montesquieu, Blackstone, Burke, etc.) the whole book is structured. It is shown that these bodies, and the privileges that they claimed, were challenged from contrary directions—both by kings or other higher authorities and by the "people" (that is, persons generally outside the governing classes, nobilities, patriciates, hereditary magistracies, etc.). Much political life consisted in the self-assertion of such bodies against a king or other superior: Whig elements in the British parliament against George III, the American colonial assemblies and the Irish parliament against the parliament of Great Britain, Dutch regents against the Prince of Orange, Belgian estates against the emperor, Swedish and Hungarian diets against their kings, general council against small council at Geneva, French parlements and provincial estates against Louis XV and Louis XVI. The demands of these bodies brought certain ideas into the arena of practical politics and debate, notably the ideas of sovereignty, the constitution, true liberty, real representation, etc. The movement became democratic, according to the thesis of the book, when in various ways in various countries certain dissatisfied persons, not content merely to liberate the constituted bodies from a superior authority, wished to reconstitute or open up these bodies themselves, make them more truly "representative" or elective, and subordinate them to the "people."

It is a secondary general idea throughout the book that what we know as conservatism first appeared not as a critique of the French Revolution of 1789 or 1793 but as a defense of parliaments, estates, diets, etc., against both royal and democratic encroachments on their established position. It is shown how Burke's philosophy was formed in opposition to parliamentary reform, notably in 1784. Contrariwise, the mounting radicalism of the democratic movement, even before 1789, is explained by the rigidity of the constituted bodies and the failure of moderate or gradual attempts at change.

Another subordinate general idea is that in no case did purely middle-class or "bourgeois" reform or revolution have any success, that successful revolution occurred only where the agricultural population generally collaborated with middle-class leaders, that this occurred only in America and France, and that the failure of democratizing efforts elsewhere—in England, Ireland, the Dutch Netherlands, Belgium, Switzerland, and in a sense Hungary and Poland—was due to the apathy or weakness of the agrarian mass or to the absence of a common ground on which urban and rural persons could work together.

The dependence of successful revolution or counterrevolution on military measures becomes also a general idea in the book. The foreign military intervention against revolution in Holland, at Geneva, and in Poland is described, and its significance is pointed out for the attempt at foreign military intervention in France in 1792 and, very briefly, for the so-called Holy Alliance of 1815. The success both of revolution and of a challenged conservatism (counter-revolution) is closely related to war: the independence of the United States in the form taken in 1783 is attributed to French intervention, the success of conservatism in Holland, Geneva, Poland, and Hungary (before 1792) is attributed in large part to armed intervention; and the ground is laid for a broad consideration, contemplated for the second volume, of the issues in the European war that began in 1792. It is argued that the needs of armed conflict in America in 1776—and it will be argued in the second volume that similar needs in France in 1792—had the effect of radicalizing and democratizing the movements in those countries beyond the intentions of original leaders. The relation of French military success to revolution in the 1790's throughout western Europe is thus also anticipated.

The American Revolution is made to occupy a central place in the book. Privileges of the American colonies within the British Empire, in such matters as tax immunity and local self-rule, are compared to analogous privileges in Europe, as in Brittany, Hungary, and Belgium. The American protest against the sovereignty or "absolute" power of Parliament is put in context with rising British radicalism that made the same protest. Whether the adoption of the federal constitution of 1787 resembled the "aristocratic resurgence" of Europe of the 1780's is considered; this is related to the Beard thesis, but it is pointed out that Condorcet and others in 1788 and 1789 already regarded the new United States constitution as "aristocratic."

The degree to which the American Revolution was a true "revolution" is examined. It is held to have been revolutionary because of the repudiation of parliamentary sovereignty, the displacement and ejection of the old colonial aristocracy, the violence between patriot and loyalist, the extent of emigration and confiscation, and the successful implementation of the idea of (as it is called) "the people as constituent power." That there is and should be a power to constitute or reconstitute organs of state and that this power lies in the "people" and eventuates in a single written document or constitution drafted by an assembly for that purpose is represented as the essential or distinctive American revolutionary idea. Issue is taken with American neo-conservatives; John Adams is sharply differentiated from Burke and set up as a leading spokesman of the democratic revolution of the time.

A long chapter details the impact of the American Revolution on Europe. It is shown that this impact was very great, that it varied from country to country, that in part it was felt at a deep psychological level, heightening the expectancy of change, the sense of a new era, and the alienation and spiritual emigration from the European old regime, and that in part it was important in a practical and immediate way by helping to form a definite public opinion on political matters, with discussion on the formation of organs of government, written constitutions, and constituent assemblies. This, of course, leads into the French Constituent Assembly of 1789 and into the various such assemblies and conventions to be traced in several European countries in the forthcoming second volume.

The distinctive features of the French Revolution are set forth with some care, for although the purpose of the book is to describe a revolutionary era as a whole, there is no thought of minimizing national or other differences in a false search for uniformities. Various economic, demographic, psychological, and other explanations of the "causes" of the French Revolution are held to be of secondary value, as not accounting for the specific forms that the French Revolution took, notably its emphasis on certain political, constitutional, legal, and civic concepts. The picture of a French Revolution that began as a "moderate" and became an "extreme" movement is likewise rejected as misleading. The true problem of the French Revolution is held to be why it was so radical or sweeping at the very beginning. In a way this is a concession to certain conservative and antirevolutionary schools of historiography, but enough has been said at this point in the book on the failure of a moderate opening-up of privileged bodies, both in France and elsewhere in Europe, to make the radicalism of 1789 seem an understandable consequence of pre-existing conservatism. This radicalism of the French Revolution in 1789 again raises the question of its resemblance to or difference from the American Revolution. The two revolutions are found to be very much alike in their principles and objectives. The difference is held to lie in the intensity and strength of opposition to these principles.

The book closes with the promulgation of the new French constitution in September, 1791. The notion, frequently heard from historians, that everything in the French Revolution had already been "accomplished" by 1791 is regarded as absurd. It is held that nothing had been accomplished except on paper, that the future of the new constitution was still very much in the balance, that intervention and restoration of the old order was a possibility in France, as shown by what happened in Belgium, Holland, Geneva, and Poland, the difference being that France was big enough to defend itself against intervention. The conservatism of Britain at this time is emphasized by the failure of parliamentary reform, even when sponsored by Pitt, and by the failure of Dissenters in 1789 to obtain equality of political rights. It is held that as of 1791, everywhere in the Western world except in America, the moderate attempts at democratization had come to nothing and that the new principles had an uncertain future in France. The first volume is therefore subtitled *The Challenge*. The second will be subtitled *The Struggle* and will deal with the Western world during the Wars of the French Revolution.

It will be seen that such concepts as I have mentioned* are those arising in close conjunction with the empirical material itself. Larger concepts on causality, influence, or human nature remain purely implicit. Economic, social, and intellectual history is used to amplify what is essentially political and constitutional history; the book may therefore seem old-fashioned to some, and the subtitle, *A Political History . . .* , is included to disarm criticism from this quarter. I am sure that the material relates closely to many concepts arising in social psychology, the sociology of the family, social stratification, the theory of power and authority, of decision-making, law, moral philosophy, justice, and much else. These questions are rarely if ever explicitly canvassed. The historian's use and awareness of questions like

---

* [Several of the concepts that Palmer has mentioned (e.g., "successful revolution occurred only where the agricultural population generally collaborated with middle-class leaders" [p. 72] and "the dependence of successful revolution or counterrevolution on military measures" [*ibid.*]) would seem to fall in the category which Wright calls "regularity generalizations" (p. 36).—EDITOR.]

these, I should think, appear in the quality of his judgments and the connections he makes in dealing with his empirical material—that is, his story.

Editor's Addendum No. 1

Professor Palmer to the Committee, June 16, 1958:

... My impression is that the possibility of validity or truth in a proposition, in the natural sciences and mathematics as in the social sciences, varies in proportion as the proposition applies to posited entities, "models," and other "unreal" or abstract concepts. Of any concrete and particular social and human situation, historical, currently political, or other, I doubt whether any significant generalization can be shown by evidence to be wholly valid or wholly invalid. To put it another way, a generalization to be accepted as valid would have to be encumbered by so many *if*s, *and*s, and *but*s as to lose some of its hoped-for scientific precision.

It is, of course, a problem of generalizations in general, not merely those arising in social science. Think of the excellent generalizations in La Rochefoucauld's *Maxims:* "A bourgeois manner may sometimes be lost in the army, but never at court." "Self-interest blinds some and gives light to others." "There are bad men who would be less dangerous if wholly lacking in goodness." I think these generalizations are as valid, useful, and illuminating as any we are likely to get in social science, and about as much or as little capable of empirical verification by scientific method. They serve their purpose if they help us to understand a particular situation and enable us to communicate this understanding to others—that is, to persuade others that the view we favor is somehow more satisfactory, enlightening, or useful.

Editor's Addendum No. 2

Professor Palmer to the Committee, January 29, 1959:

The comments of [members of the Committee] seem to me pertinent, searching, incisive, important, and clearly and carefully formulated. I believe that I have some understanding of the problems they raise, as problems. I simply do not know how to go about answering them. Potter, for example, ... finds my statement ambiguous or silent on the relation between ideas and social conditions. He finds that "ideas are regarded as secondary." Perhaps they are. I do not know. I have not settled this relationship in my own mind. I expect to die without having settled it. As for "supernaturalism," I see no particular connection between its existence or decline on the one hand and either rationalism or irrationalism or humanitarianism or aristocracy or equalitarianism on the other. As for the "Atlantic Civilization," my doubts date from the Rome meeting of 1955, where I found so many British and other Europeans opposed to the concept that I concluded that it was fatuous for Americans to insist upon it. You cannot go around publicly claiming to be married to a woman who not only denies it but shudders at the thought. And where marriage can be proved at law, community of civilization cannot. . . .

As to deterministic forces and relationship between social structure and receptivity to new ideas, I agree that these are important questions, but I simply don't know what to say about them in an abstract way. As for anti-aristocratic movements in other civilizations, of course I believe that a kind of wisdom gained from the study of one has some application to another (to deny this would condemn all history and social study to sterility), but I have no idea how this applicability can be stated with . . . rigor and precision. . . .

I know, of course, about "borrowing concepts from other disciplines" for use in history; I have at times made reasonable efforts to do so, but to tell the truth I have never felt very successful. With a few exceptions, such as "social mobility" or "functional rank," there are few such concepts that I have been conscious of employing. I do not doubt the need of concepts; but, as I remarked in the letter of June 16, the concepts of social science, with certain exceptions, have not, to my knowledge, entered much more into my work than those stated in the maxims of La Rochefoucauld. As for . . . "limited generalizations that can be proved or disproved," I am also in the dark. I do not know whether propositions about human affairs can be "proved" or not. I am not so presumptuous, or naïve, as to suppose that my book, consistent, logical, and persuasive as I hope it is, actually "proves" either its main thesis or any of its subordinate points.

VI. *Generalizations about National Character: An Analytical Essay*

BY WALTER P. METZGER

Most historians object on principle to generalizations about national character. Aware that the subject has been contaminated by the claims of chauvinists and racists, they regard these misanthropic views as signs of the failure of the genre. Some would add to Edmund Burke's pronouncement that no one should indict an entire people the far more limiting declaration that no one can depict an entire people. Others would go further and assert that national character does not exist and that even to employ the concept is to incarnate a defunct myth.

Yet the curious fact remains that historians do generalize about national character. Despite their formal objections, they do refer to Frenchmen and Germans as distinctive aggregates of human beings, they do treat Spaniards or Americans as members of a class to which psychological labels can be applied. Their reasons for doing so are manifest. General statements of this kind perform important stylistic functions: they brighten drab details and help put matters aphoristically. They also ease the task of summary by tying scattered facts together. Besides being instruments of craft, these generalizations minister to public interests. Issues such as whether Russians are more Russian than Communist or whether the character of the Congolese may change are too popular and pressing for historians fully to ignore. Thus it comes about that scholarly practice accepts what scholarly theory renounces, and a venture repudiated in program is repeatedly affirmed by act.

Intellectual consistency, if not an ultimate private virtue, is an urgent professional need. In order to satisfy that need, actions should be consonant with principles. In this case it would appear that drastic cures are quite impracticable. Historians are not likely to purge their practices or, alternatively, banish every doubt. But they may find, by reformulating their theory, that they can relent their general opposition and engage in these practices with greater confidence.

A first step in this direction would be to examine two propositions conventionally advanced in this field. The first, as presented by Boyd C. Shafer in his critical study of nationalism, is that character cannot be classified by nationality because men are basically alike.[1] The second, put forward by Adam de Hegedus in his critique of patriotism, is that character cannot be classified by nationality because every individual is unique.[2] In raising these familiar objections both writers purport to be contesting the reliability of a certain *classification*. In reality each is advancing his preference for a certain *definition*. To the first writer *character* refers to attributes shared by the entire human species; to the second the word refers to attributes which belong exclusively to the self. That there can be no *national character*—no attributes shared by groups of people—is not demonstrated but given in the premises. To show that the issue is definitional, one need only note that both these authors believe that there can be national art, national drama and literature, and national political institutions. Why not then national character as well? The answer lies not in the realm of fact but rather in the realm of meanings: to these writers, character is, by definition, either idiosyncratic or universal.

To confuse the problem of classification with the problem of definition is usually to give them both short shrift. One is apt to settle or avoid them simply by the arbitrary use of words. But these problems are too pivotal to be dismissed and much too complex to be delivered to the fiat of a casual terminology. For an adequate definition of character, it is necessary to clear a ground littered by centuries of untidy usage. For an adequate classification of character, it is necessary to assess the strength of many character-shaping forces. Both problems are difficult to resolve—which is all the more reason why they should be recognized, differentiated, and treated with the deliberateness they deserve.

1. The Problem of Definition

Traditional confusions.—In the course of its long career, the word *character*, like its synonym *personality*, acquired myriad meanings, some of them mutually contradictory.[3] Derived from the Greek word meaning "to engrave," the word *character* came to stand for a sign or symbol

[1] *Nationalism, Myth and Reality* (New York: Harcourt, Brace, 1955), pp. 215–37.

[2] *Patriotism or Peace* (New York: Scribner's, 1947), p. 152.

[3] The etymology of *personality* and *character* is considered in Gordon W. Allport, *Personality* (New York: Holt, 1937), chaps. ii and iii.

indicative of a special fact and then, through evolution, for a trait or group of traits which serves to identify an individual. One fertile source of ambiguity lies in the two meanings of the word *trait*. A trait may refer to the symbol or manifestation of distinctiveness, as perceived and defined from an external viewpoint. *Character*, in this case, would refer to something social and behavioral: a role performed in society ("he acted in his character of king"), a role played in the theater ("a character in a play") or an estimate of a person formed by others ("he received a bad character from his employer"). But a trait may also refer to a reality resident in the individual, the existence of which is not contingent on outward signs and external percepts. In the aphorism "Character is what a person is, reputation is what he is supposed to be" the word *character* carries the implication of something indwelling and essential.

Within this second category of meaning additional ambiguities arise, for psychologists have seen fit to emphasize different kinds of definitive inner traits. Some have stressed inborn endowments: in the humoral psychology of the Greeks, the truly distinguishing traits have been equated with organic temperament; in Kretschmer's constitutional typology, they have been connected with physique; in other schools that have had their fashion, they have been linked to genes, to instincts, to mental faculties. Other psychologists have stressed acquired factors, including interests, phobias, tastes, attitudes toward specific objects, basic orientations toward reality. In short, the traits that have been chosen to define *character* are as multitudinous and varied as the qualities that have been chosen to describe man. But here, by way of anticipation, we note that Freud, who belongs in this second category, did much to make his view of *trait* prevail by overshadowing competitors with his canon of insight and surmise.

In addition to arguments over kind, there has been a continuous controversy over form. In German scientific discourse *Charakter* refers to a sum of traits and sometimes to their configuration.[4] In other contexts, however, the word might refer to a single trait (like miserliness or aggressiveness) which distinguishes one individual from another and defines his fundamental type. This was the sense of the word employed by literary characterologists.

Finally, normative connotations enter and further confuse the definition. In certain usages, *character* is a neutral term—thus: "His face

[4] See William McDougall, "Of the Words Character and Personality," *Character and Personality*, I (September, 1932), 4.

shows a great deal of character" (i.e., is highly individualized) or "He is known to be quite a character" (i.e., is regarded as eccentric). But in connection with certain religious and pedagogical concerns the word was and still is used evaluatively. Thus, it may refer to the possession of moral qualities—to an ability to inhibit impulse, to demonstrate self-discipline, to exercise self-reliance, to exhibit, in short, the bourgeois virtues. Metaphors of possession and construction convey this meaning of the word. One is said to have either "less" or "more" character; to be thought of as lacking character is to be harshly judged. One may have either a "strong" character or a "weak" character; here character is closely allied with will. Education strives to "build" character; here character is pictured as an edifice shaped according to plan.

Not surprisingly, the double term *national character* absorbed the mixed assortment of meanings that clustered around the noun. Social role and essential being, patterned traits and unitary traits, normative connotations and neutral connotations—all that *character* denoted, *national character* subsumed. And more besides: the leap from the individual to the group brought additional meanings into play. On the assumption that the character of a collectivity is somehow different from the individual characters of its members, it became possible to speak of a "collective soul," a "folk genius," a "group mind." On the assumption that any fact of group existence is a fact of characteral importance, it became possible to reverse the path of inference and to say, for example, that the members of a republic possessed "republican" characters or that a population in a state at war possessed a "warlike" character. This was a major step toward confusion, for by repeated derivations of this kind the list of character traits could be endlessly expanded. On the one side verging toward the mystical, on the other side toward the redundant, the spectrum of meanings of this term stretched as far as any user's imagination.

To find illustrations of this confusion and of the errors and excesses to which it led would not be a difficult task. This confusion has been present in expository writing since the time of the ancient Greeks, when Hippocrates, Herodotus, and Aristotle—a physician, a historian, and a philosopher—first guided their respective disciplines into studies of group characteristics. It can be found in many works today.[5] But

[5] For example, the American historian Henry Steele Commager (*America in Perspective* [New York: New American Library, 1947], p. xi) has recently defined national character as "the things that are done and the things that are not done, the

perhaps the most useful illustrations of it—useful because they show what must be avoided—can be found in the accounts of travelers in foreign countries written during the nineteenth century. Though somewhat outmoded in style, these works have never lost their favor; hardly a year passes, it would seem, but a new travel reminiscence is discovered or an old memoir republished. Nor are these works mere curiosities. A historian of the American people who fails to cite Tocqueville or Bryce would be guilty of glaring omissions; a student of the American character who fails to plunder Trollope or Dickens would be remiss in his use of effective epigram.

How was *national character* used by the nineteenth-century traveler? A glance at the chapters devoted to that term reveals the extent to which he muddled meanings. Emerson in his chapter on character in *English Traits* begins by referring to temperament, physique, and mentality. The English, he writes, have "an abysmal temperament, hiding great wells of wrath, and glooms on which no sunshine settles"; they are "of the earth, earthy, . . . full of coarse strength, rude exercise, butcher's meat and sound sleep"; save for a few finest wits, they betray a "saving stupidity." He then goes on to speak of acquired attributes: the "English are intellectual and enjoy literature," they are "conservative, money-loving and lord-loving." Finally, in a climactic sentence, the author runs through a gamut of meanings, alluding in the process to manners, attitudes, and reputation: "There are multitudes of rude young English who have the self-sufficiency and bluntness of their nation, and who, with their disdain for the rest of mankind and this indigestion and choler, have made the English traveler a proverb for uncomfortable and offensive manners."[6] One wonders what, in good logic, *national character* might conceivably not refer to. However sharp-edged the style, disquisitions of this kind lack syntactical value. Each item taken separately may carry an element of truth; the discussion as a whole is as indiscriminate as a warehouse inventory.

In times of international stress, when an irate and impertinent patriotism overcame the obligations of courtesy, the foreign observer

---

attitudes toward the individual human being, the sense of responsibility toward society, the relations of the military and the civilian, the position of women and children, the role of the school and the church and that of the courts, the concepts of justice and fair play, the ideals that are held up to children and the pattern that is fixed for them, the moral standards that are accepted and the moral values that are cherished"—a definition that covers not a body of knowledge but a universe.

[6] Ralph Waldo Emerson, *English Traits* (Everyman's Edition, 1856), pp. 71-83.

judged his hosts harshly, and his hosts responded in kind. At such times, they gave the term *national character* a strongly moralistic flavor. Frances Trollope with her malicious tongue, Charles Dickens with his satirical bent, Captain Marryat with his jaundiced eye—all concluded that Americans were deficient in national character—that is, were lacking in probity and good breeding.[7] American reviewers of their works used the term in the same way when they undertook to defend their country. No one should judge another's national character, wrote one American, if he brings "a harsh uncharitable method of testing human merit." We have more national character than do our English critics, American reviewers usually concluded.[8] Ensconced in the language of moral judgment, the term came to be used as verbal powder and shot in wars of mutual derogation.

Those who refrained from making invidious judgments—and the best did strain for objectivity—often worked semantic mischief in another way. When Harriet Martineau said that Americans had no national character, she was not depreciating them; she meant merely that Americans did not yet have any common values: "There are infinite diversities to be blended into unity before a national character can arise."[9] So, too, the judicious Tocqueville:

> American society is composed of a thousand different elements newly brought together. The men who live under these laws are still English, German, Dutch. They have neither religion, nor morals, nor ideas in common. Up to the present, it can't be said that Americans have a national character unless it is that of having none.[10]

National character, to these writers, meant uniform national type.[11] They thus shut off the possibility of comparing the frequency of

---

[7] Frances Trollope, *Domestic Manners of the American* (originally published 1832; New York: Dodd, Mead, 1894), II, 12; Frederick Marryat, *A Diary in America* (London: Longman, Orme, Brown, Green & Longmans, 1839), *passim:* Charles Dickens, *American Notes* (New York: Wilson & Co., 1842), p. 302.

[8] "Captain Marryat and His Diary," *The Southern Literary Messenger*, VII (April, 1841), 259. See also "Domestic Manners of the Americans," *American Quarterly Review*, XII (September, 1832), 109–33 and J. P. Thompson, "Dickens' 'Notes on America,'" *The New Englander*, I (January, 1843), 64–84.

[9] *Society in America* (London: Saunders & Otley, 1837), III, 209.

[10] George W. Pierson, *Tocqueville and Beaumont in America* (New York: Oxford University Press, 1938), p. 114.

[11] Sometimes this definition was used for pejorative effect. Certain English Tory journalists in this period took Americans sharply to task for adhering *too much* to type. See Jane Louise Mesick, *The English Traveller in America, 1785–1835* (New York: Columbia University Press, 1922), p. 229.

specific traits in different national populations. To them, the character differences between nations were generic, not statistical.

Finally, one notes in these writings a persistent tendency to deal with cultural facts and character traits as though they were freely interchangeable. In his chapter on American national character in the *American Commonwealth*, Lord Bryce repeats what he had said in his chapters dealing with American culture. For example, after having alluded to numerous experiments in the area of social reform, he makes the facts do double duty by giving them a character twist: Americans, he concludes, are an "experimental people, as far as social reform is concerned."[12] The least that can be said against this method is that it does not further knowledge: to give one fact two phrasings is not to produce two facts. But worse faults can be charged against this approach. It leads to specious explanations. Thus, in attempting to account for the existence of only two major political parties in the United States, Bryce points to the "character of the American people": "They are extremely fond of associating themselves and prone to cling to any organization they have once joined."[13] But since this character trait was largely deduced from the very facts it was supposed to explain, the explanation is circular. The gravest offense of this method of duplication, which was employed not only by Bryce but by most writers on national character, is that it confused two orders of phenomena which analytically should have been kept distinct.[14] By failing to see character and culture as separate but interacting entities, these authors begged the theoretical questions which had to be faced for productive thinking. For example: Is everything that exists on the cultural level incorporated into the character of individuals? Does a cultural element, when internalized, retain its original meaning? How is a cultural element transmitted, and how is it transformed when absorbed? The double-entry system skirted such questions entirely.

[12] James Bryce, *American Commonwealth* (New York: Macmillan, 1888), II, 295–96.

[13] *Ibid.*, p. 51.

[14] For the sake of brevity, we have not taken up the question of the ontological status of culture and character, a matter which has been under dispute for almost a century. Recent discussions of this problem can be found in the following articles in the *American Anthropologist:* David Bidney, "On the Concept of Culture and Some Cultural Fallacies," XLVI (1944), 30–44, and "Human Nature and the Cultural Process," XLIX (1947), 375–96; Clyde Kluckhohn and O. Mowrer, "Culture and Personality: A Conceptual Scheme," XLVI (1944), 1–29.

There can be little doubt that *national character* has had to carry a heavy freight of contrary and unclear meanings, accumulated through the years. But it would be premature to conclude that the term is beyond redemption. In a sense, pessimism with respect to terms is always something of a dereliction; if it is the fate of common words to be equivocal, it is the duty of uncommon minds to make them less so. As it happens, some uncommon minds have tried to do this, not by addressing themselves to the term directly but by fashioning conceptual models and heuristic metaphors that clarify and reorder what the lax use of language has confounded.

Two of these models merit special consideration. The first is the Freudian model (as revised and applied by anthropologists); the second may be called the dramaturgical model (as used by theorists of social-role behavior). These are alternative models. They grow out of and reflect the rift that we found in the etymology of the word *character*, a rift which our culture perpetuates through its Platonic-Aristotelian dualities. Ultimately, the choice between these models may rest on metaphysical predilection, but at least the choice is between two of the more coherent options.

The Freudian model.—For our purposes the best entry into Freud's self-contained system is through his concept of character trait.[15] This concept was a product of three of his main assumptions—a belief in infant determinism, a theory of psychosexual development, and a holistic view of personality. With the first of these assumptions, Freud laid down the dictum that the psyche, once formed in the early years, admits no important innovations. By this he meant not only that early habits persist and predestine future conduct but that the entire repertoire of adult behavior, for all its seeming diversity, can be traced to a few controlling tendencies operating in the unconscious. Thus the pull of his definition of *trait* was toward the invisible and the quintessential. A trait, to him, was a latent predisposition to behave, not an item of observed behavior. Inferable from current actions, it was a precipitate of the subject's past, a clue to a buried biography.

With his maturational theory—the second of his main assumptions—Freud located the source of current traits in the libidinous life of the infant and child. He thought that all human organisms had a

---

[15] There is no concise description of this model in Freud's writings; what follows is a condensation of various ideas which he elaborated throughout his lifetime.

natural schedule of erotic development but that owing to the actions of society—which he considered the nemesis of the pleasure principle —the course could not run smooth. Constraint, frustration, and anxiety blocked or reversed this development, with indelible consequences for character.[16] In specific pleasure-giving actions that are appropriate to the early stages of development and are not successfully outgrown and integrated, Freud believed he found the prototypes for later modes of responding. Thus, the biting and sucking responses might be perpetuated, sublimated, or displaced into permanent character tendencies—into the traits of optimism or open-mindedness (the desire to "incorporate" or to "receive"), dependency or gullibility (the desire to be "taken in"), or persistent verbal aggressiveness (the use of "biting" or sarcastic language).[17] A trait was thus conceived to be a product (of an instinct and its vicissitudes), a symptom (of fixation or regression), and a lasting adaptation (to frustration and anxiety).

Third, Freud viewed character traits not in isolation but in their genetic and functional relation to the personality as a whole. In a short article that opened the subject of psychoanalytic characterology he noted that the traits of orderliness, parsimoniousness, and obstinacy usually occurred together. By dint of ingenious speculation, he related each of these character traits to the same genetic factor, the inhibition of erogenous pleasure through oversevere toilet training, and to the same psychic mechanisms, repression and reaction-formation. Under the spur of holistic thinking Freud saw these traits composing a syndrome, the syndrome evincing the total character, the total character fitting a class (the "anal-sadistic" or compulsive type).[18] In sum, character, as Freud conceived it, is a structured and concealed domain, ruled by unconscious forces, shaped by the trends of early history, taking typical forms.[19]

The great merit of the Freudian scheme is that it sets up character

[16] See Sigmund Freud, *Three Contributions to the Theory of Sex* (New York: Nervous and Mental Disease Publishing Co., 1916).

[17] We have not distinguished here between the thinking of Freud on this subject and that of his follower Karl Abraham. See Abraham, "Contributions to the Theory of the Anal Character" and "The Influence of Oral Eroticism in Character-Formation" in *Selected Papers in Psychoanalysis* (London: L. and Virginia Woolf, 1927), pp. 370–406.

[18] "Character and Anal Eroticism," *Collected Papers* (International Psycho-analytical Library, No. 8, 1946), pp. 45–50.

[19] See "Some Character-Types Met with in Psychoanalytic Work," *Collected Papers* (International Psycho-analytical Library, No. 10, 1946), pp. 318–44.

and culture (or society) as separate conceptual entities. Influence is conceived as going in two directions—from culture to character, by means of the child's incorporation of his parents' injunctions and ideals, and from character back to culture, by means of the channeling and rechanneling of the organism's basic psychic energy. At neither terminal point do the effects merely mirror their cause. The *do*'s and *don't*'s of the parents are not impressed upon character in the form of homologous traits. Rather, they form an internal monitor which must vie with instinctual drives, powerfully operative from birth, and with the cognitive-intellectual functions, which arise through transactions with reality, for control of the character of the organism. Reified in Freudian language, each of these shaping factors—the biological, the psychological, the social—is allocated an internal province, a name, and a specific goal: there is the *id* which strives for pleasure, the *ego* which strives for truth, the *superego* which strives for perfection. The basic character trend depends upon which achieves dominion: the consequence of victory by the id is a headstrong, impulsive character; the consequence of victory by the superego is a moralistic, perfectionistic character; only when the ego takes hold to synthesize and harmonize all claims does character achieve a healthy balance.[20] The fancifulness of this metaphor may be objectionable, but the thought it illustrates is worth attention. Culture, Freud was saying, does not stamp itself on character but is a party to character's internal conflicts; character embodies culture but cannot fully be described in terms of it.

According to the Freudian model character also acts as cause and alters or reinforces culture. Again, the process is indirect. Freud eschewed the kind of psychology that linked each cultural fact to a corresponding human propensity. The two groups of instincts he described—those of Eros and those of Death—he regarded as general drives capable of very diverse expressions. Despite his pessimistic notion that society demands renunciation and that civilization must beget its discontents,[21] he believed that men respond inventively to their frustrations and defensively to their anxieties and that thus they modify both. Through a process which he called *displacement*, one which he thought essential to all learning, energy may be channeled by the ego from forbidden objects of desire to more accessible object-

[20] *The Ego and the Id* (International Psycho-analytical Library, No. 12, 1927), *passim.*

[21] *Civilization and Its Discontents* (International Psycho-analytical Library, No. 17, 1949), *passim.*

choices. Through the mechanism which he called *projection*, external reality may be endowed with spurious but consolatory features and various illusions may be devised to satisfy unconscious yearnings.[22] Each individual coping with his conflicts makes an impact upon the culture; large-scale cultural phenomena—submission of the masses to a leader, widespread crusades for social justice, the institutions of religion, the growth of civilization itself—are the consequences of the cumulation of effects.[23] Thus, between character now seen as cause and culture seen as effect, intrapsychic processes serve once more as the indispensable middle term.[24]

At first the Freudian model made no provision for a character common to social groups. Freud did not focus on this issue; his interest was too much keyed either to individual neuroses or to universal psychic laws.[25] What concern he had with group-shared qualities was consumed by his character typology, which was a means of categorizing individuals according to their psychological similarities and not a device for defining the similarities of individuals in existent social groups. Group character was not fitted into the model until certain of the followers of Freud, influenced by anthropology, learned to speak of specific cultures (rather than the abstraction Culture) and until certain of the practitioners of anthropology, influenced by Freud, began to focus on personality. Eventually a new dimension of sharedness was added to the original dimension of depth.

Abram Kardiner and Erich Fromm were the prominent authors of this revision. Kardiner posited the existence of a "basic personality structure"—a common groundwork of character built by early familial disciplines commonly employed in a society. He undertook to study

[22] Freud's writings contain several definitions of *projection*. The one offered here combines two of his more important ones. See his "Certain Neurotic Mechanisms in Jealousy, Paranoia and Homosexuality" (International Psycho-analytical Library, No. 8, 1946), pp. 232–43 and *Inhibitions, Symptoms and Anxiety* (International Psycho-analytical Library, No. 28, 1936), pp. 86–87.

[23] *The Future of an Illusion* (International Psycho-analytical Library, No. 15, 1928).

[24] We have not touched here on Freud's theory of phylogenetic recapitulation. It is out of keeping with the separation of character and culture that he usually maintained. See, however, his *Totem and Taboo* (New York: New Republic, 1927).

[25] Interestingly enough, Freud's sole foray into group psychology—which took the revealing title *Group Psychology and the Analysis of the Ego* (International Psycho-analytical Library, No. 6, 1922)—was a study of the impact of the crowd on the functioning of the *individual* psyche.

the "primary institutions" of a society (methods of child nurture and care, techniques of handling aggression and dependence) in order to ascertain how the resulting "basic personality structure" (the operation of unconscious projective mechanisms) invents the "secondary institutions" (religion, folklore, ideology). One of his findings was that a society which subjects its children to consistent parental punishments and rewards will produce a basic personality which introjects and idealizes the parental image. Such a personality, he believed, will project, and such a society will find congenial, an anthropomorphic god who identifies sin with disobedience and is pleased by exemplary behavior.[26] Kardiner thus kept the Freudian model intact, except for the substitution of a different intermediate term: a common character core instead of the total individual personality.

Erich Fromm developed the concept of "social character," by which he meant a set of common motivations implanted in children by their parents, who act as the agents of society. To Fromm the object of socialization is to make individuals want to act as indeed they have to act in order to perform the tasks with which the society is confronted. As each era imposes new tasks, character must be bent to fresh necessities.[27] Thus the onset of capitalism in the West spurred the development of a social character in which the motives of acquisition and competitiveness come to predominate over any others. But the social character may be a cause as well as an end-result. In times of rapid social change, the existing social character (geared for tasks no longer exigent) may clash with the demands of the new environment; further, when the demands imposed by society violate basic human needs, character disturbances may occur which will have a repercussive effect. In *Escape from Freedom*, Fromm argued that post-medieval Western man, forced by the directives of society into postures of isolation and alienation, finds escape in symbiotic relationships of dominance and submission; these patterned modes of relating become an unintended part of the social character; this social character is in turn responsible for significant cultural change (e.g., induces the onset of totalitarianism).[28] Thus, Fromm, for all his opposition to Freud's

[26] *Psychological Frontiers of Society* (New York: Columbia University Press, 1945), p. 29.

[27] "Psychoanalytic Characterology and Its Application to the Understanding of Culture," in S. Stansfield Sargent and Marian W. Smith (eds.), *Culture and Personality* (New York: Viking Fund, 1949), p. 5.

[28] (New York: Rinehart, 1941), p. 288; *Man for Himself* (New York: Rinehart, 1947), p. 129.

biologism,[29] made use of the Freudian paradigm and placed the social character in a context of determinants and expressions, of cultural causes and effects.

We have only to consider national character as a subtype of either of these forms of common character in order to fit it into the scheme. Once it is fitted into the scheme, the term is significantly rehabilitated. It loses its mystical associations: to Kardiner and to Fromm, the common character is not the disembodied spirit of the group but a likeness in the makeup of the members. It sheds all normative implications: to Kardiner and Fromm, the common character is a product of ubiquitous socializing processes. And it assumes explanatory functions. As a link between disparate parts of culture, it explains (in Kardiner's terms) the psychological coherence of the institutions which constitute society. As an intervening variable between alterations in determinants and expressions, it explains (in Fromm's conception) the process of cultural change. Within this frame of reference, national character not only *means* something but hypothetically *does* something too.

To be sure, new difficulties partly offset these gains. Those who employ this model must locate national character in a cycle of action and reaction; merely to catalogue traits, merely to describe without explaining, is not to meet the obligation. At the same time, a "basic personality structure" or a "common set of motivations" cannot be directly apprehended. It can be shown to exist, and to exist as an effective agent, only by a devious process of inference. One must work forward from the determinants of character, backward from the expressions of character, and hope that these two roads, winding through the data of culture, will converge at the invisible Rome. Unfortunately, there are many traps along the way. There is the danger that the determinants of character will seem more homogeneous than they are—for instance, that the child-rearing disciplines of the American middle class will be confused with the national practice. There is the

[29] Fromm gave different symptomatic significance to the traits he discovered in character. What he called the "receptive" character (exemplified by such traits as overdependence and the insatiable desire to be loved), the "hoarding" character (exemplified by the traits of possessiveness and withdrawal of feeling) and the "productive" character (exemplified by the capacity to love one's self and others) suggest Freud's oral, anal, and genital types. But the underlying mechanisms that Fromm presumed to be operative in character differ from those defined by Freud. Not the frustration and sublimation of the libido but the frustration of the desire to love creatively and the use of mechanisms of escape from that frustration are what, to Fromm, produce character traits. See "Psychoanalytic Characterology," p. 8.

danger that cultural phenomena, rationally explainable on other grounds, will be assumed to be expressions of character and thus unnecessarily laden with psychological implications. And there is the danger that quite unconnected cultural elements (say, the Russian practice of swaddling children and the Russian political dictatorship) will be assumed, merely by their coexistence, to be part of a causal chain in which national character is the middle link. That these dangers are real and not imaginary is apparent to anyone who has surveyed the recent literature on this subject.[30] Yet awareness of the dangers also suggests monitory rules. Depth psychological explanations should be residual, offered only when simpler explanations have been tried and found indisputably wanting; psychological explanations should be selective and applied only to those cultural items that have obvious emotional loadings; cross-national and cross-cultural comparisons should check all presumptive causal linkages. This model must be used with care and subtlety—but this is a charge to the inquirer and not a veto on the inquiry.

The dramaturgical model.—We need not, however, rely on the Freudian dispensation to refurbish the concept of national character. We may draw on another set of assumptions—on the social behaviorism of George Herbert Mead, the developmental studies of Jean Piaget, the theatrical metaphors of Erving Goffman and other sociologists. The main idea that emerges from these varied sources is that every society, in order to achieve its goals, requires its members to play standardized roles, these being assigned in the main on the basis of age, sex, class, and occupation. Becoming a socialized person means acquiring thespian skills—knowing what the part of male or adolescent or doctor calls for, making the performance so believable that the role will seem authentic to the audience, guarding against discrepant gestures that would give the play away. These skills are acquired slowly by instructive social interactions; the novice becomes a polished actor not so much by direct tuition as by continuous practice in required roles.[31]

[30] See Geoffrey Gorer, "Some Aspects of the Psychology of the People of Great Russia," *American Slavic and East European Review*, VII (1949), 155–67, and the critical attack on Gorer's work by I. Goldman, "Psychiatric Interpretation of Russian History: A Reply to Geoffrey Gorer," *ibid.*, IX (1950), 151–61.

[31] See Erving Goffman, *The Presentation of Self in Everyday Life* (University of Edinburgh, Social Science Research Centre, Monograph 2, 1956). [For further discussion of "social role" see the essay by Cochran (pp. 103–10 below).—EDITOR.]

Generalizations about National Character

Performances, however, vary among both societies and players. Though all societies have roughly similar goals (the maintenance of health, continuity, security), they evolve different instrumental roles and weave different characteristic plots. In some societies an elaborate etiquette governs every kind of social interplay: the stage directions call for poise and an emphasis on gravity and reserve. In other societies, a warm and familiar air is required of even slight acquaintanceships. In some societies, the father plays the suzerain and lords the family from an upraised seat; in other societies, the father must accept a more equal part. Different societies present different hero-types—stellar roles to which neophytes aspire (the saint, the lawgiver, the courtier, the warrior, the tycoon). Different societies present different villain-roles that arouse antipathy in the audience (the usurer, the witch, the stranger). Moreover, though many dramatic presentations are routinized and many roles are prescribed, there is always room for personal interpretation. Each individual gives something of his own to the roles that society manufactures—a nuance of inflection, an attitude of confidence or stage fright, a characteristic front, a talent for improvisation. The personal side to these impersonations is the phenomenon we call "style."

And so to new definitions. Let character *trait* denote the style with which an individual plays a specific social role, and *character* the style that infuses the individual's playing of his many roles. Then, *national character* may denote the style which the troupes constituting the nation bring to the roles within their repertory. In pursuit of national character one asks: Do French parents, unlike American parents, sharply differentiate their roles, so that authority adheres exclusively in the father and the nurturing function in the mother? Do American teenagers, in comparison with their German counterparts, place more emphasis on roles involving social skills than on those involving intellectual achievement? Do English teachers succeed, where American teachers fail, in serving as models for their charges? Or, to turn to a single style that may be evident in a number of role-performances, are we as likely to find in other settings the plays that Americans often witness—housewives currying favor with their maids, parents propitiating their children, ball players insulting umpires? Does this suggest uneasiness or incompetence in the assertion of prerogative? Is there then a mode of acting which Americans find especially to their taste, rather the way the American theater proper developed the Method School of acting in preference to the style of the Royal

Academy? A world full of interest beckons when we start our quest at this intersection of what society prescribes with what people do.[32]

An interesting world—but not one entirely free of pitfalls. It would be all too easy to assume that anything that happens on the social stage is characterologically significant. But such an assumption would be costly, for it would assimilate psychology to sociology, make character traits synonymous with customs, and reintroduce the duplications we deem it wise to avoid. Consequently, to be prudent we must delineate in this as in the Freudian model a set of character determinants and a set of character expressions. We must find the roles which, when played, do most to shape the character of the performers, and the performances which, when observed, best reveal the character of the players. There is some dispute over which social roles may serve these several functions. Some psychologists, like Sears, Maccoby, and Levin, stress the character-forming roles of early childhood by means of which the child imaginatively assumes the parent role, admonishes himself from that perspective, and develops an internalized sense of right and wrong.[33] Mead puts particular emphasis on the games of older children, during which each participant implicates himself in the others' roles and acquires a generalized understanding of the nature of role-playing as such.[34] As for the roles which best exemplify character, there may again be a number of candidates. In general, one may reasonably assume that these should be the roles in which the player invests a good deal of emotion, in which he has a vital stake, and which he plays consistently and often. Other criteria of selection may be possible, but the important point is that some criterion is necessary.

The foregoing touches on the trouble one encounters in David Riesman's *Lonely Crowd*, a study of changes in the American character.[35]

[32] Among the interesting studies of national or ethnic patterns in social-role behavior one may cite Ruth Benedict, *The Chrysanthemum and the Sword* (Boston: Houghton Mifflin, 1946); Mark Zborowski, "Cultural Components in Response to Pain," *Journal of Social Issues*, VIII (1952), 16–30; Arthur M. Schlesinger, Sr., *Learning How To Behave* (New York: Macmillan, 1946); and Harold Nicolson, *Good Behaviour* (New York: Doubleday, 1956).

[33] Robert R. Sears, Eleanor E. Maccoby, and Harry Levin, *Patterns of Child Rearing* (Evanston, Ill.: Row, Peterson, 1957).

[34] George Herbert Mead, *Mind, Self and Society* (Chicago: University of Chicago Press, 1934).

[35] David Riesman, Reuel Denney, and Nathan Glazer, *The Lonely Crowd* (New Haven: Yale University Press, 1950). For a translation of Riesman's concepts into role-theory terms, see Sheldon L. Messinger and Burton R. Clark, "Individual

Though the author acknowledges his indebtedness to Erich Fromm, it would not be difficult to show that he works within the dramaturgical framework. He draws his evidence from the social stage—from what passes between children at play, between parents and children at home, between teachers and students at school, between business executives at work. He finds that there has been a recent change in the style of all of these role-performances. Riesman gives special emphasis to the shift in the parental style from strong authoritative guidance to weak unstable manipulation, to the shift in the teacher's role from that of judge and mentor to that of social director, to the shift in objective among business managers from that of impersonal efficiency to that of the maintenance of group morale, and to the growing significance of the peer-group, whose plays require of the actors a capacity for feckless imitation, a reluctance to trust to self-direction, and a talent for a dialogue devoted to expressions of consumer taste. Shaped by these experiences, the American, Riesman believes, has changed his national character—that is, has changed his entire style of acting. The older "inner-directed" character, after internalizing his early roles, appeared on the adult stage as a complete, self-motivated person. His promptings were from within, and he projected a sense of self that brooked no tampering by the audience. By contrast, the modern "other-directed" character brings to his roles no sure identity but seeks to define himself through his roles. He constantly scans his audiences for cues as to how he should behave and constantly tailors his part to his view of his audiences' expectations. He is not, however, miscast: the society that creates him also requires and is sustained by him.

Riesman, as we can see, makes a variety of social roles serve the dual purpose of revealing and forming character. He thereby exaggerates their significance. Roles sometimes shape the man, but men also sometimes opt their roles. To describe the "other-directed" man as he is found in the bureaucratic echelons of business is not necessarily to depict a man who has been created by his job but possibly to depict a man who has been selectively *chosen* for his job. The distinction is important, for the great proliferation of such offices may not prove that the new character is more frequent but simply that this particular character (possibly long established) now has an expanding medium for expression. On the other side, Riesman does not distinguish be-

---

Character and Social Constraint: A Critique of David Riesman's Theory of Social Conduct," in Seymour Martin Lipset and Leo Lowenthal (eds.), *Culture and Social Character* (New York: Free Press, 1961), pp. 72–85.

tween roles that are purely ceremonial and roles that are charged with vital feelings. Yet it is likely that many roles are played in the ordinary round of life perfunctorily, opportunistically, and merely for the occasion. Undoubtedly, one cannot play an intimate role with another without infusing it with emotion; for this reason, what Riesman has to say about parent-child relationships strikes at something quite significant. But many of Riesman's examples taken from the job and the playground may deal with encounters of façades. His underlying idea —that modern man does not dissemble but gives his all to the company and surrenders his soul to the group—ignores at the expense of reality the vast amount of simulation that enters into social intercourse. An indiscriminate use of social roles to describe the national character inevitably rests on the tenet that people always are what they seem.

What we have said so far comes down to this: the concept of national character need not remain hopelessly ambiguous; to the extent that *character* can be more clearly defined, *national character* can be too; when the latter term is more clearly defined (by means of a conceptual model or a metaphor), many objections to it dissolve (though new complications may arise).[36]

Up to this point, our emphasis has been on the noun in the term *national character*, not on the qualifying adjective. We must be, however, as much concerned with *national* character as with national *character*. We must, therefore, turn our attention to the second problem—the problem of classification—which raises, in its own right, difficult though separate issues.

2. The Problem of Classification

One usually challenges a national classification by favoring an alternative classification: a supranational, a subnational, or an international one. The first of these generally alludes to a culture-pattern

[36] The reader's attention is called to an attempt, not treated here, to define national character as the statistically modal character and to require the study of national character to be a psychological investigation of adequately large and representative samples of persons, studied individually. See Alex Inkeles and Daniel J. Levinson, "National Character: The Study of Modal Personality and Sociocultural Systems," in Gardner Lindzey (ed.), *Handbook of Social Psychology* (Cambridge, Mass.: Addison-Wesley, 1954), chap. 26. Our slighting of this approach is not intended to be a comment on its significance but, rather, a recognition of its unfeasibility for most historical research. It would involve projective tests, intensive interviews, and psychoanalytical excavations—clinical techniques which, even if they work, can be applied only to the living. Historians by and large must study character from afar.

or culture-complex which stretches beyond any single nation. Thus one critic of national character writes: "It is in relation to a particular culture pattern that one might expect to find a particular character structure."[37] The subnational category usually refers to regional peculiarities within a nation. "The Picardian differs from the Gascon, the Norman from the Savoyard," contends an opponent of the concept of a Gallic entity.[38] The third category points to class affinities which unite the peoples of different nations. "The similarities between a German and a French physician, a German and an English naval captain . . . are much greater than the community between a German physician and a German naval captain" writes one who places greater stress on the international line of cleavage.[39] Whatever their classificational preference, these writers all invoke the same argument: the nation, they hold, is less important than some other primary matrix in producing a distinctive common character. It should be noted that this argument is not concerned with the properties or *components* of character, a matter which, as we have seen, is germane to the problem of definition. Rather this argument is concerned with the *influences* exerted upon character. And this is what goes to the heart of the problem of classification.

One way of answering the argument is to *identify* the national matrix with one of the preferred alternatives. This is what David Potter tries to do in his defense of national character in *People of Plenty*. Potter argues that "because the culture tends to realize itself politically through the process of national unification," the cultural matrix and the national matrix tend to become synonymous. As he puts it: "If a French national character exists, it is not because common citizenship or common residence in France made the French people alike but because the French people were alike, and, being alike, achieved a national framework for their culture."[40] But this argument, however plausible, goes against the facts. A culture or culture-complex often does not realize itself politically. Certain cultures, like that of the Jews, have existed for long periods without achieving

[37] Maurice Farber, "The Problem of National Character: A Methodological Analysis," *Journal of Psychology*, XXX (1950), 307–16.

[38] Walter Sulzbach, *National Consciousness* (Washington, D.C.: Public Affairs Press, 1943), p. 36.

[39] M. Ginsberg, "National Character," *British Journal of Psychology*, XXXII (January, 1942), 183–205.

[40] David M. Potter, *People of Plenty* (Chicago: University of Chicago Press, 1954), p. 14.

national expressions. Moreover, cultural and national boundaries often do not exactly overlap. The Scandinavian culture has three or four political embodiments. Also the boundaries of nations have been often drawn by dynastic marriages and wars, rather than by cultural affinities. It is true that self-induced cultural isolation may work, as in the case of Japan, to make culture and nation coincide. But such cases of perfect congruence are certainly exceptional.

But why not pursue the possibility that a nation in its own right, by exercise of its powers, creates an important crucible of character? It is not apparent why this should be discounted in favor of the other possibilities. If it be objected that the nation, because it has geographic dimensions, subsumes and cuts across other matrices, the same could be said about the region and the culture-complex, which are also territorial in scope. If it be argued that the modern nation is a recent creation, while character-formation is timeless, the same could be said in the main about recent social stratifications and recent occupations. Perhaps most of the animus against the idea of a national matrix springs from ideological considerations, from the desire of modern thinkers to deflate the pretensions of modern nationalism and to advance more ecumenical allegiances. If so, the rejoinder is plain: to acknowledge the importance of the nation is not to plead its desirability. Finally —and this is a point around which much confusion has developed— to shape is not the same as to bind. It should be obvious that the direction sentiments take does not explain their source. Whether English naval captains feel closer to German naval captains than to English sailors would be a matter of considerable import to English and German history, but it is barely relevant to the question whether English and German naval captains have a similar character structure and says very little indeed about the factors that created their characters. Were consciousness of kind the test, we might say that brothers who felt a closer kinship with their friends than they did with one another prove by that very fact that they lacked common progenitors!

Perhaps another reason why some critics resist the idea of a national matrix arises from the common assumption that a nation, from a functional standpoint, is not a character-forming agency but "simply a governmental unit, having jurisdiction over the people within a recognized area."[41] But this assumption, even if true, is not as limiting as it seems. With respect to character-formation there is nothing "simple" about government, nothing moderate about its "jurisdiction." This

[41] *Ibid.*

hardly needs proving for totalitarian nations, where the political authorities are empowered to set the nation's character goals and to muster toward the attainment of them almost every character-influencing device. But government is also influential in democratic nations, where character goals are diverse and the main character-forming agencies are private. Even the most limited democratic governments take part in the forming of character (for example, by training military conscripts) or do so indirectly by regulating private agencies (for example, by separating public school and church, by maintaining a censorship apparatus, by exempting institutions from taxation). In a larger sense, hardly anything such governments do fails to have some effect on character. A fiscal or economic program that accelerates social change, increases social mobility, or redistributes wealth touches the character-making process. It is true that under a federal system, like that of the United States, certain matters of key importance (education, marriage, divorce) lie formally beyond the scope of the central power. Even so, the trend in modern times is toward the enlargement of the functions of the central government and the contraction of the exclusive functions of subordinate units. To be sure, there are some concerns which no political authority touches. In this country, for example, the government does not organize youth clubs or control the uses of leisure. But this does not weaken the argument: *not* doing is also a form of doing; no nation would be more distinctive as a molder of character than the one which adhered completely to laissez faire.

In this view the nation is regarded only as a government and power system; a nation, however, is much more than that. It is also a community of peoples who are exposed to *common experiences*. Some of these experiences grow out of national wars—the efforts and dedications, the dangers and deprivations. Other experiences grow out of peace—the heroisms of sport, the national ceremonials. Some experiences shock, like the enormous event of occupation or revolution or civil war; some experiences are continuous, like relationships with neighbors. Some experiences fade and are thereafter symbolically encountered, like the impact of frontier conditions; some experiences periodically recur, like the diversions of a national election. Some experiences are directly felt, like going to the nation's public schools; some experiences are shared vicariously through the nation's media of communication.[42]

[42] See Karl W. Deutsch, *Nationalism and Social Communication* (New York: Wiley, 1953).

The foregoing is but a sketch of a matter that deserves more detail, but it may be enough to establish the idea that growing up and living in one country rather than in another is a matter of characterological importance. Once this is conceded, however, the real analytical difficulties begin. For now we would want to know, how important is the national matrix *relative* to the others? This knotty question would not have to be asked if the national matrix replaced the others, and it would not be such a perplexing question if all the matrices were separate. But we must conceive of a national matrix as both comprising and competing with all others. For members of a nation are simultaneously members of regional, occupational, and other groups as well. It may be that a character trait exhibited in a national population owes more to these subgroup experiences than to the over-all national experiences. How, then, can these interpenetrating factors be parceled out and their relative influence appraised?

Let us phrase the issue somewhat differently. It is clear that if there were an equal proportion of subsidiary memberships in each nation—say, if 35 per cent of every national population were Catholic, 15 per cent highly educated, 60 per cent middle class, and so forth—any relatively high frequency of trait in one nation would have to be ascribed to nationality. This is to say, if all other factors were held constant, whatever the contribution they made, any discrepant result would have to be attributed to the remaining variable. If, in reality, subgroup memberships were equally proportioned, we would not have to grapple with this issue any further. We would have the answer to such quandaries as David Potter posed when he noted that "if the compatriots of Thomas Jefferson were self-reliant and individualistic, it was perhaps as much because they were landowning, subsistence farmers as because they were Americans."[43] If the farm population in England and the United States in Jefferson's day constituted the same percentage of the whole population, the occupational factor which Potter stresses could be discounted, and nationality would account for any difference that would appear. But, of course, the proportions were not the same: around 1800 a greater percentage of Americans than Englishmen were farmers. Similar disparities would be found to exist were we to compare most other submemberships. A higher percentage of Italians than of Americans is Catholic. Americans belong in much higher proportion to the middle class than do Indians or Indonesians. The question, reformulated, is therefore this: How can we account for

[43] Potter, p. 17.

national character differences when there are many possible contributing factors *of greatly unequal strength?*

It is not possible here to explore fully the statistical and conceptual issues presented by this formulation. But we can, within our limits, suggest an approach that holds some promise. For a guide and encouraging example, let us turn to a study in a quite different field: Samuel Stouffer's *Communism, Conformity and Civil Liberties*, an investigation of American political tolerance.[44] By breaking his national sample into regional divisions, Stouffer found (1) that the western region of the United States had a larger proportion of tolerant people than the southern region of the United States. He also discovered (2) that city-dwellers were more tolerant than farm-dwellers. He knew as well (3) that a larger proportion of westerners lived in cities. With these three sets of facts in mind he posed a question: Are people more tolerant because they are westerners or because they are city-dwellers (and there happen to be more city-dwellers in the West)? If we substitute national groupings for these regional groupings, and character traits for these attitudes, we can see that at this point Stouffer had reached the stage at which we confronted our dilemma.

A simple trick of the sociological trade (one familiar in this discipline but surprisingly little appreciated by historians) enabled Stouffer to come to some conclusion. The trick was to hold the urban-rural factor constant by comparing *urban* westerners with *urban* southerners, likewise *rural* westerners with *rural* southerners, and by estimating in percentage terms which group in each pair was more tolerant. These comparisons revealed that among urban people, westerners were more tolerant than southerners; similarly rural westerners were more tolerant than rural southerners, though there was a smaller difference between the two rural segments than between the regions compared as wholes. Before jumping to final conclusions, however, Stouffer paused to ask: Might not still a third factor, as yet disguised under the regional rubrics, account for these persistent results? Educational level was possibly such a factor, since it was assumed to be correlated with tolerance, and fewer southerners than westerners achieve high academic levels. But again, better-educated westerners proved to be more tolerant than better-educated southerners when put to the tabular test.

The time to draw conclusions was still not yet. Would the same results appear if *both* of these possibly important factors—the educa-

[44] New York: Doubleday, 1955.

tional and the occupational-residential—were artificially controlled? To test this hypothesis, Stouffer constructed eight categories and made four more comparisons. Once more the same result: urban, better-educated westerners were more tolerant than urban, better-educated southerners; urban, less-educated westerners were more tolerant than urban, less-educated southerners; and so on down the line. Now he could say with greater confidence that the regional factor was important. He could not say just how this factor operated to produce the differences in results, but this much he knew: if the members of the urban, more-educated group or of the rural, more-educated group or of the less-educated urban and rural groups had been divided at random, no difference as to tolerance would have appeared, yet when the members of these groups were divided regionally, significant differences did appear. The members of each group were exposed to certain common experiences, but those members who lived in different regions were exposed to different total experiences.

What can be learned from this procedure? First, that matched comparisons may indicate whether the character differences between nations are really national character differences. To return to our illustration: if in the days of Jefferson, American *farmers* were more "individualistic" than English *farmers*, and—another check—if American non-farmers were more individualistic than English non-farmers, we would know that the factor of occupation cannot fully explain the disparity. We would have an answer to Potter's dilemma, for we would have achieved artificially what we bemoaned did not occur naturally—the neutralization of the influence of unequal and overlapping group memberships.

Of course, we would have to have the characterological information to start with. If nothing is known about character in the first place, this technique cannot be applied. It is also true that the closer we come to the present, the fuller and more accurate such evidence is likely to be. But we need not insist on a finicky standard of proof. Concessions to imprecision can be made without greatly damaging the design; a gross difference need not be put into exact numbers in order to convey its import. And this much may be added as a hope-inspiring general rule: if we can venture to say anything about the character differences between two nations, we can probably venture to say something about the character differences between two subgroups within those nations. It takes little more effort (and conceivably somewhat less) to prove a statement about American farmers and English farmers than to prove a statement about Americans and Englishmen. If we can or wish to say nothing, very well and good. But if we can say *something* about national character, then we can say a little more.

This procedure has theoretical implications that are also worthy of consideration. It will be recalled that Potter placed only two factors—the occupational-residential and the national—in opposition. Theoretically, however, many factors may be operative. Americans may have been more individualistic because they adhered to certain religious sects that stressed or inculcated that trait or because they dwelled in sparsely settled places and were made to shift for themselves. Obviously, these are hypotheses and must be verified by matched comparisons. At the same time, it should be understood that the operation promises only to test, not to create, good hypotheses. Knowledge, insight, and wisdom—the architects of a fruitful hunch—are not rendered obsolete by perfected methods.

Is this technique distortive because it serves to sunder what society brings together into one interrelated whole? The partisans of *Gestalt* in our midst may say *yes*, and oppose its use for this reason. But what may be implied by their objection? If they mean that everything exists in a context and can be understood only in a context, the objection has little merit in this case. It is, of course, true that an American farmer was not the same sort of person as an English farmer because each lived in a different context of values, traditions, and beliefs. But we are not ignoring contexts when we isolate these individuals for comparison. We *would* be ignoring contexts if we compared various farmers irrespective of their nationality. But if we compare rural Americans with rural Englishmen and a character difference appears, it is because the difference in context is being registered, not because the comparison is inapt.

Quite possibly, however, something else is implied by this objection, namely, that whereas no factor in isolation accounts for a national difference, many factors in combination—religion, occupation, education, and the rest—do account for a national difference. The procedure advocated here provides for only a limited number of categories, whereas the possible permutations are almost infinite. To a certain extent, this is indeed a valid argument. Only a limited number of factors can be handled by this method. A category combining three factors will probably hold fewer persons than a category combining only two—there were fewer pietistic rural Americans than there were rural Americans. A point must soon be reached beyond which it would be futile to invent new categories, because there would be too few subjects to fit them for really significant results. But there is a reason for limiting the number of categories aside from the reason of convenience. If all the factors one could think of were put into every possible combination, they would *constitute* the factor of nationality, fractured into numberless parts. It is not, however, our purpose in using this method to rip the whole into parts so that the whole completely disappears but, rather, to keep the whole intact while gauging the importance of the parts.

It goes without saying that no procedure should be disqualified merely because it originates in another discipline. "Outside history, no salvation" is poor professional doctrine; "Neither a borrower nor a lender be" was never meant to be a rule to govern scholarly conduct. At the same time, it would be a mistake for historians to assume that the behavioral sciences now divulge full and finished solutions to these problems. Historians will not find in adjacent fields any certain deliverance from quandary, but they may find across the way a salutary open-mindedness, a taste for conceptual analysis, and a good deal of intellectual pluck. For the study of national character, all three ingredients are essential.

VII. *The Historian's Use of Social Role*

BY THOMAS C. COCHRAN

Social role is the part played by an individual in response to an understanding shared by members of a group as to the attitudes and behavior that should normally follow from his occupation of a given position or status.[1] Thus *social role* involves a formalized conceptual system for explaining why and to what extent people in similar situations tend to act in similar ways. For example, when after his inauguration as vice-president (March 4, 1901) Theodore Roosevelt wrote Leonard Wood that he had "taken the veil" and revealed his plans for studying law on the side or "perhaps becoming a scholar,"[2] he was describing his concept of the social role of the vice-presidency.

In fact, it is hard to write history or formulate social theories without at least implicitly assuming role continuities or social norms of behavior as expressed in such phrases as *Roman patrician*, *Texas rancher*, or *factory worker*. The concept of *social norm* indicates the same type of uniformity as *social role*, but the latter has the advantage of providing a theoretical structure capable of explaining how and why norms are effective. In his essay (above) entitled "Generalizations about National Character" Walter Metzger discusses two major systems for analyzing action—that stemming from Freud and that built around the concept of social-role behavior. "*National character*," he says, "may denote the style which the troupes constituting the nation bring to the roles within their repertory."[3] The concept of *social role* is widely recognized and used also by sociologists and other social scientists. Professor Robert K. Merton, for example, says: "Sociological theorists are largely at one in adopting the premise that social statuses and social roles comprise major building blocks of social structure."[4] Since social role involves a subtle and rather elaborate family of constructs dif-

---

[1] A number of writers use the term *role* (alone) to indicate the abstract concept. They then have to use *role behavior* or *role attribute* to refer to actual role-playing. See Neal Gross, Ward S. Mason, and Alexander W. McEadwin, *Explorations in Role Analysis* (New York: Wiley, 1958).

[2] George Mowry, *The Era of Theodore Roosevelt* ("New American Nation Series" [New York: Harper, 1958]), p. 109.

[3] P. 91 above.

[4] "The Role-Set: Problems in Sociological Theory," *British Journal of Sociology*, VIII (1957), 110.

ferently defined by different writers, it seems necessary to discuss some of the problems in the use of these constructs in historical research.

One problem is the danger of ambiguity between the abstract or normative concept and the role actually played by an individual. The way in which a person in fact carries out a series of related actions will be called here his "personal role" or his "individual role." Many factors—such as childhood conditioning, experiences of private life, or other positions or statuses occupied simultaneously—which influence the playing of this personal role are usually inaccessible to the historian. Outward behavior, however, can presumably be known, as can influential events and details in the surrounding situation. In general, study of behavior, particularly in formal organizations, indicates broad areas of uniformity in the playing of personal roles. Executives in business or government, for example, try to act in such a way as to preserve harmony and good morale among their staffs. One of the strongest pressures for such uniform action is the desire to live up to the expectations of the group involved.

These group expectations of how the actor will normally play his role define the social role. The fact that such expectations exist is testified to continuously in every group. *Social role* is in the first instance a general term for what lies back of commonly held knowledge concerning how a person will act under given circumstances—why, for example, a clergyman in a wealthy parish is not likely to preach against the rich.

A major difficulty of role analysis is the identification of the many factors that define a given social role. While a generalized set of expectations regarding behavior attaches to the position or status of the actor, the exact playing of the expected role by a particular individual is modified both by his own necessarily unique conditioning and other statuses and by the relevant behavior and varied expectations of other people. The latter consideration means that what appears to be one role is really a system of roles reciprocal among the players, perhaps much alike but varying in detail. "Social role," Leland H. Jenks writes, "is primarily a function of a social group, not of any particular individual or unorganized aggregate of them; moreover it is a function of the degree of social communication in such a group."[5]

[5] "The Role Structure of Entrepreneurial Personality," *Change and the Entrepreneur*, ed. A. H. Cole (Cambridge, Mass.: Harvard University Press, 1949), p. 143.

The Historian's Use of Social Role

The ideal for a clearly and simply defined social role is that it represent the expectations of only one group fully informed on the performance in question and with definite and uniform attitudes regarding it. In such a case there would be a single "defining group," and all aspects of the social role would relate to its expectations.[6] Military hierarchies may foster this type of relationship, but in general history such situations are the rare exception. If social role is to be a useful tool of analysis for general history, there should probably be in each situation under examination at least a major defining group whose normal expectations determine the general characteristics of the role. There may also be minor defining groups, as small as one individual, whose expectations set certain segments of the role but toward which the major group is indifferent or not in agreement.[7] For example, in a corporation with directors composed partly of the chief officers of the company, the board, led presumably by the officer personnel, will be the major defining group for the chief executive roles, but in each of his operations the top executive deals also with subordinates who form minor defining groups for segments of his role, though such subordinates may never be considered by the board of directors as forming defining groups for them. Large suppliers, customers, or public officials may also constitute minor defining groups. The complete description of a social role in organizations requires knowledge of the expectations of the several groups involved.

Merton has called this "complement of *role-relationships* in which persons are involved by occupying a particular social status" a *role-set*. He is concerned, however, "with social arrangements integrating the expectations of those in the role set, . . . not primarily . . . with the familiar problem of how the occupant of a status manages to cope with the many and sometimes conflicting demands made upon him."[8] Since such "social arrangements" are a problem in the mechanics of social structure, while the present discussion is of the behavior of role players, I will not follow Merton's theoretical analysis beyond his definition of the term.

[6] In my *Railroad Leaders, 1845–1890* (Cambridge, Mass.: Harvard University Press, 1953) I used the term *prescribing group* for those who set the expectations for the role. In the interest of a uniform vocabulary the term *defining group* used by Gross, Mason, and McEadwin is substituted here.

[7] Gross, Mason, and McEadwin (p. 74) point out that consensus in expectations should be treated as a variable. It must be carefully defined for each group in relation to a role player and a situation.

[8] Merton, pp. 110–12.

Defining groups in a role-set are those which because of their status can exercise effective power on the performance of the role in question. If the major defining group, which may be very small or infinitely numerous, governs a large part of the role and exercises ultimate censorship over all aspects, the concept of social role should have utility for historical analysis. But in some roles there is no defining group that affects all of the actors or most of the actions. In such cases each performer may evaluate his defining groups differently, and hence no important uniformities will emerge in the playing of the role. There are probably few real situations that conform to the conditions for either of these two extreme examples. But whenever a new type of operation has to be performed, one for whose conduct there can be only imaginary conceptions, an unstructured social role is approached. Hence, innovation, by breaking away from established norms, fosters further innovation in role-playing. The pioneer small manufacturer starting his own business in a new type of product and buying and selling in an impersonal market would approach this situation. He could seek his own economic gain and behave in a strictly instrumental way without response to social pressures. In practice he would probably modify his performance to fit the expectations of associates in his community and of his chief employees, but lacking effective sanctioning force, these would be weak defining groups.

If one finds, however, in any given situation a significant defining group, its character is of primary importance. Its determining effect on social role, how much it can make variously motivated individuals conform to the commonly held group expectations, would be a function of frequency of communication, uniformity of attitudes, and effectiveness of power. The small board of directors or the officers' conference tends to maximize all the positive characteristics. But there is no reason, in theory, why the usefulness of the concept of social role should be limited to situations in which there is a high degree of conformity in the expectations of a single defining group. Roles, that is, may be sharply and uniformly defined in certain respects by all defining groups even though they differ regarding other segments of the role. Reverting to the Theodore Roosevelt illustration, we find both Democrats and Republicans apparently in agreement that political impotency was a characteristic of the social role of vice-president, although they undoubtedly differed regarding what other aspects of the role were desirable. Much of the value of history, whether viewed aesthetically or scientifically, depends on assumptions or generalizations regarding anticipated uniformities in role-playing. It would otherwise be more confusing than it is anyway to use such "types" or "labels" as the Athenian citizen, the medieval monk, or the American president.* An element of drama is nevertheless introduced either by an actor playing his role as expected in the face of unusual pressures, as Buchanan did in 1860, or by an actor innovating and moving beyond the expectations, as Wilson did in 1913.

There is a great difference in the force of the sanctions that define a social role. Some are merely conventional, as the matter of whether or not the president personally reads his messages to Congress. Others are as strong as the basic structure of society—for instance, the sanction against political assassination. Obviously, these extremes offer little interpretative aid to the historian. The utility of the role concept depends on defining intermediate sanctions of varying force such as those arising from class or status.

When one examines the force of various sanctions against deviation in the playing of social roles it becomes clear that in some directions the role is "open-ended." Or, put another way, either the defining group has no fixed expectations or all of a range of alternatives are equally acceptable to it. Generally sanctions are unlikely to bar adopting more efficient means for achieving goals pleasing to the defining group. The location of these open-ends or the potential areas of change reflect the approved personality types and pervasive themes of the culture. In the United States individual innovations that depart from the social role in the direction of increased efficiency are likely to occur and to be accepted, whereas both occurrence and acceptance of innovation are less likely in some other cultures.

Other than the groups whose expectations should be met if role performance is to be successful, there are groups that are normally passive in relation to the role if it is played within conventional limits but are able to bring *censoring* pressures against actions that exceed these limits. Law enforcement officers are obviously of this character. Censor groups are likely to become important when basic changes in role-playing occur, as in revolutions or in military or economic crises.

One of the most elusive problems of role theory results from the fact that the actor not only tries to live up to the expectations of the defining groups and avoid reprisals from censor groups but also has inner guides or admonitions affecting his action. Consciously or unconsciously he

* [For further comment on such "types" (or "aggregates," as Potter calls them), see the article by Potter, pp. 184 and 187–88 below.—EDITOR.]

tries to satisfy what psychoanalysts might call "the imperatives of his super-ego." In role language this internal sanctioning authority is called his *reference group*. The historian must take account of this tendency for conduct to be modified by inner drives not necessarily deducible from the situation, but in many cases empirical evidence short of that from interviews by skilled psychologists will not suffice to establish a reference group. Occasionally such information is plausibly given in autobiographies. For example, Andrew Carnegie, recalling a difficult and unpleasant role that he played as a young man in a bobbin factory, writes: "I was not beyond asking myself what Wallace [the Scotch hero] would have done. . . . A real disciple of Wallace or Bruce could not give up; he would die first."[9] From one standpoint the reference group is a focused summation of the characterological peculiarities of the actor. In most historical research relating to aggregates of actors these are the kinds of data that must be treated as random and averaged out over a large number of cases.

A further ambiguity is introduced by the fact that defining groups may be only analytically distinct from reference groups. Perhaps the most successful role players, those best adjusted to their situation, tend to have their major defining group also as their reference group, but clearly this is not always the case, and therefore it is desirable to define *reference group* strictly as "the inner sponsoring or censoring authority for the individual."[10]

When attention is shifted from the role player to the situation in which he acts, the reciprocal roles of others or, in Merton's terms, the *role-sets* become important. The executive who frames a policy decision, for example, must take into account not only the character of the information available to him, the expectations of his major defining group, the possibility of censorship, and the structure of the organization through which the decision must be implemented but also the role characteristics of the men who will operate the policy. These characteristics will include not only the men's social roles but also those unique aspects of individual roles that create unique reciprocal attitudes among his confreres. Thus social and individual roles in a given

[9] *Autobiography of Andrew Carnegie* (New York: Houghton Mifflin, 1920), pp. 35–36.

[10] R. M. Cyert and J. G. March in "Organizational Structure and Pricing Behavior in an Oligopolistic Market" say that "a reference group for a given individual consists in those other individuals with whom he perceives himself sharing common evaluative criteria for judging an attitudinal position" (*American Economic Review*, XLV [March, 1955], 133 n.).

situation are modified by each other, because for each role other roles are part of that situation.

Regardless of individual personality traits, the reciprocal interaction of roles presents problems in the operation of a formal organization. Each role is adapted to certain instrumental needs that create general attitudes toward the work of the organization. Role segments derived from specialized tasks are likely to conflict with over-all policy—or, in more specific language, harmonious reciprocal adjustments among the roles are not immediately achieved. Part of the trouble may come from differing evaluation of evidence by groups with different orientations. For instance, government administrators on a board may see things differently from men representing business. But violent conflicts between reciprocal roles in administrative hierarchies are usually avoided by the process of selection of the players. A man too poorly adjusted to the social role entailed will not seek that kind of position, and those having the power to select will choose only men who seem likely to do well in the role.

Such considerations suggest that social roles seen as tendencies toward predictable behavior depend on (1) the instrumental necessities of the task with their psychological and cultural correlates and (2) the expectations and power of the defining groups. But the historian who believes his evidence indicates certain characteristics of a social role must always be prepared to find eccentric behavior arising from individual motivations, including reference-group imperatives, in the actor.

Even from the highly simplified model presented above one can see the difficulty of finding relevant source material in forms suitable for historical generalization. Yet, in spite of its demands for data rarely if ever completely available from past records, the concept of social role has historical utility. While role systems are subject to infinite variation and subdivision, closely defined social roles such as exist in some professions or among elected politicians or corporate executives establish uniformities of attitude that can be important building blocks for larger historical interpretations.[11]

Role analysis applies to a central problem of the historian: What makes for permanence and for change? Sharply defined roles with strong defining groups make innovation more difficult, while loosely defined roles invite variations in behavior. This difference in roles

---

[11] See Cochran, *Railroad Leaders*, pp. 218–28.

gives meaning to such clichés as "a young country" and "an old country." In new situations social roles are still fluid; in old, traditional situations they tend to be well defined. The American promoter on the unsettled frontier governed his conduct largely by expediency, while the Congregational minister in New England knew rather precisely what was expected of him.

The point, therefore, of this brief discussion is that while the historian familiar with the intricacies of social role may find it difficult wholly to define any single role, the concept is useful for systematically examining situations involving well-defined status and group relationships. Knowledge of the intricacy of role analysis can also guard the historian against overly simplified views of the pattern of social interaction.

PART II

VIII. Categories of Historiographical Generalization

BY LOUIS GOTTSCHALK

The articles that make up this volume without exception consider it a fact, whether for better or for worse, that historians (and others using the historical approach) frequently do make generalizations, whether knowingly or unknowingly. Their authors seem fairly agreed, to use Wright's terms (p. 36), that "labeling" generalizations are common and that "regularity" generalizations are far from unknown. They also render plain enough a conviction that generalizers tend to fall into several different groupings. At least six categories seem to be implied: (1) those who make generalizations only if they are unaware that they are doing so and try to eliminate the ones of which they are aware; (2) those who make generalizations knowingly but intend to limit their generalizations strictly to the exposition of the historical subject matter under investigation and of that subject matter only in its own setting; (3) those who make a deliberate effort to go beyond the historical subject matter in hand in order to indicate its interrelations with antecedent, concurrent, and subsequent events and who thus risk broad interpretative syntheses but still limit their interpretations to interrelated trends; (4) those who with a similar readiness to go beyond the subject matter in hand draw parallels and analogies to it in other times or places of the past, whether or not otherwise interrelated; (5) those who venture propositions about past trends or analogies in such general or abstract terms as to leave the implications, if they do not indeed state explicitly, that their propositions may well be extrapolated to events in the future; and (6) those who propound philosophies that are intended to provide a cosmic understanding of the course of human events past and to come.

For the sake of brevity at least (and perhaps of clarity) each of these categories can be identified by its membership. Category No. 1 I shall call "the school of the unique," inasmuch as those who fit into it are prone, whether or not they consider scholarly generalization possible in historiography, to maintain that the historian's purpose should be to emphasize differences rather than similarities, to deal with the special and unique rather than the comparative and general. I shall contend below that only compilers of documents and chroniclers of unselected events truly belong in this category. Category No. 2 is "the school of the strictly limited generalization," in which I place the purely narrative-descriptive historians. Category No. 3 is "the school of generalization on the basis of trends," to which belong the interpretative historians, those who strive to establish some hypothesis or theory that will help to explain a number of interrelated historical events. Category No. 4 is "the school of generalization on the basis of comparisons"—that is, the comparative historians. Category No. 5 is "the school of generalizations that have validity for prediction or control"—that is, the nomothetic historians. Category No. 6 is "the school of cosmic philosophies of history"—that is, the philosophers of history.

The writers of the articles that precede and follow this one agree that adherents of the school of the unique are likely to be beguiled if they think they can avoid generalization. The arguments in support of this agreement seem to run essentially as follows: (1) language consists largely of verbal and written symbols which by their very nature must have general denotations and connotations; (2) the method by which the historian examines testimony and other evidence to arrive at the unique historical fact comprises in itself a set of rules (i.e., generalizations); (3) what is special, segregate, or unique cannot be understood except by comparison with the average, the normal, the aggregate, or the general (and vice versa). Even if a member of the school of the unique were to make a most strenuous effort to avoid generalization, he would first have to test his evidence for its authenticity and credibility by some set of recognized general rules such as are set forth from time to time in manuals of historical method. Then, to avoid using words or other symbols freighted with general meaning, he would be obliged to present only the duly tested evidence itself and in a strictly chronological order without comparisons, interrelations, reflections, or interpretations.

No doubt, such an array of testimony in chronological order is possible. Begging the question of the degree of generalization involved in a choice of subjects, one may grant that a historian might well undertake, for example, to present all the available letters written by Lafayette to Washington. Having searched for, found, and authenticated such letters, he would not even have to assay their contents for credibility. By presenting them in chronological order, he would have accomplished his task without any obligation to make further comments by way of comparison, interpretation, or generalization. Nor would he have to face the relatively but not altogether simple kind of generalization required in making decisions concerning the arrangement and selection of his material, since a chronological arrangement would by professional consensus be regarded as most appropriate and availability would solve the problem of selection. Some very useful historical work now going on in the United States—the editing of the Adams, Burke, Franklin, Hamilton, Jefferson, Madison, and Walpole papers, for example—is of this nature (though not quite, since the editors have not always contented themselves with presenting the text, the whole text, and nothing but the text).

The compiler-editor is perhaps the most consistent adherent of the school of the unique. Once, however, a compiler departs from the principle of giving the *full* text of *all the available* documents in a *prescribed* area and in *chronological* order without interjecting *any words of his own*, he comes face to face with the risk of inconsistency, for he must employ at least the sort of generalization involved in fixing criteria for selection from among his compiled materials and for the use or avoidance of descriptive language of his own. He has to ask, for example: Is picturesqueness of language in a document more worthy of selection for quotation than quantitative data? Should repetitive material be omitted? What about trivia? What are standards of importance, anyway? Is the use of space to give variant readings justifiable? Should introductory remarks or footnotes be used to present the several documents' contexts and, if so, what tests for their wording, length, relevance, etc.? To be sure, the compiler-editor rarely has to make his own decisions on such matters, since the processes of compilation have become largely conventionalized. But conventions of this kind are themselves generalizations, and unexamined acceptance of them does not avoid generalization but avoids only awareness of generalization, though in the supposed case perhaps only generalizations of historical method and linguistic connotation. If the historian of the school of the unique seriously means to run the risk of generalization only at this level, he should rest content with compiling documents with as little editing as possible.

Most historiographical work, however, is not compilatory-editorial. It is descriptive, narrative, or expository or a combination of these and requires a more or less skillful use of language. As soon as the historian uses his own language, he has to cope with the general notions conveyed by certain words. Finley shows above (pp. 21–23, 30–31) that words applicable to one time may, even without context, mislead when applied to another time; Wright shows (pp. 53–56) how the same holds true for isolated words applicable in one place when applied to another place. Readers need hardly be reminded that the common meaning of the same words may differ in English usage from American usage. Thus, studied selection of words may well be required to avoid comparative connotations or, as Palmer (p. 71) indicates that he has done, to suggest them. Words in a context may be still more compromising. I have elsewhere explained why a simple sentence like "Columbus discovered America on October 12, 1492" is loaded with comparative and general terms (of chronology, philology, exploration, geography, biography, etc.); only some of the difficulties are avoided by a less simple wording such as "On a day conveniently labeled 'October 12, 1492' a group of sailors captained by a man known in English as 'Christopher Columbus' landed on an island which was apparently the one now called 'Watling Island.' "[1]

Leaving out of consideration the philosophical question, raised by Starr above (p. 3) and Aydelotte and Potter below (pp. 149–51 and 183–87, respectively), whether there actually is a difference between historical fact and historical generalization, I have also indicated elsewhere that generalizations are particularly prone to lie hidden in certain kinds of words and phrases that historians and others use commonly. I did not (and do not) mean simply that common collective or plural nouns like *Moscow* or *Americans* or descriptive adjectives like *national* or abstract nouns like *character* imply general meanings without which communication would be extremely difficult if not impossible, though I meant that, too. I meant also that some words presume (or should presume) a conscious comparative, evaluative, or generalized connotation in the mind of the user. Such words include superlative adjectives, emphatic adverbs that single out the words they modify from the general run, and all adjectives and phrases which indicate that the words they modify designate a regular or normal class of beings or mode of behavior.[2] A historian who wishes to do more than quote documents,

---

[1] *Understanding History: A Primer of Historical Method* (4th [rev.] printing; New York: Knopf, 1956), p. 17. (I would now be inclined to still greater doubt about Watling Island.)

[2] "The Historian's Use of Generalization," in Leonard D. White (ed.), *The State of the Social Sciences* (Chicago: University of Chicago Press, 1956), p. 447: "I speak rather of the category of generalization that is implied by certain kinds of words that for lack of a better name I call *singularizing words* and *generalizing*

who prefers to narrate, describe, or expound in his own words and who yet adheres to the school of the unique might conceivably avoid these hidden generalizations as well as others, whether explicit or implicit, whether by comparison or interrelation, but he can do so only if he also avoids all standards (i.e., generalized notions) of relevance for his selection of the data, of importance for his assay of the relative emphasis he gives them, and of interrelation for his arrangement of them in some revealing order. In other words, if he rests content to be a chronicler of discrete events (to present what may be called a qualitative time analysis in a binary number system), he can with assiduous attention reduce to a minimum the risks of departure from the unique.

So far I have dealt only with the problem of generalization as faced by the historians of the school of the unique (though some at least of his unavoidable problems will confront other historians as well). When the historians who subscribe to the principles of the other schools face the same problem, they are likely to do so with less effort to avoid, and perhaps with some express effort to find, a comparative or general thesis. Their sins, if sins they be, thus become those of commission rather than of omission.

Let us begin with the school of the strictly limited generalization. What does the historian do who is willing to generalize but wishes to go no further than the limited data in hand? He is likely to take at least two steps: (1) apply generalizations borrowed elsewhere than from the documented historical knowledge under investigation in order to fill the gaps in it, and (2) classify or categorize at least those parts of his data that lend themselves to some kind of comparison, contrast, regularity, or generalization, however circumspect. I shall illustrate these two steps from my own investigations.

When one arranges the isolated bits of information derived from the sources pertaining to a single career in a biographical (i.e., chronological) order, one often finds some details relatively difficult to explain. For example, the Marquis de Lafayette wrote a letter dated September

---

words. Singularizing words comprise not only adjectives in the superlative degree, like *best*, *most*, and *first*, but also emphatic adverbs like *even* and *especially*, verbal phrases like *single out*, and phrases like *par excellence*. Generalizing words comprise adjectives like *every* and *all*, adverbs like *naturally*, and phrases like *as usual*." Examples of the use of such words in actual historical writing follow (*ibid.*, pp. 447–48). For a discussion of "latent generalizations" based on kinds rather than levels of generalization, see the essay by Potter below, especially pp. 186–91.

18, 1787 (and apparently late in the day), from Paris, and on September 19 he wrote another to an American merchant from Varennes, roughly one hundred and fifty miles away. Since both letters are authentic and error in dating them is highly improbable, the question arises how such apparently contradictory pieces of evidence can both be credited. Note that already a generalization has been applied—viz., in 1787 for a man to be in two places one hundred and fifty miles apart within a period of probably no more than twenty-four hours required a special effort, a generalization which is based, in turn, upon a series of other generalizations about the means of transportation in the 1780's. Putting together such a set of generalizations and applying them to a particular historical episode is sometimes placed under the heading of "historical imagination," or what Finley (p. 29 above) calls "extrapolation"—that is, the kind of thought process needed to fill in the gaps between the explicit testimony and what-must-have-been in order to make the several parts of that testimony dovetail. In this instance there seems to be no choice but to assume that Lafayette, "spurring his horses throughout the night and most of the next day," reached Varennes from Paris "at the end of a gruelling journey."[3]

The process of filling the gaps in the testimony sometimes requires and frequently invites comparison. If, as is true, the investigator finds several other gruelling trips of a like nature in the career of Lafayette, he might well generalize—not that Lafayette was a good horseman, for the information is inadequate for such a generalization, but perhaps that Lafayette did not allow the prospect of traveling rapidly over distances that might well have daunted ordinary men to daunt him in the accomplishment of his aims. Such a comparison sheds light on the idea of uniqueness. For what is it, limited though it is to one career *sui generis*, if not (1) a generalization about a single character, (2) a statement comparing that character with a generalized concept of the character of ordinary men, and—consequently (and, what is more, suspect if not derived *after* such a comparison)—(3) a statement about the uniqueness of Lafayette? In brief, it is hard to conceive of an assertion about the unique that would not demand a comparison of some sort or other.

[3] *Lafayette between the American and the French Revolution (1783-1789)* (Chicago: University of Chicago Press, 1950), pp. 337-39. (The historian who did not, mentally at least, compare the conditions of this ride with those of the celebrated flight of King Louis XVI to Varennes would certainly be lacking at least in imagination; the king, with every reason to hurry, required about twenty-four hours.)

So far our hypothetical historian of the school of limited generalization has limited himself strictly indeed—that is, to a concatenation of chronologically close or similar events in one man's career. Suppose that, still subscribing to the limited-generalization school, he were willing to make a broader generalization about the carefully tested data in hand—say, for example, about the revolutions in which over a long lifetime Lafayette participated. He might then come out with some such generalization as: "Lafayette participated in every revolution from the 1770's to the 1830's of which he knew." Or: "Lafayette consciously tried to model his action in revolutionary situations on his concept of how Washington would have acted in similar circumstances." If carefully made, these generalizations (which I think are true, though the question of their truth or falsehood is not really relevant to the present discussion) should result from a classification or set of classifications of Lafayette's behavior, a hypothesis that his behavior falls into a definite pattern. If true, they are good examples of explicit concepts knowingly and strictly limited to a specific set of historical data. But they cannot avoid being also implicit methodological prescriptions to future historians. They say in effect: (1) in any investigation of Western revolutions between the 1770's and the 1830's, look for Lafayette, and (2) in any investigation of Lafayette's motivations look for his "father-image" of Washington.

If the biographer in the instance under consideration above were not in the school of limited generalization but were prepared to be among the bolder generalizers, he might come fairly close to using the broad concept of *social role* that Metzger (pp. 90–94) and Cochran (pp. 103–10) deal with in their articles above. He might go so far as to say: "In any investigation of any revolution, past or to come, consider the possibility that the role of a leader may at times be deliberately or subconsciously patterned, by both his internal drives and the expectations of those about him, after that of an admired leader of an earlier revolution." A truism? Perhaps, but so are many of the more familiar "laws" of physics and the social sciences (Newton's, Boyle's, Gresham's, for example), for today's truisms sometimes are only convincing and well-known articulations of once unarticulated inklings— "what oft was thought, but ne'er so well expressed." Generalization from a single instance? Yes, but a generalization from a single instance is not necessarily wrong and, if properly qualified in the light of further instances, may well prove to be right for any number of instances.

Such a generalization can, of course, be made also—and perhaps just as well—from contemporary experience and observation, without any knowledge of history; in that case it may be tested by its applicability to historical events, becoming more convincing or being made more precise or being discarded altogether as it is respectively corroborated, conditioned, or found wanting by applicable events in the past.

There is no reason why the maxims of a La Rochefoucauld or any other wise man, as Palmer contends (p. 75 above), should not be equally useful as sources of historical insight. Like proverbs, the maxims and aphorisms that endure may articulate the folk experience. The test of time is likely to have value, as Nichols insists (p. 141 below), also for the studied generalizations of historians. But until thoroughly examined—that is, until carefully checked and strictly conditioned by contrast and comparison with the verifiable experience of mankind, as Aydelotte suggests (pp. 171-72 below)—maxims, aphorisms, and proverbs are likely to be not only too general but also too contradictory to be useful to either the historian or the layman hoping to benefit from the teachings of history. The fables of Carolyn Wells about the two brothers or the two farmers or her several other groups of two pointed up the contradictory nature of proverbs: "This Fable teaches that In a Multitude of Counselors there is Safety, and that Too Many Cooks Spoil the Broth"; or "This Fable teaches that Absence Makes the Heart Grow Fonder, and that Out of Sight is Out of Mind"; or "This Fable teaches that a Bird In The Hand is worth Two In the Bush, and The Patient Waiter Is No Loser"; or "This Fable teaches that a Rolling Stone Gathers No Moss, and a Setting Hen Never Grows Fat."[4] But folk experience and wise men's sayings provide fairly good starting points for the historian—loose generalizations to be tightened and refined or discarded.

If a historian were willing to go so far as to generalize about the roles of leaders in a revolution, he would no longer belong in the school of limited generalization. He would then be a comparative historian (belonging in the school numbered 4 above) or a nomothetic historian (belonging in the school numbered 5 above). But let us not overlook

---

[4] *The Wit and Humor of America*, ed. Marshall P. Wilder (New York: Funk & Wagnalls, 1911), II, 7-8, 16, 48, and 72. Cf. Lazarsfeld as cited by Finley (p. 33, n. 14, above): Lazarsfeld tricks the "common-sense" reader into accepting as plausible exactly the opposite of what he then shows to have been proved true by careful investigation.

Categories of Historiographical Generalization

school No. 3, the interpretative school, those historians who, while trying to provide a hypothesis that will explain much of history, mean to apply it only to a trend or tendency within a limited set of past events without pronouncing upon its applicability to other events of the past and still less to future events. Weber's thesis concerning the Protestant ethic, Pirenne's concerning medieval disruption, Mahan's concerning naval warfare, Turner's concerning the American frontier, Beard's concerning the American constitution, and Becker's concerning the heavenly city of the eighteenth-century philosophers are well-known examples of theories based on such trends. When offered in the spirit of Pirenne, they are tentative, intended only to suggest further investigation: "Every effort at synthesis," said Pirenne, "however premature it may seem, cannot fail to react usefully on investigations, provided one offers it in all frankness for what it is."[5] The extent to which the Weber, Pirenne, Mahan, Turner, Beard, and Becker theses are still fighting symbols around or against which historians rally and fight leads to the patent historiographical generalization that historians are at least as much interested in syntheses that explain possibly interrelated events as they are in portrayals of the unique.

If a historian were an interpretative historian—that is, one concerned with deriving a theory that would provide a synthesis of interrelated events of the past—even though he based his study on a single and unique historical figure like Lafayette, he might venture the hypothesis that the revolutions of the late eighteenth and early nineteenth centuries were a chain of revolutionary interactions regardless of whether they were in the Eastern or the Western Hemisphere, eastern or western Europe, North or South America (which is, in fact, a thesis that Acton, Faÿ, and Mornet suggested long before I examined it in part and which Palmer has more fully developed in the book some of whose general assumptions and conclusions he discusses in his paper above).[6] This sort of synthesis perhaps suggests itself by the

---

[5] Quoted by James L. Cate, "Henri Pirenne, 1862–1935," in *Some 20th Century Historians*, ed. S. William Halperin (Chicago: University of Chicago Press, 1961), p. 28.

[6] Lord Acton, *Lectures on the French Revolution* (London: Macmillan, 1910), pp. 20–38; Bernard Faÿ, *L'esprit révolutionnaire en France et aux États-Unis à la fin du XVIIIe siècle* (Paris: Champion, 1925); Daniel Mornet, *Origines intellectuelles de la Révolution française, 1715–1787* (Paris: Colin, 1933), pp. 389–99; Louis Gottschalk, *The Place of the American Revolution in the Causal Pattern of the French Revolution*

process that Finley (p. 33) calls "professionalism." Sooner or later one or more investigators of a period or area begin to suspect some kind of nexus within the matter of their historical investigation. Though such "hunches," "insights," "guesses," "hypotheses"— whatever you may call them—may be rejected out of hand by some of them, the bolder or rasher among them venture to examine the possibility of the objective reality of such a nexus, and then it is likely to become a subject of debate, and perhaps of eventual refinement to the point of wide recognition in the learned world. This process is not very different from the way analytical scholars in other fields proceed —Darwin, for example, or Freud. If this process serves no other purpose, it at least may furnish propositions upon which to focus future investigations and debates. In historiography such investigations may sometimes lead a historian to apply the thesis in question to other episodes in the past deemed analogous, in which case that historian becomes *ipso facto* an adherent of the comparative school (the one numbered 4 above).

But do not these historical syntheses, no matter what their authors' intention, invariably have a wider applicability than to the single set of data from which they rose? If Weber is right, isn't it implicit in his concept of the Protestant ethic that where a certain kind of religious attitude prevails, there the spirit of capitalism will, or at least may, flourish? If Pirenne is right, doesn't his thesis imply that a culture of long duration may more confidently be expected to collapse as a result of sudden invasion than of seriatim penetration. If Mahan was right, couldn't victory in war (at least, before the invention of the airplane) be regarded as dependent on maritime control? If Turner is right, won't his frontier thesis apply to some extent to all societies that have frontiers to conquer in the future as well as it has applied to American society in the past? Whether he believed it at the close of his life or not, didn't Beard's book inevitably raise the question in the inquiring mind whether written constitutions are not at all times likely to be reflections of the desire for stability on the part of vested interests? Isn't Becker saying by implication that no matter how antireligious a set of intellectual reformers may appear to be, they can hope for a

---

(Easton, Pa.: American Friends of Lafayette, 1948); Robert R. Palmer, *The Age of the Democratic Revolution: A Political History of Europe and America, 1760–1800* (Princeton: Princeton University Press, 1959).

better world only if they substitute one set of articles of faith for another?

Theses like these, I believe, are more often initially derived from their authors' personal experience (including cogitation and book learning) than from the study of purely historical data. Once derived, however, they may be tested and given precision by studied application of them to vicarious episodes or circumstances.[7] While the dignity of historiography may perhaps dwindle in such a mental process, the validity of the generalizations so derived and tested may be enhanced. Yet, whether suggested by purely historical data or by relevant observations in the historian's personal life, the principles upon which an interpretative historical synthesis is based may, if valid at all, be valid *mutatis mutandis* for more than the data to which the historian *qua* historian has applied it. The major significance of such a synthesis lies, of course, in whether and to what an extent it may be valid rather than in how it is derived. Addressing themselves to this major problem, Metzger (pp. 99–101 above), Nichols (pp. 141–44) and Aydelotte (pp. 172–77), among others, suggest ways of refining or testing historical generalizations so that they may be more stringently applicable if only to more strictly defined circumstances.

We come now to the nomothetic historians, those who candidly seek, by drawing historical parallels, delineating regularities of past behavior, or extrapolating sequences of past events into the future, to derive from history abiding lessons or laws of universal behavior or, at least, some basis for prediction or possible control of future behavior. To the extent that these historians examine seemingly comparable sets of past events, they belong also in category No. 4, the comparative school of historians. A distinction must be made between two kinds of historians who venture upon universals. One kind limit themselves to probing for generally applicable lessons or rules that the examination of well-defined and known activities of the past may teach about interrelated events of the actual past or about similar eventualities, whether unknown, purely conjectural, feared, or hoped for. The other kind propound cosmic philosophies of history that have a teleological or eschatological coloration. The former include students of history like Machiavelli, who examined political behavior of the past in order to

[7] See my "The Historian's Use of Generalization," pp. 442–45.

derive lessons (or, perhaps more accurately, to bolster convictions otherwise derived) for the conduct of the rulers of Italy, and Montesquieu, who examined the history of various kinds of governments in order to discover (or, perhaps more accurately, to argue for his preconception of) the national character and institutions necessary for the perpetuation of the French monarchy. The cosmic philosophers include Augustine, Joachim of Floris, Condorcet, Hegel, Marx, and numerous other historians or users of history interested in the over-all course and the end-product of the historical process.

The latter school, the propounders of panoramic ideologies or historical determinisms, form the category numbered 6 above, the philosophers of history. Aydelotte speaks (pp. 154-56 below) about some modern masters of this school. I deliberately choose to deal with it only in passing on the ground that its practitioners are more or less consciously special pleaders, belonging to the disciplines of theology, philosophy, or political speculation rather than to that of history as a branch of learning, no matter how well they use historical knowledge and no matter how much more important they may be to the world than academic historians. The tests of their hypotheses are not conformance with historical evidence and plausibility or probability alone; they require other standards than, or in addition to, the canons of historical investigation and other kinds of convictions than those derived from historical research and tight inference from testimony. Yet, as everyone knows, these all-pervasive interpretations of history have been the fountainheads of some productive streams of historical investigations aimed at proving or disproving them.

The nomothetic historians (category No. 5) concerned the Committee more than did the philosophers (category No. 6). The historian who specializes in a more or less well-defined field of history may himself detect phenomena recurring or presumed to recur from time to time or from place to place. Most often, however, they are presented to him as ready-made labels—such as (to borrow examples from Wright's article alone) feudalism, Caesars, baroque, "the dynastic cycle." "Classificatory" or "labeling" generalizations, as Finley (p. 21) and Wright (p. 36), respectively, call them, whether or not recurrent, are or can be themselves categorized in ways that derive from the very nature of historical evidence.

The nature of first-hand verbal testimony and vestigial artifacts (as distinguished from hearsay, judgments, or inferences) is such that they can bear direct witness only to four things—*who, doing what, where, and when.* Except to the extent that they are revealed as motives or influences by introspective autobiography and revealed or betrayed by outward manifestations that fit into some general pattern, answers to *why and with what consequences*—causes and effects—can only be inferred but cannot be directly witnessed. And *how* can be witnessed directly only insofar as the relevant testimony applies to processes— relatively simple means and operations—that can be subsumed under *doing what.*[8] If we try only to answer the four questions implied in *who, doing what, where, and when* (and, for the moment at least, leave causality and process out of consideration), we may more or less objectively classify historiographical labels into four, though often overlapping, kinds. I shall specify and then illustrate each kind by examples mentioned in one or more of the articles comprising this report: (1) biographical entities or aggregates that answer the question *who?*—e.g., Athenian individualists, "bad-last rulers," constituted bodies, and urban, educated American southerners; (2) group behavior or activities that answer the question *doing what?*—e.g., engaging in revolution, waterworks bureaucracy, *n* Achievement, slavery, and social role; (3) geographical interrelations that answer the question *where?* —e.g., in the Central Kingdom, classical Rome, Atlantic Civilization, nineteenth-century England; and (4) chronological interrelations, or periodizations, that answer the question *when?*—e.g., in the reign of Justinian, the T'ang Dynasty, the age of the democratic revolution, the American Civil War. The chances of overlapping among these four kinds of labels or classifications are obvious; almost every one of the examples given under any one of them could easily be fitted into the other three, though sometimes only with additional specifications. In sum, any historical datum may and frequently must fit into all of four kinds of classification—biographical, behavioral, geographical, and chronological—and it would be a rare datum for which classifications under all four headings would not be easily available in relatively conventional labels.

The historian's problem, it would seem therefore, seldom is the paucity of ready-made labels or classifications, even when he eschews the problem of causality, but rather the accuracy and fittingness of the

---

[8] For an indication of some of the historian's problems in dealing with the problem of causation and explanation see the article by Potter below, especially pp. 179–83; also Meyerhoff as quoted above (pp. vi–vii, n. 2).

available ones. If he is interested in causality, process, and explanation, the same holds true for general laws, perhaps a fortiori. Every article submitted to the Committee is more or less avowedly concerned with the problem of accuracy of generalization—a fact which suggests that at least some historians, whichever of the above six schools they may prefer, agree that one of the major functions of the historian is to examine and confirm, to modify or refine, and to use or repudiate the concepts (whether labels or laws) that come to him ready-made. Such concepts come from many sources—from primary historical material (e.g., "the bad-last ruler") or secondary historical material[9] (e.g., "slave" and "division of labor" as applied to ancient Greece); from the philosophy of history (e.g., "geographical determinism" and "class struggle") or the history of art (e.g., "the baroque period"); from anthropology (e.g., "culture diffusion" or "kinship") or sociology (e.g., "n Achievement") or psychology (e.g., "social role") or economics (e.g., "price curve" and "business cycle") or any other of the social disciplines that exploit historical data; from the clichés of his own day (e.g., "national character" and "capitalist class") or the distilled wisdom of his most talented contemporaries (e.g., "inferiority complex" or "challenge and response").

It would follow, then, that many, if not most, of the generalizations that historians intentionally venture take the form of refinements of those he has encountered in the course of his own experience whether in his capacity of professional historian or in that of educated layman, whether personally or vicariously. Finley, Wright, Bodde, and Metzger by insisting upon a careful semantic analysis of the terms involved; Aydelotte and Potter by describing the need for strict and systematic examination of the things historians talk about; Nichols by pleading for a careful examination of the genealogy of general interpretations; and Aydelotte by asking for the application of quantitative methods where feasible—each has indicated some of the steps by which such a refinement can in some instances be obtained. And along with them, Starr, Palmer, and Cochran have scrutinized some more or less refined concepts with varying degrees of receptivity or skepticism.

Historians of the nomothetic school often are not content merely to refine borrowed generalizations but seek, sometimes unawares, to

---

[9] Cf. the essay by Nichols (pp. 130–44 below) on the genealogy of generalizations.

Categories of Historiographical Generalization

derive additional ones that are at least partly original. In the course of a few weeks in January, 1961, preparatory to writing the first draft of this article (and with no effort to read especially appropriate literature, though with special attention to the problem here under discussion) I gathered the following generalizations having some claim to originality and avowedly based on an examination of history:

A. "A politically satisfied populace might well accept an administration less than perfect whereas a politically dissatisfied one could always find fault with even the most laudable intentions."[10]

B. ". . . wherever a European state which is not now free may gain or regain political freedom, there the parliamentary system of government is sure to be established."[11]

C. "And history is witness again and again that size and prestige have no fixed correlation. Indeed, its first lesson is that true prestige has always been the product not so much of genuine power as of genuine excellence."[12]

D. "It seems far more probable [than an explanation in racial terms—Celtic and Germanic] that geographical factors determined the kind of settlement the peasants [of medieval Europe] made."[13]

E. "The religious art of all peoples and periods has always been the expression in visual form of their belief in unseen supernatural powers governing their lives and destinies."[14]

F. "But the driving force behind the innovations in outlook and methods of these European scientists [of the seventeenth century] came in no small degree from the immense confidence they possessed in the powers of the mind to find truths concerning the universe which was then almost universally believed by learned Europeans to be the creation of God, as Christ had revealed him."[15]

These six generalizations are not of the same kind: some are by historians, others by persons in other disciplines using historical data;

[10] Arthur G. Haas, "Metternich, Reorganization and Nationality, 1813–1818" (Wiesbaden: Franz Steiner Verlag, 1963), p. 10.

[11] R. K. Gooch, *Parliamentary Government in France: Revolutionary Origins, 1789–1791* (Ithaca, N.Y.: Cornell University Press, 1960), pp. 1–2.

[12] Barbara Ward, "The Highest Resolve—True Prestige," *New York Times Magazine* (Jan. 1, 1961), p. 37.

[13] Jerome Blum, *The European Peasantry from the Fifteenth to the Nineteenth Century* (Washington: Service Center for Teachers of History, 1960), p. 3.

[14] Benjamin Rowland, "Religious Art East and West," in the papers submitted for the Second Conference of the Frank L. Weil Institute for Studies in Religion and the Humanities (manuscript; Cincinnati, 1961).

[15] J. U. Nef, "Can There Be a New Christian View of History?" *ibid*.

some are about historical data exclusively, others on the basis of historical data mean primarily to lay down norms for prediction. All of them, however, are intended to have universal validity, for, to recast a point already made, even when they deal with agricultural institutions or religious art of the past, they lay down general factors by which institutions or art may be affected (and understood) in the future.

Whether or not these generalizations are valid (and doubts readily arise about some of them), they seem to shed light on how their authors arrived at them. Some of them may well have come by outright borrowing, but it is also possible that others were originally glimpsed from a single instance or a group of instances which came to the author's attention (no matter whether directly through personal experience or vicariously through his study of history) and then, having been compared with similar historical instances and having been modified and qualified to fit all the relevant instances of which he knew, were ventured as a generalization true of the past and, implicitly if not explicitly, potentially applicable also in the future wherever the same conditions may prevail. Reasoned bets and other "calculated risks" are frequently determined by a similar procedure.

This procedure is one that I think may also have validity in generalizations upon causality. At any rate, in the few attempts I have made seriously and avowedly to propound a generalization about causes I have proceeded that way. For example, I once tried to analyze the causes of revolution. Beginning with the revolution that I knew best, no matter how inadequately, I derived for it a set of causes (in eclectic and general terms) from many suggestions that had come to me from many sources. I then tested them against the causes of other revolutions of which I knew, categorizing, qualifying, hedging, and shaping the terms in which I thought, as I went from revolution to revolution and back again, until I felt prepared to risk an interrelated set of causes in print.[16]

It is obvious that the same historian can belong at one time or at different times in more than one of the schools described above. For my own part, I have tried to be editor-compiler, narrative-descriptive historian, interpretative historian, comparative historian, and nomo-

---

[16] "Causes of Revolution," *American Journal of Sociology*, L (1944), 1–8. Apparently this is also the way Nichols (pp. 130–44 below) has proceeded with regard to his generalizations about the genealogy of generalizations.

thetic historian, and I make no promise not to engage at some future time, if I should think I have anything worth saying, on some philosophic explanation of all history. The world has room and the profession has need for all kinds of historians.[17]

[17] Letter of Professor Meyerhoff to the author, July 26, 1961: "What *kind* of generalization is this report dealing with? (1) Generalizations derived from non-historical disciplines: common sense or the sciences, both natural and human, or (2) generalizations which are characteristically and specifically historical? This distinction, I think, undercuts your 'categories.' . . ." If, as some philosophers maintain, there are no characteristically and specifically historical generalizations (see pp. vi–vii, n. 2 above), then, Meyerhoff continues, "the only problem would be to discuss (*a*) how far the historian must (or should) go in falling back upon these non-historical disciplines . . . or (*b*) how far the historian is (and must be) limited in this respect because he is always falling back upon common sense assumptions and truisms." But, Meyerhoff adds, "on the other hand there is the view, chiefly held by the comparative and speculative students of history, according to which it is possible to formulate characteristically and specifically historical generalizations—even though these generalizations do not satisfy the standards set by a quantitative or statistical analysis. Advocates of this view would fall into your categories 4, 5, and 6 (possibly 3)."

Farther on Meyerhoff adds: "A statement such as 'Ideas follow trade routes' or 'Economic depressions produce a revolutionary situation'—whether true or false—is (or presumes to be) a genuine explanation in the logical sense. These are generalizations which *explain* the particular phenomenon, say, of a revolution by subsuming it under, or deriving it from, a general law. It is these explanations in terms of general laws which I think are of major concern for your project. . . . It might be helpful to focus more specifically . . . upon this type of historical explanation and distinguish it more clearly from the . . . more spurious type which you call 'labeling generalizations' and which does not pose a specifically historical problem."

IX. The Genealogy of Historical Generalizations

BY ROY F. NICHOLS

The construction of historical generalizations is a cumulative process, leading to formulations that are often unstable and subject to frequent change. An understanding of the conditions determining this instability, which include a succession of creations, modifications, and eliminations, may contribute significantly to the historian's proficiency and effectiveness in practicing his intricate art.

The first historical account of any development or period may present facts and events in the form of generalizations, and subsequent generalizers tend to build on this foundation. In reality no historical generalization is ever wholly lost. The interpretations of a given epoch at different times, however, may evoke a series of generalizations which are the reverse of uniform and, in many cases, are conflicting. The passage of time and changes in environment and persons work to produce this variety. Under changing circumstances generalizations are modified not so much because new evidence is discovered as because new minds are at work in a different cultural atmosphere.

Some of these changes produce a succession of generalizations which bear a traceable relationship. In such a succession one generalization determines another somewhat as the genes determine the characteristics of new biological generations. Therefore, generalizations can be said to have genealogies. This genealogical succession complicates the formulation of generalizations, and a clearer understanding of it is essential if the historian is to construct effectively a type of generalization which will have long life and more lasting validity.

The nature of this genealogical process can be conveniently illustrated by reference to the work of the first Committee on Historiography of the Social Science Research Council. This committee in its report, *Theory and Practice in Historical Study* (New York, 1946), published an article entitled "What Historians Have Said about the Causes of the Civil War" by Howard K. Beale, which may be used as a base for further analysis. The now rounding century of generaliza-

Genealogy of Historical Generalizations

tion regarding the American Civil War reveals certain characteristics of the cumulative process of historical generalization.

Generalizations about the Civil War began with the clash of arms. At the primary stage of the conflict official spokesmen, reporters, and participants for one reason or another felt called upon to account for what was happening or had happened. The first to give utterance to such accounts were political leaders rallying the contending communities to their respective causes. Their generalizations were later to have particular historical significance because of the men who made them. The Federal government had a superb spokesman in the person of President Abraham Lincoln, whose words became immortal. Jefferson Davis, his Confederate counterpart, was an able interpreter, but his utterances were never to receive anything like such acclaim. Lincoln laid the foundation of generalization when in his first message he referred to the conflict as both a "giant insurrection" and a "rebellion," a struggle "to preserve the Union against those who would destroy it and to maintain in the world a government whose leading object was to elevate the condition of men." Shortly before this, Senator Stephen A. Douglas, out on the stump rallying the nation to its defense, declared the war to be the "result of an enormous conspiracy formed . . . by the leaders in the Southern Confederacy more than twelve months ago." President Davis, in contrast, reported to the Confederate Congress that the contest was a fight "for our common defense against the unprovoked war of aggression," a cause "just and holy" for "honor and independence." It was, he said, the result of a "persistent and organized system of hostile measures against the rights of Southerners," of the "determination of the North to gain control," of the "insistence upon the absolute right of the majority to rule and to maintain a theatre of agitation and aggression against Southern rights." Statements by officials of such stature established the basis for what may be called that "tyranny of initial formulation" from which historians seldom entirely free themselves.

A second group that contributed generalizations at this primary stage were journalists and other writers who began their reporting with the outburst of gunfire. Right after the First Battle of Bull Run they commenced their work. The initial fruits of their labors came from the pen of Orville J. Victor, the inventor of the dime novel, who worked for the publisher Erastus D. Beadle. They put to use the idea of the cheap paperback as a means of reporting the conflict. Victor began immediately after Bull Run to write what he called *The History*,

Civil, Political and Military of the Southern Rebellion, which was published in monthly installments. His readers did not get beyond the title and the first page before coming upon one of the earliest of this group of historical generalizations: "Never since the revolt of Lucifer has there been a more causeless rebellion against a justly-constituted and beneficent government." One of the Confederacy's principal journalists, Edward A. Pollard, editor of the *Daily Richmond Examiner,* undertook to be its historian. He began generalization in his *Southern History of the War: The First Year,* which was followed by other annual volumes. The South had seceded, he claimed, because an "open and avowed consolidationist" interest in the North was insisting that the majority must govern. This interest having gained the election of 1860, there was "no longer any guaranty for ... rights or any permanent sense of security." Institutions, property, life itself were in danger. The North was fighting because it knew the value of the Union to that section and believed that it would be ruined by secession. The South was being coerced to gratify Northern selfishness and "worse lusts of revenge and fanaticism." Speakers and writers like these, Union and Confederate, were obviously following the "official line."

A third group contributing to this primary stage of generalization was composed of participants. Statesmen, soldiers, sailors, and journalists undertook to tell the story, reveal the truth, justify their own conduct, and reap financial gain from the rising interest of a new generation of the reading public. Their principal concepts were neatly phrased in certain of their titles: *The History of the Rebellion, The Great Conspiracy, The History of the Rise and Fall of the Slave Power in America, The Lost Cause,* and one of later coinage, "The Needless War." The authors of these works included James G. Blaine, John A. Logan, Joshua Giddings, Henry Wilson, Horace Greeley, and Pollard. As the quantity of memoirs of the military and naval commanders on both sides grew, the United States government did its part by beginning the publication in 1880 of a massive collection of the official records of Union and Confederate armies and navies. The title of this series supplied the official generalization; they were the record of the *War of the Rebellion.* The former vice-president of the Confederacy, Alexander H. Stephens, supplied the countervailing generalization in the title of his memoirs, *A Constitutional View of the Late War between the States.* And "the War between the States" it has remained to the largest group in the region of the late Confederacy.

The tone of the generalizations of the participants was determined

Genealogy of Historical Generalizations

in large part by the immediate outcome of the conflict. The Union forces won, and the Republic was restored. The fact of victory inevitably invited a moral implication. Righteousness had triumphed. Not only had a good, the Union, been preserved but evils, slavery and the so-called right of secession, had been destroyed. The contending forces were likewise identified with moral tags. Wicked Southern conspirators had plotted destruction of a superior government. This treasonable combination had been resisted by a valiant host aroused to defend the right. Northern patriots had flocked to the colors to crush rebellion and had brought traitors to book. This interpretation was written into the canon of American history within a quarter of a century after 1865.

To this judgment certain of the defeated entered a caveat, developing a romantic counter theory of the Lost Cause. To them the culture of the South had been a way of life based upon a concept as old and hallowed as the Athenian democracy with its slave base, though smeared by hypocritical Harriet Beecher Stowes. The chivalrous efforts to maintain it had been frustrated by superior numbers of materialistic philistines who could not appreciate a higher civilization. The war had, therefore, been a brave struggle to preserve cherished constitutional rights and liberties against the greedy aggression of jealous Northern politicians.

These generalizations obviously formulated not one history but two, one Union and the other Confederate—which produced a paradox. The purposes of both sides were described as idealistic and, to a certain extent, identical—that is, insofar as they were both dictated by a determination to defend constitutional rights. Each side was contending for "liberty" to enjoy its "rights." The Union was fighting to preserve the "rule of the majority." The South was fighting to protect the rights of the minority, the constitutional rights of the states. Northern historians rejoiced in the victory of righteousness. Southern commentators admitted defeat in arms but not in ideals; the "Lost Cause" would someday be regained. Some few, applying a greater amount of critical observation, wrote of the contest as one which might have been avoided; to them it was a "needless war." The latter historians were generally Southerners or Democrats or both.

Writers such as those of the three groups described above represent types which inevitably appear at a time of historical crisis, and their work provides the first stage of generalization about that crisis. This stage develops within twenty or thirty years after the event and is formulated by participants in it, whose immediate acts, observations, and emotions dominate their thinking. This first stage of generalization is followed by a second.

The contributors to the second stage are not observers or participants. They are of a new generation, coming forward after the record, in a sense, has been made available. This generation, brought up in the atmosphere of the event, has been affected by it but has taken little if any part in it. They probably, therefore, will approach the task with greater detachment even though the views of each of them must in general be largely dominated by his cultural situation. These men and women must make a selection from the mass of source material mobilized for them by those who labored in the primary phase. The sources of the second generation are the accounts prepared or the documents preserved by the first generation.

The historians in this second stage of generalization on the American Civil War did most of their significant work between 1885 and 1910. They were stimulated to greater objectivity and selectivity not only by the very mass of the record but also by advances in technique which were now at their disposal. In the preceding decades a concept of scientific history had been developed in the graduate schools of American universities, just coming into being. Rules carefully formulated regarding the critical use of evidence were taught in specially organized seminars to candidates writing theses for the degree of Doctor of Philosophy by faculty members themselves actively engaged in research and writing. Historical journals were at the same time growing in number and providing vehicles for communicating the work of the new scholars. Wealthy amateurs as well as trained professionals were busily occupied in historical research. Amateurs like James Schouler and James Ford Rhodes, together with John William Burgess and John Bach McMaster in the universities, were setting a new pattern of writing and incidentally of generalization.

These writers and their disciples sought to apply rules of criticism, to discover facts, and to tell a complete story, often in great detail. They were men of scholarly interests, even when they themselves had not had the training they were giving their students. They were compelled to be critical, because often conflicting accounts and much more detail than they could use were available. They had to be selective as well as critical; they had to exercise judgment. Their generalizations, however, were usually simple and did not depart very radically from those formulated in the primary phase. To Rhodes, for instance, although he substituted the designation "Civil War" for "Rebellion," slavery was still its sole cause and the war was, therefore, not the product of a conspiracy but the natural consequence of the sectional concentration of this evil institution. These authors' attention (except in the case of McMaster) was almost exclusively devoted to military and political events and sequences. The struggle was interpreted from the Union point of view. The Confederacy was held to be an unfortunate error, its government inept and its president bumbling. Except in a few instances, sympathy for the South among Northern scholars and other writers did not emerge in this age, while Southern-born historians, such as Woodrow Wilson, William Garrott Brown, William E. Dodd, and John Spencer Bassett, leaned over backward to keep their sectionalism from showing, and with reasonable success. The historians in this stage produced a full and comprehensive narrative dominated by generalizations which they hoped would be "definitive," a term dearly loved by these "scientific" historians. This second stage of historiographical generalization may, indeed, be described as a search for the definitive.

A third stage of generalization starts when an extensive and inclusive narrative has been scientifically established. (In the case of the American Civil War it came after the First World War.) At this point, approximately half a century after the event, more sophisticated scholars begin to explore new paths of interpretation. They ponder the canons of history previously established and find new meanings. Earlier generalizations may be revived and given fresh prominence, but broader and more abstract concepts also are set forth. This process becomes cumulative; it is never static, and it never ends. This third stage is a period of revision. Some sacred cows are slaughtered and what is known as "debunking" appears.

At this stage in the reconsideration of the history of the Civil War many judgments were revised, and even Lincoln was dragged from his lofty shrine. Scholars were no longer satisfied with such interpretative concepts as "rebellion," "conspiracy," "lost cause," and the like. To them human behavior was understood to be more complex, motives more mixed, causes more intricate, meanings more elusive. To them impersonal forces seemed at work but not always obviously. Men were more often considered as unconscious instruments than as directing agents. Their actions were neither to be praised nor blamed, neither defended nor justified; they were to be understood and sometimes "exposed." The conceptualist dedicated himself to the task of making this understanding possible and sought new generalizations through which to communicate his new understanding. Certain examples may be cited.

Frederick Jackson Turner in the course of his thinking on the significance of the frontier saw a new dimension in the Civil War. He defined a more complex sectionalism: the West as well as the North and the South must be reckoned with. This new section had developed with great speed during the nineteenth century. It was demanding a place in the sun of national politics, and much of the strife between North and South was sparked by rivalry over control of the institutional pattern of the West. A complex variety of folkways in a series of sections and subsections did much to condition the conflict.

Edward Channing conceived of the struggle as a phase of evolving nationalism. The growing nation's aims were ambiguous: Which definition of aims should prevail, that of the North or that of the South? When the South concluded that its definition was doomed, it determined to follow the example of the colonies in 1776 and work out its own destiny. The Civil War to Channing was a War for Southern Independence, a war to ensure to the South freedom to organize a nation after its own design, free from the implications of Northern definition.

Charles and Mary Beard in their writings during this third stage thought more in economic terms. Northern capitalists and enterprising developers in their eyes were seeking to take control from the Southern agrarians, who had been in control since the adoption of the Constitution. Northern interests wanted to be free from the Southern veto, free to secure the protection and the subsidies which they so much desired and to develop the national wealth. The Beards characterized the struggle as a Second American Revolution, a revolt against the rule of the South.

A concept of wider acceptance than those just cited was suggested by an ante-bellum tag made popular by William H. Seward. He had spoken of an "irrepressible conflict" between slavery and freedom. Now, in order to give emphasis to the concept of a contest determined by impersonal forces, various interpreters wrote of the Civil War as "The Irrepressible Conflict." This designation emphasized man's helplessness in the grip of such forces. He was their victim. Conflict could not have been avoided, and the fact should be recognized.

Such a generalization offered scholars an opportunity so tempting that quite a few embraced it. In this era of conceptual probing, under something of a Hegelian inspiration they advanced the idea of a "Repressible Conflict." Ulrich Phillips and Avery Craven were prominent in this school of thought. As the South improved its educational system and its universities flowered, its scholars and publicists developed a school of Southern apologetics proclaiming new truth. Slavery, they contended, had reached its limits in 1861, it was dying. Had there been a little more patience and consideration, the problem would have been solved without war. Greed, bad manners, and lies had so roused the passions of men that honor bound them to reach for the sword under the goading of slick Northern Machiavellis. If the Confederacy had had a little better luck or more men and guns, America would have been spared the robber barons and the world would now be a better place. To them the Civil War was needless, fought by a blundering generation.

The South, in the midst of a literary renascence, fought and won a new war—on paper. Twelve "young" Southerners, united, "took their stand" in this third stage and declared that when the Confederacy fell, a fine and noble thing succumbed to philistine materialism, and the nation and the world were the poorer. Walter P. Webb put forth the need of something like regional autonomy and advocated experiment therein. Inspired by excellent writing and impressed by cogent argument, certain commentators began to speak of "The Lost Cause Regained."

During this phase of generalizing, certain other historians had lost their interest in delivering merely moral judgments. They wished also to understand dispassionately in order to be practically useful. Experience in world war had provided them with a new motivation: War was evil, and history should teach men how to avoid it. Furthermore, they held that historians must rise above emotional paradoxes; they must reject the concept of two histories, one Northern and one Southern. Contrasting views like these must be fused into a larger conceptualization.

At this point again new tools became available, and a fourth stage of generalization about the Civil War may be discerned. The increasing sophistication of social scientists made it possible for them to supply helpful concepts. The basic disciplines in this realm—anthropology, economics, political science, psychology, and sociology, together with the cognate fields of psychiatry and geography—had always had some limited influence on historical thinking. Now, however, scholars in these areas were becoming more analytic and perceptive in their study of the "behavioral sciences," particularly in cultural anthropology, social psychology, demography, and human ecology. Their knowledge of race, family, group dynamics, roles, and behavior of small groups contributed new skill to generalizing about the Civil War. Likewise, their better understanding of co-operation and competition and of the relation between personality and culture provided broader concepts to the historian who might choose to generalize about cultural conflict.

The perils and exactions of the two world wars of this fourth period stimulated further insight. The concept of power struggle gained greater currency. A school of psychiatrically oriented political scientists contributed an analysis of democracy which emphasized the influence which the American pattern of frequent elections may have had upon emotions—the reciprocal relation between frequent electoral choice and fear and ambition. Could anyone expect a "house divided" to stand? Under these influences the political contests which had so much to do with arousing emotions to fighting pitch might be viewed in terms of the operation of group dynamics, of role-playing and status-seeking.

The new social-science concepts likewise opened the way for exploring the nature of the conflict in the light of kinship conflict, leading some historians to revive the older concept of "The Brothers' War" and follow its scientific implications. Conflict within a family is not the same as warfare between tribes and nations. In kinship conflict the fight is for control or security within the family, and there is desire neither to break up the old group nor to form a new one; independence is not really wanted. In the Civil War, according to this analogy, the main motive of the South was to reform the United States and obtain therein an autonomous position of power and security. As the secessionists really did not want independence, their alleged determination to secure it did not galvanize them to the greatest effort. In fact, ambivalence and mixed motives weakened their drive and may accordingly have been a major factor in their defeat. Such reconsideration invited new generalizations.

These concepts, furthermore, opened a whole new vista of generalization in yet another direction. Much of historical thinking has been circumscribed by geographical, cultural, and particularly national limits. American thinking about civil war has been conditioned by its cultural complex, by American nationalism or nationalisms, in a fashion pervasive and oppressive. But historians are becoming increasingly conscious of universal phenomena common in the analysis of behavior which is not trammeled by nationalism and which may be said to exist in a new realm. As the philosophers found metaphysics essential in their search for meaning, so historians are discovering an area of speculation which can be thought of as metanationalistic.

Such historians as leap the barriers of nationalistic thinking and transcend cultural limitations[1] can enter a new phase of generalization, a conceptualization within the framework of universal history, and produce generalizations of a more comprehensive nature. This holds true for those studying the American Civil War. They can discover that that conflict was not unique, it was but one of a class of social wars which may occur anywhere in any epoch. Some such phenomenon, for one example, has been an element in the Anglo-American experience about once in every century. At various times in the nineteenth and twentieth centuries, to cite further examples, there has been the common phenomenon of national unification, generally including a phase of social war, notably in Germany, Italy, and the Dual Monarchy. Similar struggles on the field of battle or over the negotiation table have resulted in division as well as unification, in such instances as the separation of Belgium from Holland and of Norway from Sweden and as the breakup of the Ottoman Empire, the Russia of the tsars, and the Austro-Hungarian monarchy. There have been revolutions in Germany, the Balkans, Portugal, Spain, and China. The British Empire has become the British Commonwealth of Nations, and a process of separation is going on in Africa in various areas of British and French influence. The American Civil War was perhaps only an example of this type of metanationalistic action.

There appears indeed to be a continuous process of cultural integration and disintegration, marked by revolution, social wars, and other phenomena which are phases of a seemingly universal experience. Comparison of generalizations about each of these produces new generalizations related to the history of cultural unity and particularly to the nature of the process which promotes, discourages, or destroys cultural unity. Answers to new general questions about civil war are constantly being sought. At what points are tensions likely to cause disruption? What means best promote unity? How can tension be re-

[1] See Robert Palmer, *The Age of Democratic Revolution* (Princeton: Princeton University Press, 1959) and his article (pp. 66–75 above).

laxed? Is it true that the process of operating democratic government or any other kind of government invites disintegration? How can group hostility be overcome? Must internal conflicts and bloodlettings recur with a certain degree of regularity just as do international conflicts?

In the instance of the American Civil War was it inevitable that a democracy so huge and with such ecological and demographic diversity should develop so much social tension as to threaten its growing nationalism and in the course of this growth produce two incompatible patriotisms and two moralities? Did the armed conflict that ensued so mark the restored culture that it is still really two cultures, with certain degrees of incompatibility? Is it true that dwellers in these two cultures have not yet been able to free themselves sufficiently from their birthright bias to generalize objectively? Or can the scholar by constructing a table of comparative Northern and Southern generalizations achieve a balance of interpretation which may establish an objective generalization? Can he compare generalizations relating to the American conflict with others formulated in regard to similar experiences outside American culture? With these comparisons in mind can he construct a calculus of generalization which will enable him to correct for bias and produce a new series of more valid concepts?

The historiography of the Civil War thus can be used to illustrate a process of generalization that may be applicable as a system of analysis. Regardless of what event, series of events, or epoch may be under consideration, generalization seems to pass through the phases described—through two certainly, each about a quarter of a century in duration, and probably through two others that follow, each representing (to date in the twentieth century) a type of conceptualization. One of these types of conceptualization is philosophical and theoretical, dominated by men and women of interpretive genius, such as Turner, Channing, and the Beards, or by lesser revisionists, and the other is formulated in terms of behavioral science with its more exact analysis of cultural limitations. Generalization thus advances from the simple to the increasingly complex. Events originally viewed as unique eventually are discovered to have duplicates in other cultural patterns. Formulations have changed from narrative descriptions, literary in character, to increasingly complex analyses of human behavior in the technical language of the most advanced findings of the social sciences.

The process of generalization, in fact, never ceases. New variations of old concepts are being constantly presented. Yet it is striking how persistent some of the initial concepts prove to be. It can be ventured that old generalizations never die, nor do they even fade away. Just as more perceptive formulations are constantly appearing, so old ones are repeated and ratified. Let us cite but one example—the comprehensive reconsideration of the Civil War projected by Allan Nevins in ten volumes. Though the six volumes of this work that have already appeared[2] present a wealth of new material and a much broader perspective than earlier studies of such matters as he considers, Nevins' basic generalizations maintain ground early taken. Slavery is still the cause, conspiracy the vehicle. He remains deliberately interested almost exclusively in the Northern phase and circumscribes his analysis within the limits of only one of the contending cultures.

The sequence of historical interpretations, passing as it does through identifiable stages, invites the formulation of a quasi-law for the expanding tendency toward generalization: the expansion tends to increase in direct proportion to the distance in time from the event itself. The rate of expansion, however, is frequently modified or limited by the persistence of past pronouncements. There is likewise a probability of recurrence at intervals, not regular, of various older formulations. The strength and frequency of these recurrences depend more on their emotional than on their logical attractiveness. The sequence of historical interpretations, as time passes, unfortunately becomes more confused by the possibility of accidental or unpredictable developments. Whereas the process during the first two generations of generalization after an event is to a degree orderly, thereafter there may be confusion such as has developed in twentieth-century Civil War historiography. There it has been caused by the acceleration of social-science conceptualization. Many new generalizations have come from certain new social-science attitudes rather than from any compulsion caused by mere temporal distance from the events. The perceptive historian will leave room for such accidents in his calculus.

The reason for insisting on rigorous "genealogical" thinking, on thorough research in the history of a given generalization, is that one of the few means which the historian has of judging the probable degree of validity of a generalization is to examine its age and the degree to which it has stood the scrutiny of succeeding generations. But this is

[2] *Ordeal of the Union* (2 vols.; New York: Scribner's, 1947), *Emergence of Lincoln* (2 vols.; New York: Scribner's, 1950), *War for the Union* (2 vols.; New York: Scribner's, 1959–60).

no infallible criterion. The age of an idea may well provide a measure of its truth, but long life may indicate only respectability—i.e., that the generalization is acceptable to a particular culture. Such respectability does not necessarily insure truth, but it may supply a presumption to be tested.

The understanding and use of the genealogy of the changing constructs that help to shape a historian's thought thus may greatly increase his capacity to discover the meanings which he seeks. But this genealogical method is a sophisticated technique, and many a historian is either ignorant of it or persuades himself that it is superfluous. The reason for this neglect is that many historians can be satisfied with a definition of their responsibilities and with techniques which have limits unfortunately narrow. All historians are prone to read primary and secondary sources. Some interview participants in the events they deal with. All who interview ask questions; some who read likewise ask questions of what they read. On the other hand, there are those who ask no questions at all but propose to let the sources tell the story. They put their notes, generally transcripts, in a pile and let the pile dictate what they write.

As no historian can discuss everything and as, at times, sources are contradictory, scholars perforce add to their techniques those of selection and criticism. But as the processes of selection and criticism have been refined by the advance of specialization and fragmentation which has marked the past century of historical scholarship, much of the more comprehensive meaning of history has been obscured and the historian's power of generalization has been severely limited. The historian has perhaps become more and more fearful of using the instrument of generalization itself, let alone the insights contributed by knowledge of a generalization's genealogy. But if the writing of history is to have its greatest significance and be more than a mere narrative of events, it ought to attempt to communicate the meaning of what men have done. This meaning can be most effectively supplied only by the most carefully constructed generalizations, which to be most comprehensive require the conscious use of techniques of formulation, certain elements of which have been illustrated in the foregoing analysis.

Within the framework of this analysis let us conclude with some generalizations regarding the process of generalization. The basic element in this process is, of course, a critical and scientific search for fact. But such a search will be guided, and its meaning conditioned to some extent, by insight, hunches, and flashes of inspiration. Some of the emerging interpretations will be susceptible of testing by critical methods; others, the product of dreams and prejudices, will be unprovable but may be suggestive and may often lead to new search and discoveries in the sources. Furthermore, the capacity of the historian to generalize depends upon such variables as his knowledge of his own relation to the work in hand, his life experience, his status in society, and his own psychological organization as an individual. The capacity to generalize, therefore, must be understood to vary with the historian, the effectiveness of his use of the process depending upon his self-knowledge. In view of this situation those using any generalization must acquire as much information as they can about its author if they are to form an adequate judgment about the validity of his construct.

Finally, the capacity of the historian to make effective generalizations depends in large part upon his skill in exploiting the genealogy of earlier generalizations. Whatever generalizations a historian derives he presents in the form of reports upon an explanation or interpretation or meaning which he has attained. These reports will subsequently arrest attention for varying lengths of time depending upon his skill of presentation or the cogency of his ideas. Many of such arrests of attention may have only a limited justification and a short life. At the given point of time at which these subsequent arrests are communicated in the form of a book, an article, a lecture, or a conversation, they may establish a general meaning or explanation of the events considered. The historian who communicates such a generalization has made history for someone besides himself. His generalization may not, however, stand for long; it will stand only so long as it is unmodified, but modification is almost inevitable. Though certain generalizations have long life, countless others are ignored and some may even seem lost or dissipated by continuous modification. The fact is that anyone confronted by a generalization, even though he may not recognize it as such because he absorbs it without conscious thought, almost immediately begins the process of generalization over again, bringing on new arrests of attention in his turn.

One of the hazards which on occasion blocks the historian's progress is the temptation to omit consideration of what his predecessors have done. We teach, and rightly so, that the investigator should start with the sources and only from them proceed to generalize, if he generalizes at all. Frequently, however, others have worked with the same sources and have likewise generalized, though in another context of time and environment. If the latest generalizer does not give attention to previous formulations and their reception, he may well miss implications which occurred to others nearer in time to the events in question but which he, because of his chronological distance, might not perceive. He ought to make a special effort to consider and judge these implications as well as his direct insights stimulated by study of the sources so that he can decide whether and which previous generalizations should be part of his foundation or be disregarded as bare excrescences. The process of writing history merely by consulting the primary and original sources and omitting study of previous secondary treatments is like building a structure without an architectonic framework, merely by piling stones one upon the other. But history is not a pile of notes.

X. *Notes on the Problem of Historical Generalization*

BY WILLIAM O. AYDELOTTE

The problem of historical generalization is slippery and evasive. If historical generalizations are, as they are often said to be, qualified, tentative, and difficult to substantiate, these reservations also apply, with perhaps even greater force because of the second degree of removal, to the generalizations about generalizations attempted in this collection of essays. A discussion of historical principles can easily degenerate into a mere statement of good intentions or into an arid didacticism that has little bearing on the concrete problems of research. It seems especially presumptuous to try to prescribe for a field like history, since the practices and objectives of historians vary, and legitimately, with the field of study, the nature and quantity of the evidence available, the problems that seem important in a particular context, and the concerns and interests of individual historians. The subject has become to some extent a congeries of different disciplines, and one might hesitate to dismiss peremptorily any one of them as unimportant. One cannot well say what "the historian" should do, for "the historian" is a fiction.

It is probably better, therefore, that anyone who discusses historical generalizations should speak so far as possible from his own experience. My interest is in quantified or statistical research, and it is this concern that I shall have chiefly in mind in the following remarks. The problems of statistical generalization, however, do not in essence differ from those involved in other kinds of generalizations—in a strict sense all generalizations are statistical, whether this is made explicit or not—and I hope that what I have to say about my own difficulties may bear on the problems of those who place a different emphasis in their research and that it may prove directly related to issues raised in some of the other essays in this volume.

On the question of historical generalization some of the most acute modern historians have taken a very cautious position. Anyone who wishes to maintain, as I do, that such generalizations are both feasible and desirable must face impressive arguments that have been marshaled for the contrary opinion. Of these arguments I wish particularly to consider four: (1) that a "generalization" can take the form only of a general law, detachable from its context and applicable in all comparable situations and hence, because of the complexity of historical materials, entirely beyond the historian's grasp; (2) that no final proof can be given of any general statement because of the complexity of historical events, the limitations on the amount of information that can be recovered by the historian or digested by him, and the inescapable bias imposed either by the historian's own predilections or by the assumptions of the society in which he lives; that, since historical generalizations cannot be proved, historians who claim they can are merely deceiving themselves; that for these reasons no agreement can be achieved among historians about any general proposition; and that all generalizations, because of their inevitably flimsy character, should be relegated to a role wholly subordinate to the main business of the historian, which is telling a story based upon the facts; (3) that historians should address their chief efforts to insight and speculation, not to the hopeless objective of achieving demonstrable generalizations; that the best of their insights have been achieved and will be achieved not through labored documentation but through judgment, wisdom, and a maturity that comes only with experience; and that, therefore, such general statements as historians can make will be and should be personal, subjective, intuitive, speculative, and impressionistic; and (4) that, for these reasons, little can be gained from formal procedures, the hope that a recital of statistical evidence can take us deeper into the heart of reality is illusory, and the results of attempts to formulate general statements by these means have been trivial and inconsequential.

Though these four arguments are related they can be roughly distinguished for purposes of discussion. None of them can be lightly dismissed. The reservations they express serve in several ways to chart the limits of our knowledge. One may well wonder whether these difficulties are not so formidable as to deter historians from attempting to generalize in any extensive or ambitious fashion. My own view, however, is that this line has been rather overdone. My objection to these various points is not so much that they are unsound in themselves as that they have sometimes been pushed too far, into a context to which they do not apply, and have been made to yield inferences that do not necessarily follow. Reservations about the finality of historical knowledge are valid enough, but there is a danger of erecting them into a general law against any generalizations in history except on a subjective and intuitive plane. This forces the argument further than our experience warrants or than our practice assumes. It is in itself a generalization to which some of the above objections might legitimately be taken. I hope to show that this position is vulnerable at various points: that significant general statements need not be universal laws; that the problem of verification is not altogether insuperable; that intuition need not be the historian's final resort; and that effectual means exist whereby both the scope and the reliability of historical statements may be somewhat extended.

1. The Problem of Nomenclature

Disagreement about the feasibility of historical generalizations may rest, as many intellectual disputes do, on nothing more than an ambiguity in stating the problem. The dispute may be more one of theory than one of practice. Certainly some historians who express a formal skepticism about generalizations make them very briskly when they come to present their own findings. This scarcely settles the matter, however, for to show that a man's practice does not coincide with his theory is still not to answer his argument. The point is rather that historians who are optimistic and those who are pessimistic about the possibility of generalizing may simply be talking about different things: the optimists may be referring to contextual statements of limited scope, the pessimists to universal laws. Quite possibly the optimists and the pessimists would not differ greatly on the merits of a substantial number of historical propositions. Perhaps historians concur more on what kinds of statements they are prepared to make themselves or to accept from others than on how they describe these statements. If this is the case, the controversy over historical generalizations may be unreal, and the issue may have been played up beyond its actual importance.

If a "generalization" were defined as a general law, detachable from its context and applicable to all comparable situations and if this were adopted as an exclusive definition, it would have to be granted that historians do not often make generalizations and probably should not. Such a definition has occasionally been advanced. It has been said that a generalization must be an implication that holds true for all things of a certain kind, an "if, then always" statement, and that what we mean by explaining an observed fact is incorporating that fact into a general law.[1] By this view a generalization should be not a description of a finite set of cases which has no predictive claim but a statement about an unrestricted class of cases which comprises an "inductive leap" and which implies a prediction for all undescribed cases of the type that may ever exist, past, present, or future. Certainly the practice of most historians falls short of this. Historians, apart from the creators of the great historical systems, do not generally seek to formulate universally valid laws of historical development. Most historians restrict themselves to particular contexts and do not traffic much in universals, except perhaps for an occasional rhetorical flight.

It seems clear enough, however, in view of the many different senses in which the word *generalization* has been used, that to insist on the above definition as an exclusive one would be merely whimsical. The notion that a historical generalization can be only a statement of this character has been ably disputed by William Dray in his attack on what he calls the "covering-law theory."[2] Louis Gottschalk holds that it is sufficient to define a generalization merely as "a proposition that describes some attribute common to two or more objects."[3] David Riesman distinguishes between the "classic" approach aimed "primarily at generalizations that could in principle be true at any time and place" and the "romantic" approach which "is concerned with a particular people, in a particular time and place."[4] Others have sought to distinguish generalizations from other statements not in terms of scope but in terms of structure or purpose—by drawing lines that separate generalizations from trends, from hypotheses, from inferences, from classifications, and so on. The *Oxford English Dictionary* offers a string of definitions of *generalization* and *generalize* which, with the illustrations that accompany them, provide accommodation for almost every position that has been taken.

In view of these variations it seems unlikely that much would be gained by attempting a more refined definition of *generalization*. The

[1] Hans Reichenbach, *The Rise of Scientific Philosophy* (1951; new ed.; Berkeley and Los Angeles: University of California Press, 1958), p. 6. Cf. the quotations from the letter of Hans Meyerhoff to the Committee given on pp. vi–vii and 129 above.

[2] *Laws and Explanation in History* (New York: Oxford University Press, 1957).

[3] "The Historian's Use of Generalization," in Leonard D. White (ed.), *The State of the Social Sciences* . . . (Chicago: University of Chicago Press, 1956), p. 437. See also Gottschalk's comments on pp. vii and 115–16 above.

[4] "The Study of National Character . . . ," *Harvard Library Bulletin*, XIII (1959), 7.

word, like other key words, has in the course of time acquired a number of different meanings. The difficulties created by vagueness of usage cannot be escaped by elaborating a more precise vocabulary. To assign a single meaning to the term and to insist that all who did not use it in that sense were in the wrong would not only be arbitrary but would also render the ensuing argument highly vulnerable, since it could at once be rejected by all who did not accept the definition that it presupposed. An attempt at definition can become a kind of shadow-boxing that has little practical value.

If it is difficult to agree on what a generalization is, it may not be profitable to try to distinguish generalizations from other kinds of historical propositions. Doubtless a "generalization" is ordinarily conceived to be a statement broader than some other statement, but the term *broader* is relative. Putting it differently, one might say that all statements are generalizations but that some, those which we commonly and as a matter of convenience refer to by that designation, are broader than others. By this view, even the distinction between factual statements and generalizations is merely one of degree.

This point may be a stumbling block to many, for the distinction between facts and generalizations has been one of the most persistent and most cherished in historical theory. Not only Chester G. Starr in his contribution to this volume (pp. 3–4) but other historians as well have insisted on the line between fact and theory, between particular and general statements, between statements that recite the data immediately observed and statements containing inferences and generalizations based upon them—between, for example, the information presented in a census return and the manipulation of this information to establish general propositions. Thus Sir Isaiah Berlin writes: "The same facts can be arranged in many patterns, seen from many perspectives, displayed in many lights, all of them equally valid. . . . Yet through it all the facts themselves will remain relatively 'hard.' " He adds in a footnote: "Criteria of what is a fact or what constitutes empirical evidence are seldom in dispute within a given culture or profession." Berlin concedes that a boundary between facts and generalizations cannot be precisely established but regards this as of no importance. "We shall be reminded," he says, "that there is no sharp break between history and mythology; or history and metaphysics; and that in the same sense there is no sharp line between 'facts' and theories: that no absolute touchstone can in principle be produced;

and this is true enough, but from it nothing startling follows. That these differences exist only metaphysicians have disputed."[5]

No doubt a distinction between generalizations and facts, even if it cannot be defended in strict argument, may still serve as a convenient short cut in referring to statements of greater or less complexity, and I shall occasionally employ it in this loose manner in these notes. Such a usage, though imprecise, is not wholly misleading: a difference in scope does matter and it is absurd to pretend otherwise or to regard the most simple and the most inclusive propositions as being on a par. The theory of natural selection is a generalization in a sense that the detailed findings of paleontology are not.

Yet the distinction between facts and generalizations has become increasingly unacceptable as historians have examined more explicitly and systematically their assumptions and their own mental processes. The difference seems one of degree rather than of kind and the line separating the two classes of statements, as even Berlin admits, must be arbitrary. "The distinction . . . between data and inferences," says Raymond Aron, "has a deceptive clarity. No one denies that in the most advanced natural sciences yesterday's inferences are today's givens. Propositions established mainly by means of inference become the data of which the scientist speaks. Theories and facts are integrated in such a manner that one would attempt in vain to separate them rigorously."[6] To argue as Berlin does that facts exist independently, as unchanging building blocks available for a variety of theoretical purposes, is to oversimplify. A "fact" cannot be apprehended or described by itself alone: a "factual" statement implies a predicate and cannot refer to something in an intellectual void with no points of reference around it. As Sidney Hook says: "Every fact which the historian establishes presupposes some theoretical construction." He adds: "There is only a difference of degree of generality and validity between facts and hypotheses and theories."[7] If what we commonly refer to as "facts" can be used as building blocks for a variety of purposes, so can low-level generalizations, and even high-level ones. The category of "generalizations" can include very simple statements, the

[5] *Historical Inevitability* (New York: Oxford University Press, 1954), p. 70.

[6] "Evidence and Inference in History," in Daniel Lerner (ed.), *Evidence and Inference: The Hayden Colloquium on Scientific Concept and Method* (Glencoe, Ill.: Free Press, 1959), p. 19.

[7] "Problems of Terminology in Historical Writing—Illustrations," *Theory and Practice in Historical Study* (SSRC Bulletin 54), p. 124.

category of "facts" very complex ones, and one would be at a loss where to draw the line between them.

It is better understood now than it used to be that the "facts" do not speak for themselves and that what we loosely refer to as factual statements turn out, when we consider them closely, to be based on an intricate chain of comparison, hypothesis, and verification, though these steps take place so rapidly that they are not always remembered or perceived. This applies even to our simplest observations, the "evidence of our own eyes." The point has been neatly illustrated by J. Z. Young in his account of experiments conducted on persons who, though born blind, were later operated on and received their sight.[8] The difficulty of training these individuals to interpret what the evidence of their own eyes actually was affords a striking example of what complex processes of deduction, inference, and speculation men go through when they perceive even the simplest "fact." The information gathered by a census-taker is sometimes cited in discussions of these problems as the simplest kind of raw data. Yet this information is recorded, and has little meaning unless it is so recorded, in categories which imply much previous thinking and generalizing. This may be why the techniques of census-taking have been greatly changed and improved over the last hundred years, as the basic assumptions that underlie them have been more clearly worked out.

The lack of any common agreement about what a generalization is and the ambiguity of the boundary separating generalizations from other statements are not, as Berlin suggests, trivial matters. On the contrary, they point the way to a reformulation of the problem. It follows from this line of argument that all historians generalize in that the statements they make cannot be distinguished from generalizations by any defensible criterion and that the claim made by some historians that they merely recite the evidence and permit the facts to speak for themselves is unallowable. Written history, like any other coherent or intelligible presentation, is not a simple record but something far more complex. Hence, the question whether historians should generalize or not is meaningless: as several essays in this volume insist, they must generalize if they are to say anything worth saying. In this sense the controversy over the propriety of generalizing is indeed unreal, and it is pointless to argue about it.

---

[8] *Doubt and Certainty in Science: A Biologist's Reflections on the Brain* (New York: Oxford University Press, 1951), pp. 61–66.

In another sense, however, the problem is real enough. Variations in practice, in the kinds of generalizations historians have tried to make, indicate an extensive disagreement about what may properly be done with historical materials. This disagreement is no mere matter of semantics or of talking at cross purposes; it is concrete and substantial. General propositions offered by historians range in scope from the simplest to the most complex, from the narrowest to the most inclusive. Illustrations of the lower part of this range are scarcely needed. Since, however, it is sometimes said that historians habitually restrict themselves to "low-level" generalizations, cautious and limited statements of which they can be reasonably sure, it may be useful to cite a few illustrations drawn from the more rarefied upper part of the range which will show that this is by no means always the case:

1. "All the wars here discussed were preceded by a fall in prices on the London Stock Exchange and by a rise in the number of trade union members reported as unemployed."[9]
2. "The Speaker was a power in the House, but, as the Elizabethan period went on, his power was on the wane."[10]
3. "The prime minister replaced the sovereign as actual head of the executive when the choice of the prime minister no longer lay with the sovereign; the sovereign lost the choice when strongly organized, disciplined parliamentary parties came into existence; and party discipline depends primarily on the degree to which the member depends on the party for his seat."[11]
4. "A new Constitution does not produce its full effect as long as all its subjects were reared under an old Constitution, as long as its statesmen were trained by that old Constitution. It is not really tested till it comes to be worked by statesmen and among a people neither of whom are guided by a different experience."[12]
5. "All classes which have ever attained to dominion have earnestly endeavored to transmit to their descendants such political power as they have been able to acquire."[13]

[9] Hook, p. 127. Hook uses this quotation to illustrate his definition of the term *generalization*.

[10] Wallace Notestein, *The Winning of the Initiative by the House of Commons: The Raleigh Lecture on History* (London: Oxford University Press, 1924), p. 17.

[11] Lewis B. Namier, *Monarchy and the Party System: The Romanes Lecture* (Oxford: Clarendon, 1952), p. 4.

[12] Walter Bagehot, *The English Constitution* (1867; new ed.; London: Oxford University Press, 1928), pp. 260–61.

[13] Robert Michels, *Political Parties: A Sociological Study of the Oligarchical Tendencies of Modern Democracy* (English trans.; New York: Hearst's International Library, 1915), p. 12.

6. "Modern technology created free society—but created it at the expense of the protective tissues which had bound together feudal society."[14]
7. "The man of the nineteenth century had a sense of *belonging* (deeper than mere optimism) that we lack."[15]

The first of these statements deals with a limited number of cases and is formulated in such a way that it could presumably be verified with some exactness. The second and third are broader in scope but still restricted to particular contexts. The fourth and fifth are couched in general terms and appear to be intended to apply to all cases of the type indicated. The sixth and seventh are contextual in that each purports to describe a single train of events but are so sweeping that it might be difficult to verify them or perhaps even to say what they mean in any concrete or explicit sense.

It is in terms of this divergence in practice that the problem may be reformulated. It is pointless to ask whether historians should "generalize" if we cannot affix any distinguishing meaning to that word. It is not, however, pointless to ask how far historians should generalize: how broad or inclusive they can make their statements without departing too far from the standards customarily accepted for demonstration and verification. This question may not be easy to answer, the answers may be different for different kinds of historical enterprises, and perhaps no definitive answer can be given. The question is not meaningless, however. On the contrary, it seems the most profitable way of formulating the issue, and the rest of this article will deal with some of the points that should be raised if one is to take a position on it. The question of scope depends, in the first place, on the question of reliability. The problems of historical generalization and of historical proof are directly connected, and it is impossible to deal adequately with the first without considering the second.

2. *The Problem of Proof*

A major objection to historical generalizations is that they cannot be proved. By this view, which is certainly widely shared, it is naïve to suppose that the evidence can be arranged in a clear pattern whose validity can be demonstrated, and attempts to do this rest on a misunderstanding of the kinds of materials with which historians must work

[14] Arthur M. Schlesinger, Jr., *The Vital Center* (Boston: Houghton Mifflin, 1949), p. 51.
[15] Crane Brinton, *Ideas and Men: The Story of Western Thought* (New York: Prentice-Hall, 1950), p. 442.

and the kinds of problems they face. Robert R. Palmer, for example, agrees that a kind of wisdom gained from the study of one civilization "has some application to another (to deny this would condemn all history and social study to sterility), but I have no idea how this applicability can be stated with . . . rigor and precision. . . ." He says also, "Of any concrete and particular social and human situation, historical, currently political, or other, I doubt whether any significant generalization can be shown by evidence to be wholly valid or wholly invalid."[16] Starr holds that generalizations cannot be verified, though facts can, and that historians may reach agreement about facts but do not at present possess the means of reaching agreement about generalizations. He is all for more generalizing, since to forego it would impoverish historical literature, but he insists that it be done on an admittedly speculative basis.[17]

Criticisms of this kind have been directed particularly against the most daring generalizers of modern times, the builders of the great systems in history and the social sciences. Many of these systems were offered not as speculations but as "proved" sets of propositions: their authors claimed for them the precision and finality that they thought they observed in the natural sciences. Hobbes proposed to assimilate political theory to the state of perfection attained by the exact physical sciences and claimed to be the Galileo of the science of politics. Gobineau spoke of "making history join the family of the natural sciences, of giving it . . . all the precision of this kind of knowledge," and described himself as the Copernicus of the historical world.[18] Henry Thomas Buckle hoped to accomplish for history something analogous to what had been effected for the natural sciences and to show how apparently capricious events were in accord with certain fixed and universal laws.[19] Toynbee maintains that the course of history is governed by laws which can be empirically discovered and defined.

Though some of these schemes have great interest and represent impressive achievements both of learning and of systematic thought,

---

[16] Letters to the Committee, Jan. 29, 1959, and June 16, 1958, above, pp. 76 and 75, respectively.

[17] Pp. 3 and 15–18 above.

[18] Quoted in Ernst Cassirer, *The Myth of the State* (New Haven: Yale University Press, 1946; new ed.; Garden City, N.Y.: Doubleday, 1955), p. 282.

[19] See the discussion by James L. Cate, "Humanism and the Social Sciences: But What about John de Neushom?" in White, pp. 429–30.

they have on the whole been rejected, as adequate accounts of the historical process, by most historians today. The grounds for their rejection have been much the same: that their claims to be empirical or "scientific" have not been made good, that they are not based upon the evidence, not in accord with the evidence, or not testable by the evidence. Toynbee's assertion that he has discovered general laws by empirical means has been vigorously disputed in a series of brilliant polemical articles by Pieter Geyl, who regards this claim as utterly unconvincing.[20] Professional opinion seems to incline toward Geyl's side rather than Toynbee's. All attempts to trace a structure of history, writes Isaiah Berlin,[21] "from the days of Herder and Saint-Simon, Hegel and Marx, to those of Spengler and Toynbee and their imitators," have been "always *a priori* for all protests to the contrary." General schemes of history have been notoriously vulnerable targets, and hardly any have withstood the test of critical examination over any long period of time. The disparity between the pretensions of the system-builders and the professional reception of their works might well serve as a caution against any effort to offer proof of general historical statements.

It is true, of course, that the reservations of historians toward these general schemes are by no means shared by many of those outside the profession. Geyl made a survey of reviews of Toynbee and found that those condemning him were mostly written by historians and those praising him mostly by non-historians. To historians Toynbee's work is unacceptable; to non-historians it is "an immortal masterpiece," "the greatest work of our time," and "probably the greatest historical work ever written."[22] Geyl will not allow Toynbee's claim that he reached his conclusions empirically; to Pitirim A. Sorokin, Toynbee's work displays "the technical competence of a meticulous

[20] *Debates with Historians* (1955; rev. ed.; New York: Meridian, 1958), chaps. v–viii and "Toynbee's Answer," *Mededelingen der Koninklijke Nederlandse Akademie van Wetenschappen, afd. Letterkunde*, XXIV (1961), 181–204.

[21] *Op. cit.*, p. 69.

[22] *Debates with Historians*, p. 283. See, for similar cases, the contrast between the learned and the public reaction to Spengler described by H. Stuart Hughes, *Oswald Spengler: A Critical Estimate* (New York: Scribner's, 1952), pp. 1–2 and the contrast between the scientific and the popular reception of Robert Chambers' *Vestiges of Creation* discussed by Milton Millhauser, *Just before Darwin: Robert Chambers and Vestiges* (Middletown, Conn.: Wesleyan University Press, 1959), pp. 116–40.

empiricist."[23] The popular appeal of the systems, however, is, properly understood, no argument in their favor and no ground for disregarding our present reservations. This scarcely seems a case where the public is right and the experts are wrong. It is more probable that the uncritical acceptance of cosmologies by the lay public represents the desire, apparently implanted in most men, for an easy formula, a unified pattern in the confusion of life's experiences. Popular enthusiasm for these systems may not even reflect a historical judgment; it seems at times to have more of a religious or eschatological character. As Perez Zagorin says, "Many people read Arnold J. Toynbee . . . as the Roman augurs read the flight of the birds."[24] Such enthusiasm, from an audience that does not comprehend the ingrained difficulties of the problem, is actually a ground for additional caution. The craving it reflects may appear within the profession as well as outside it, even if in a more sophisticated form, and a generalization may serve as a wish-fulfillment fantasy at a high intellectual level as well as at a low one. Perhaps historians have some reason to pride themselves on their resistance to this impulse and to pressures from outside their guild and on the caution and objectivity which they have shown as a profession.

Certainly the impossibility of final proof of any historical generalization must be at once conceded. Our knowledge of the past is both too limited and too extensive. Only a minute fraction of what has happened has been recorded, and only too often the points on which we most need information are those on which our sources are most inadequate. On the other hand, the fragmentary and incomplete information we do have about the past is still far too abundant to prevent our coming readily to terms with it: its sheer bulk prevents its being easily manipulated, or even assimilated, for historical purposes. Further, historians deal with complex problems, and the pattern of the events they study, even supposing it to exist, seems too intricate to be easily grasped. Doubtless, finality of knowledge is impossible in all areas of study. We have learned through works of popularization how far this holds true even for the natural sciences, and, as Crane Brinton says, the historian no longer needs to feel that "the uncertainties and inaccuracies of his investigations leave him in a position of hopeless

[23] "Arnold J. Toynbee's Philosophy of History," *Journal of Modern History*, XII (1940), 374. It should be added, however, that Sorokin is also highly critical of certain features of Toynbee's work.

[24] "Historical Knowledge: A Review Article on the Philosophy of History," *Journal of Modern History*, XXXI (1959), 247.

inferiority before the glorious certainties of physical science."[25] Nevertheless, these difficulties present themselves with greater weight in some fields than in others, and there is no use in deceiving ourselves by pretending the contrary. In history and other subjects that deal with the study of man in society they appear peculiarly intractable. The complexity of the historian's materials and problems, the number of variables he has to consider, the difficulty of isolating or successively eliminating these variables for purposes of inquiry, and the apparently unavoidable imprecision of his fundamental concepts all serve to make his larger formulations difficult either to achieve or to defend.[26]

In addition, historians are fallible for reasons often beyond their control. Bert J. Loewenberg regards it as undeniable that "every intellectual effort is limited by the psychology of the person making it and the sociology of the conditions under which it is made."[27] A man's bias, personal concerns, interests, and proclivities may color, may impart a subjective distortion of which he is unaware not only to his selection of the facts but also to his notion of what constitutes proof. As Proust writes: "The facts of life do not penetrate to the sphere in which our beliefs are cherished . . . ; as it was not they that engendered these beliefs, so they are powerless to destroy them; they can aim at them continual blows of contradiction and disproof without weakening them." Arthur M. Schlesinger, Jr., quotes this statement to describe the soft-minded liberals of present-day America.[28] Yet there is no reason why it should not apply to others as well—Proust certainly couches his remark in general terms—and it is quite possible that those who pride themselves on being tough-minded may fall into the same trap. Certainly we can all recollect examples from our own experiences of people who are willing to hold to beliefs despite the evidence or who derive what seem clearly mistaken conclusions from the facts before them. One thinks of Samuel Butler's anecdote of the man whose religious faith was restored by reading Burton's *Anatomy*

---

[25] "The 'New History' and 'Past Everything,'" *American Scholar*, VIII (1939), 153.

[26] Morris R. Cohen, "Reason in Social Science," in Herbert Feigl and May Brodbeck (eds.), *Readings in the Philosophy of Science* (New York: Appleton-Century-Crofts, 1953), pp. 663–69; Edgar Zilsel,"Physics and the Problem of Historico-Sociological Laws," *ibid.*, pp. 715–16 and 720.

[27] "Some Problems Raised by Historical Relativism," *Journal of Modern History*, XXI (1949), 17.

[28] Schlesinger, p. 49.

of Melancholy because he thought he was reading Butler's *Analogy of Religion.*

A bias can also be cultural as well as personal. Even if a historian manages to identify his assumptions and his colleagues endeavor to correct his conclusions, the climate of opinion that surrounds them may impart a slant from which they can never fully emancipate themselves. Even the most carefully formulated statements may be *zeitgebunden* in ways that contemporaries will not perceive.

It must be remembered that "proof" is not something external to the human mind. The validity of a historical statement depends not simply on the arguments and evidence adduced in its support but on the acceptance of these arguments and evidence by one or more individuals, presumably those competent to judge. Further, since men's judgments of their own work are notoriously liable to error, the approval of others has come to be accepted as the sounder, though not necessarily infallible, test. By this view a generalization is valid to the extent that it is communicable or acceptable to others, and the historian (or anyone else) ultimately rests his case not on logic but on persuasion, though the former may be a means toward the latter. If, however, we have no better test of "proof" than consensus, the possibilities of finality seem to be rather remote. Professional opinion may be fragmented, so that the consensus is not clear. When there is general agreement, matters may actually be worse, for the consensus of professional opinion has often proved mistaken and has, further, often been singularly unwilling to approve new ideas upon their first appearance. Sir Lewis Namier has written that a new historical interpretation should, once it is formulated, appear so obvious as to command instant acceptance; this did not happen, however, in the case of his own very considerable innovations, which were not appreciated in anything like their full significance until some years after their publication. Intellectual history is full of instances where contemporaries failed to understand the value or even the meaning of some of the most important intellectual enterprises of their own day. Some works were slighted for reasons that later proved irrelevant; others were for a time estimated more highly than we now think they deserved. Nor is it always clear whose consensus is wanted. It would hardly do to say that the validity of a statement should be measured on the simple democratic basis of the number of its adherents. Such a principle would at once reinstate Toynbee and throw his critics out of court. A historian seeks to convince not all men but a learned audience, though its boundaries cannot be very clearly discerned. A criterion of consensus can also, and perhaps often does, lead to a debasing of the historical craft: a historian may become "other-directed" and say not what he himself believes or considers most important but what he thinks will appeal to his audience; or, again, he may become a kind of sophist, concentrating not on the art of discovery but on the techniques of persuasion.

These ambiguities are well understood today and historians seem highly alert to the complexity and evasiveness of historical problems. Hans Meyerhoff in a note in his recent anthology on the philosophy of history comments on the fact that the philosophers whose essays he includes "are primarily concerned with defending the possibility of an objective history," whereas the historians who join the debate "are conscious, to different degrees, of the ineluctably subjective factors ... that seem to intrude upon the subject of history."[29] Geyl finds modern historians overcautious rather than overbold: "This much is certain: the quality which the academic and specialized study of history tends to develop is that of caution. ... The prevailing mood among professional historians nowadays is a chastened one in the face of the immense mass of material and the infinite complexity of the phenomena."[30] Perhaps many contemporary historians would agree that they spend their time in an atmosphere of intellectual twilight in which they can only dimly discern the outlines of even their most immediate surroundings and can be sure of nothing.

My argument here is that the lack of finality of historical proof, though incontestable, is an improper objection to attempting historical generalizations. In the first place it presupposes non-existent alternatives: it suggests there is a choice between making admittedly vulnerable generalizations or making other statements that are somehow sounder. Yet, by the logic of all that has been said, no such choice exists. The objection of lack of finality applies to propositions of all kinds. The choice is not between making proved statements or unproved ones but between making unproved statements or keeping silent.

In the second place, and this is the nub of the matter, the darkness is relative. To say that all statements are uncertain is not to say that they

[29] *The Philosophy of History in Our Time* ... (Garden City, N.Y.: Doubleday, 1959), p. 161.

[30] Pieter Geyl, *Use and Abuse of History* (New Haven: Yale University Press, 1955), pp. 60–61.

are equally uncertain. We may not be completely sure of anything, but we can come nearer to making a convincing case for some points than for others, and we can bring some arguments to a stage where our doubts and reservations are no longer very serious and we do not feel uncomfortable in provisionally accepting certain conclusions, pending the production of evidence to the contrary, in order to get on with the work. Palmer's assertion (p. 75 above) that the epigrams of La Rochefoucauld are as much or as little verifiable as any derived from social science would appear to imply that all generalizations are verifiable, or rather unverifiable, to the same degree. Such a view disregards the fact that, measured by the admittedly necessary standard of professional consensus, some statements can be asserted with more security than others. Even if it is not possible to escape bias altogether, it may still be possible to escape it to some degree. As Ernest Nagel writes: "The very fact that biased thinking may be detected and its sources investigated shows that the case for objective explanations in history is not necessarily hopeless."[31] Though a man's own idiosyncrasies may distort his views, he must still satisfy his professional colleagues. Their personal quirks may go some distance to counteract his, and a pooling of opinions may result in rubbing away the misconceptions of individuals. This seems most likely to occur in a situation where controversy exists and where, when a man takes a position, there will be opponents on the alert to catch the loopholes in his argument. Correction of this kind seems less probable when the mistaken assumptions of an individual are shared by his entire generation. Yet even here perhaps a historian can do something to put himself on his guard by seeking to clarify his thought and purpose or to formulate his interests in propositional or categorical terms.[32] Though it is misleading to assume that proof can be final or that bias can be entirely avoided, it is also misleading to assume that the problem is impregnable on all fronts and that no inroads upon the difficulties can be made.

[31] "The Logic of Historical Analysis," in Meyerhoff, p. 213. Willson H. Coates has acutely suggested: "Once we have stamped finality as the great heresy for scholars, we can see the concept of the relativity of knowledge as a movement in the direction of greater objectivity." The relativists, he says, by successfully challenging historical "objectivity" put history "in a philosophic perspective which is a nearer approach to the objectivity which they deny is possible" ("Relativism and the Use of Hypothesis in History," *Journal of Modern History*, XXI [1949], 24).

[32] See "Proposition VIII" in SSRC Bulletin 54, pp. 135–36, and also Thomas C. Cochran, "A Survey of Concepts and Viewpoints in the Social Sciences," *The Social Sciences in Historical Study* (SSRC Bulletin 64), p. 85.

Such inroads have been made in many cases, and Starr's view (p. 15 above) that historians "do not now have methods by which they can reach agreement on the generalizations obtainable from a given mass of facts" seems to me too sweeping. I cannot, of course, accept his distinction between provable facts and unprovable generalizations. The point appears rather to be that such matters are relative. It might be more useful to think in terms of a scale or ladder of propositions passing from very simple statements of which we feel practically certain to increasingly complex and far-reaching statements of which we are increasingly less sure. This is not the whole story, of course, for there are other things to consider, particularly the availability of the evidence. This varies among different projects and it may actually happen that, because of better evidence, we can make a more convincing case for a complex statement on one point than for a simple statement on another. It is an objective of research design to achieve this condition, to select a problem that is not only worth studying in itself but on which, also, sufficient evidence can be found to enable the researcher to make some progress. Yet perhaps there is a rough truth, with allowance for modifying circumstances, in the notion of an inverse relationship between certainty and significance, and it may be useful to regard the question of historical generalization as revolving around this relationship.

The problem, then, is where to draw the line, how to define the most advantageous middle position between these two extremes. The proposition that generalizations should be neither too broad nor too narrow may be a defensible theoretical position, but it is not of much practical help. Yet it seems almost pointless to try to lay down any general rule. The stopping place will vary for each project: it will depend on the kind of evidence that can be found, and it will also depend on the interests and concerns of the individual, what he thinks most worth doing. Nor need the degree of reliability be the same in all cases. Some questions are important enough to be worth discussing even if our ground is not secure. There is clearly a place for intelligent speculation based on very little evidence. Perhaps it is legitimate to make generalizations at any level if they can be shown to serve a useful purpose and if no misrepresentation is made regarding the degree to which they can be substantiated.

I cannot offer a general formula in answer to this question nor can I prescribe for the profession as a whole, but I should like to express a personal opinion. This is that we may have more to gain not by extending our generalizations but by restricting them, by pursuing limited generalizations on which we have some prospect of reaching tenable ground. It seems proper to emphasize this, since there has been a certain amount of talk on the other side. It is sometimes said that it is the historian's job to explain the world, for he is in a better position to do so than anyone else, and that if he will not draw conclusions from his evidence others less qualified will step in and do it for him. Geoffrey Barraclough writes: "The failure of the historian to provide an interpretation of history, to say what it is all about, is another example of the notorious 'trahison des clercs', of the refusal of the specialist to live up to his work," and cites Miss Wedgwood to support his opinion.[33] Similarly, it is often urged as a criticism of the social sciences that they have increasingly abandoned the attempt to formulate large general laws, a theory of society, and now tend more to direct themselves to the detailed and often highly technical study of limited situations.

Yet I cannot see the advantage of attempting to pronounce on matters which we do not yet understand and on which our thinking and research have not progressed far enough to make a general formulation possible. I do not suggest that we should ignore the larger questions relating to the structure of society and politics that have always fascinated men. The hope of shedding some light on these points is an incentive with which we could ill afford to dispense. On the other hand, these questions are so complex that it may be better strategy to divide the enemy, to break the problems down to a point where they become more manageable. In this sense, the restriction of objectives, in history and the other social sciences, may be a sign not of degeneration but of maturity. The increased attention to smaller, more sharply defined problems which are nearer to the bottom than to the top of the scale of complexity may reflect a clearer awareness of the possibilities of these subjects and of the level at which generalizations can be most advantageously attempted.

Robert K. Merton puts the point felicitously when he speaks of focusing attention on *"theories of the middle range:* theories intermediate to the minor working hypotheses evolved in abundance during the day-by-day routines of research, and the all-inclusive speculations

---

[33] *History in a Changing World* (Oxford: Blackwell, 1955), p. 222. H. Stuart Hughes advances a similar argument in "The Historian and the Social Scientist," *American Historical Review*, LXVI (1960), 45.

comprising a master conceptual scheme."[34] Contemporary sociologists who have shortened their sights and addressed themselves to the investigation of concrete problems and particular populations, who try to study simple things with high-powered instruments rather than complicated things with crude instruments, may well have strengthened their position. Though they have not offered simple solutions for complex problems, they have illuminated more limited questions in regard to which, hitherto, singularly erroneous conceptions prevailed.

Historians also may find themselves on better ground if, instead of dealing with large general problems which cannot be exactly formulated and the answers to which must be largely speculative, they consider questions on which they can hope to reach a more secure footing. The larger questions may orient our research, and it is proper that they should. They cannot, however, be solved all in a moment. We shall be digging around their roots for some time to come, and during that time our answers must continue to be incomplete and provisional. The most helpful approach to them lies in careful study, doing what we can and making sure of our ground. Little will be gained by attempting to force an answer to questions which, however important they may be, cannot be answered in the present state of our knowledge. As Paul F. Lazarsfeld has pointedly though hyperbolically remarked: "Kings who have wanted the philosopher's stone or immediate cures for currently incurable diseases have usually advanced charlatanism not knowledge."[35]

3. The Problem of Theory

Here I wish to deal with the proposition that generalizations should be suggestive rather than demonstrable and that they should appeal to the imagination rather than to the external facts. Such a position does not, as I mean it, imply that the historian should fail to examine the evidence, disregard it or openly flout it. The case is rather that, in view of the difficulties of adequate proof and the impossibility of final proof, the key to understanding the past is not the pedestrian pursuit of documentation but imagination and vision. Somewhat along this line Palmer has argued that the main purpose of a generalization should be to present an insight that helps in the understanding of a particular situation

---

[34] *Social Theory and Social Structure* (1949; rev. and enlarged ed.; Glencoe, Ill.: Free Press, 1957), pp. 5–6.

[35] Rose K. Goldsen *et al.*, *What College Students Think* (Princeton: Van Nostrand, 1960), p. xi.

and to communicate this insight to others, "to persuade others that the view . . . is somehow more satisfactory, enlightening, or useful." He suggests further in a passage to which I have already briefly referred that the penetrating observations of a brilliant man, even if subjective or impressionistic, may be more helpful than labored demonstrations which within an inevitably limited framework make some attempt at proof, and he argues that the maxims of La Rochefoucauld constitute generalizations "as valid, useful, and illuminating as any we are likely to get in social science, and about as much or as little capable of empirical verification by scientific method."[36]

No reply to this view will be adequate which fails to take account of the important role of unproved statements in any serious historical inquiry. It might indeed be argued that, just as the line between generalizations and facts cannot be established, so the line between proved and unproved statements, what we sometimes call generalizations and hypotheses, is also difficult to discern. If proof is merely a matter of degree, the distinction between proved and unproved statements cannot be an absolute one. Possibly all our statements, even the simplest ones, are in this sense merely working hypotheses. Some of the most useful, indeed, may not be proved or provable but merely theories of how things might work which help to explain the known evidence and do not conflict with it. It is relevant that Darwin looked at his own theory of natural selection in this light. He wrote to Herbert Spencer on February 23, 1860: "Of my numerous (private) critics, you are almost the only one who has put the philosophy of the argument, as it seems to me, in a fair way—namely, as an hypothesis (with some innate probability, as it seems to me) which explains several groups of facts."[37] It might be argued, along the same line, that the words *empirical* and *doctrinaire* are customarily used rather loosely and that probably no purely empirical research in history has ever been done and no purely doctrinaire history has ever been written, though certainly impressive efforts have been made in both directions. The two terms constitute a kind of theoretical model, a pair of "ideal types," never realized in practice but convenient for purposes of analysis.

But the case may be put even more strongly. It is quite possible to produce generalizations that are wholly unverifiable and that may nevertheless prove to have considerable value. A good example can

---

[36] Letter to the Committee, June 16, 1958, p. 75 above.

[37] Quoted in David Duncan, *Life and Letters of Herbert Spencer* (2 vols.; New York: Appleton, 1908), I, 128.

be found in the formulations of classical economics. From the foundation of modern political economy, says M. M. Postan, the tendency to abstract theorizing became increasingly predominant, so that economics formerly "tried to solve the largest possible problems from the least possible knowledge" and the ingenuity of theoretical economics was "only rivalled by the unreality of some of its conclusions." Yet modern efforts to inject larger doses of empiricism into the subject have, in the opinion of several distinguished economic historians, not helped to the degree that was expected in establishing a new formulation. The majority of these empirical studies, Postan finds, do not verify the conclusions of economic theory because most of these conclusions were so derived as to be incapable of verification or so constructed as not to require it; yet, even though unverifiable, they are illuminating and important. Commenting on the historical school of economists in Germany, Edwin F. Gay wrote that we can see now that their full hopes of inaugurating a new and more realistic stage in the development of economic science have not been realized and are not realizable. Sir John Clapham related in his inaugural lecture in 1929 that when he read Gustav Schmoller's *Principles*, a work that sought to illustrate the doctrine that "historical delineation can become economic theory," he noted on the flyleaf of his copy of the book the words, "He solves nothing." Clapham added that, "as economists, I believe that the German historical school have gone bankrupt."[38] The point I wish to make here is that there will always be things which seem important to say but which cannot be proved by the limited means of verification available to us and yet are not irresponsible or misleading but may on the contrary be significant and illuminating. We will not come to grips with the problem of generalization unless we realize that some of the most important statements we want to make must of necessity be extremely speculative.

Furthermore, it is a commonplace, not only in statistics but also in other areas of research, that an overemphasis in the direction of simple-minded empiricism is not an adequate approach and that any investigation that is worth anything must be brought under some theoretical control at an early point. As Lazarsfeld puts it: "Statistical

---

[38] M. M. Postan, *The Historical Method in Social Science: An Inaugural Lecture* (Cambridge: At the University Press, 1939), sections I and II; Edwin F. Gay, "The Tasks of Economic History," *Journal of Economic History*, I, Supplement (December, 1941), 9–16; J. H. Clapham, *The Study of Economic History: An Inaugural Lecture* (Cambridge: At the University Press, 1929), pp. 30–31.

results can be obtained only as answers to preceding speculations,"[39] and as Whitehead puts it in more general terms: "No systematic thought has made progress apart from some adequately general working hypothesis, adapted to its special topic."[40] Theory plays an essential role in intellectual advance; collection of facts by itself is inadequate and may, if theory is neglected, actually retard or impede understanding. It is unfortunately the case that a number of empirical studies have not produced results proportionate to the labor expended on them, since they were not addressed to significant problems and the objectives for which they were undertaken were insufficiently considered in theoretical terms. Indeed, the assiduous pursuit of an ostensibly strict empiricism may act as a soporific and prevent our giving critical consideration to more general problems of interpretation. It can even become a kind of escapism, a lazy man's way out, a means of avoiding the most important tasks. The mechanical parts of research are easier than the thinking parts, and the accumulation of data is easier than writing it up. An obsession with the mechanical part of the job can become an excuse for not attempting the necessary thought that should underlie it. As A. C. Bradley has said: "Research though laborious is easy; imagination though delightful is difficult."

The answer to the line of argument summarized at the outset of this section is not a flat-footed reassertion of the virtues of empiricism. It is rather, I think, the insistence on a distinction, which is not always remembered, between two kinds of intellectual activity, both needful for generalization and yet wholly different from each other: the means by which we arrive at or formulate a proposition and the means by which, once having obtained it, we attempt to assess its merits. A confusion between these two processes may lie behind a good deal of the disagreement. Those who make a great point of external checks and empirical methods may be thinking of the second stage, verification. Those who attack the uninspired collection of data, who resent quantitative techniques, who insist that historical thought must be speculative and intuitive, may be thinking of the first stage, getting ideas rather than testing or confirming them.

[39] Paul F. Lazarsfeld *et al.*, *The People's Choice* . . . (New York: Columbia University Press, 1944), p. 42.

[40] This quotation from Alfred North Whitehead is used by Lee Benson as an epigraph to his book, *Turner and Beard: American Historical Writing Reconsidered* (Glencoe, Ill.: Free Press, 1960).

For the first step, deriving a generalization, no rules and no standardized procedures can be laid down. To assert that the most significant general statements are simple inductions from the evidence quite misrepresents the character of historical thinking. A generalization is not simply something logically derived from the evidence, the result of hard work effectively directed. It is also a comment on the evidence, a happy idea, an "inspiration," a new way of looking at things which helps us to understand the materials we have collected, an arrangement of the evidence in a new way so as to suggest something unexpected and important about it, the pointing-out of similarities and relationships hitherto unappreciated. The most challenging problem of research is often not to collect or recite the evidence but to display the context in which it is significant, to show how results that are trivial or meaningless in one frame of reference may become useful or even decisive in another.

We know relatively little about the mechanism through which ideas occur to us. They appear to grow in the mind as we become acquainted with the material, or perhaps as we do other quite different things, by a process that cannot be exactly charted. A man may reach his most important generalizations in a semi-intuitive fashion on the basis of his general judgment of many different things which he might find it difficult to identify. The creative process is a tangle of contradictions, and an analysis of it may be more a matter of psychology than of logic. It seems clear, however, that, while certain technical or routine tasks can be pushed ahead in almost any circumstances, what is needed for a real intellectual advance, for the solution of problems, is a more intimate kind of activity and one less subject to control. Ideas come from a variety of sources, often quite unexpected or unpromising ones. They may be stimulated or crystallized by reading or conversation, sometimes on matters remote from and apparently quite unconnected with the subject of inquiry. It seems, then, unwise to close off any possible avenue of suggestion: we should be receptive to ideas from any source and cast our nets for them as wide as is practically possible.

I should like to mention here that, in my own research, I have found monographic studies in the social sciences a particularly fruitful source of inspiration and ideas. Although an interest in co-operation with the social sciences has been identified as one of the important shifts of emphasis in recent American historiography,[41] this change in orienta-

[41] SSRC Bulletin 64, pp. 13–14 and 21.

tion has been bitterly resented by many in the profession. It is curious that a main objection to the use of the social sciences for historical purposes has been that they impose mechanical and mindless methods, techniques that are inappropriate to the complexity of historical materials, and choke up the sources of imagination and ideas. My own experience has been precisely the opposite. I have found in this literature little that I could borrow in the way of technical devices, with the one exception of the technique of scalogram analysis. What I have principally gained from these materials, on the contrary, have been new ideas and new perspectives which have enabled me to appraise my own problems differently and which have suggested questions that it might be profitable or illuminating to investigate. It seems to me unfortunate that professional limitations of outlook have prevented many historians from exploiting more fully the leads they could obtain from this impressive accumulation of ideas and findings in a related field. It appears pedantic to insist that historians must play the game according to a set of rules, that they cannot use certain procedures or approaches because they have been pre-empted by other disciplines and that to attempt such borrowings is to distort by newfangled methods the clear, pure stream of historical narrative. To limit our search for ideas and methods to sources of acknowledged professional or departmental orthodoxy places an unnecessary restriction upon our efforts and serves to defeat our ultimate objectives.

As a source of ideas there is also, I like to think, a real place for the speculative essay, even if its conclusions are undemonstrable or unacceptable. Such essays, even when we disagree with them, can provide insights, suggestions, or pointers to further research. I have heard it said that we all condemn the philosophers of history—and then crib from them. This is not true, I believe, at least on any large scale, but the overemphasis illustrates the point I am trying to make. Even Pieter Geyl, Toynbee's most notable critic, has something like this to say in his essay reviewing Toynbee's last four volumes: "If one could only accept the work as a collection of stories, and glimpses of life, and dissertations on aspects and problems, from the history of the world, what a mine of curious and out-of-the-way information . . . , what flashes of insight, what instructive juxtapositions even—what learning, what brilliance!"[42] Books whose conclusions are controversial or vulnerable may, despite this, be provocative and illuminating

---

[42] *Debates with Historians*, pp. 181–82.

and make in their own way a contribution to the progress of historical thinking that is not to be disregarded.

The second step—testing, verifying, and appraising our ideas and inspirations once we have obtained them—is obviously quite a different kind of procedure. The means by which we derive generalizations are irregular and unpredictable. The means by which we verify them are, if not altogether controlled by formal rules, at least subject to sets of assumptions and techniques that are fairly widely accepted. It has been well put that "the methods and functions of discovery and proof in research are as different as are those of a detective and of a judge in a court of law."[43] It is the essence of my argument here that in making historical generalizations the second step is as necessary as the first, that bright ideas are not enough by themselves, that generalizations even if reached intuitively should also meet the test of external verification to the satisfaction of others and that we must reject the position that, in Sidney Hook's trenchant words, "the adequacy of the historical understanding is determined not by external criteria . . . but by a self-certifying insight."[44]

It is a common experience in research that insights, though indispensable, are not always reliable. An insight may be merely euphoric and commend itself, though this may not be at first perceived, because it fits our prejudices or our present beliefs. "What is called an 'understanding' of history or of historical events is often merely the feeling of satisfaction which comes over us when a new impression or treatment of history falls easily into one or another of the categories already accepted and established in our minds."[45] Insights generally prove of unequal value, a proportion of them have to be rejected on further consideration, and many investigators have testified how large this proportion is and how many of the ideas and hypotheses that occurred to them had eventually to be discarded. The advancement of knowledge depends not only on getting ideas but also on trying them out and sifting the good ones from the bad ones.

Though theory can be a help it can also constitute a hazard. The formulation of one's ideas at too early a stage can result in a rigidity of thought from which it is difficult to escape. It is only too easy to be-

---

[43] W. I. B. Beveridge, *The Art of Scientific Investigation* (1950; rev. ed.; New York: Norton, 1957), p. 123.

[44] *Op. cit.*, p. 128.

[45] "Proposition XIII" in SSRC Bulletin 54, p. 137.

come the prisoner of one's own preconceptions, or even of the preconceptions of the system one is attacking. The mind has a tendency to fill in, when a step in the argument is missing, with speculations or pseudo-explanations which may blind the researcher to the significance of his findings and actually impede discovery. Something like this has unquestionably happened in my own field of British political history in the nineteenth century. The developments of this period have been too often dismissed in catch phrases, and it is only recently, by hard digging and hard thinking, that some scholars have been able to advance beyond this level. Though I believe there is a place for the speculative essay, I would add to this that speculation, at least in my experience, does not prove very helpful unless it is based on considerable familiarity with the evidence and some careful thinking about it. I do not at all agree with Stuart Hughes's view that the system-builders, since they "are alone in a position to give free play to their speculative propensities, are the writers who actually operate on the 'frontiers' of historical thinking."[46] A man who tries to cover all fields is not likely to know enough about any one field to take him very far into the inwardness of events. The contributions of such writers to the problems I am interested in seem to me jejune and insipid, a secondhand rendering of the most common, if not the latest, clichés. The general studies from which I have profited have been rather different in character. For example, the explorations of Max Weber, Robert Michels, Maurice Duverger, Hannah Arendt, or David Riesman are all in part speculative and to some extent vulnerable, but they are based on significant accumulations of detailed knowledge and are directed to problems sufficiently restricted in scope so that some progress can be made in dealing with them.

The need for testing one's insights seems obvious, but it is not always remembered. My own impression is that, on the whole, historians have paid too little rather than too much attention to the problem of verification of statements of any complexity. Though demanding standards of exactitude unquestionably obtain in the profession, these seem to have been addressed principally to statements of a fairly low conceptual level. As Stuart Hughes says, paraphrasing Marc Bloch: "The historian's scrupulous care in ascertaining whether an event had in fact taken place contrasted painfully with the amateurishness the same historian manifested when he came to explaining it."[47]

[46] "The Historian and the Social Scientist," p. 27.
[47] *Ibid.*, p. 21.

On the other hand, the argument against pedestrianism has served as a pretext for historical methods which it seems difficult to justify by any considered standard. There still prevails a tradition of "literary history" in the bad sense, in which large, general statements jazzed up with a little swingeing rhetoric take the place of careful analysis, a procedure that seems irresponsible in the present state of our ignorance. H. A. L. Fisher in his tribute to the Whig historians writes that a good history is more likely to emerge "from a few first-class authorities cleverly interpreted by a fresh mind than from a vast and exhaustive miscellany of unequal value."[48] The implications suggested by this statement—that an exhaustive investigation is incompatible with a balanced presentation and that a historian is likely to have more insight if he has not delved too deeply into his sources—give some food for thought. Perhaps not all "literary historians" would so frankly avow the basis of their work, but there seems to be more acceptance in practice of Fisher's dictum than there probably would be in theory.

Historians are sometimes criticized for not venturing far enough in the direction of generalization. A juster criticism of many historical writers might be that they have gone too far, further at least than their evidence warrants. Many historical works, textbooks especially, contain fairly wild, impressionistic general statements for which the evidence is not, and is not likely to be, forthcoming. Nor are such statements restricted to textbooks; writers of monographs sometimes commit the same offense in sections where they try to orient the immediate subject of inquiry in a larger context. My own interest in problems of verification springs in part from exasperation with such goings-on. I could not bring myself to accept many of the statements I found in the history books. It was not merely that these statements were occasionally inconsistent; I also wondered how the authors knew or how they could know.

For these reasons I cannot agree that the most significant statements we can make are insights and nothing more or that the epigrams of La Rochefoucauld, though I read them with pleasure, are as good as we can do by way of historical generalization. I think, on the contrary, that we can do better. La Rochefoucauld's maxims are perhaps more fun to read than many historical monographs, partly because the author was intelligent and witty, qualities that are unfortunately not universally distributed in the academic profession, but partly also be-

---

[48] *The Whig Historians: The Raleigh Lecture on History* (London: Oxford University Press, 1928), p. 28.

cause he was under no particular obligation to worry about the validity of his generalizations and could cheerfully disembarrass himself, perhaps with a qualifying adverb, of the reservations that inevitably clutter the writings of social scientists and historians. He was free to make impressionistic observations and, if he wished, to point them up for effect, to call attention to a particular feature of a situation by humorously exaggerating it. Perhaps, however, the humdrum results of painstaking scholars who have surveyed all the available evidence and bring us a report on it may be, though less prepossessing or less glamorous, actually more useful for gaining an understanding of the historical process. It should be added that it is by no means inevitable either that the professional scholar is always pedestrian or that the amateur is always inspired.

4. *The Problem of Procedure*

The argument is sometimes made that, since historical understanding is a matter of insight, judgment, wisdom, and maturity, formal techniques are not particularly helpful and it is illusory to suppose that an orderly recital of the evidence, whether the order is statistical or of some different kind, will take us much further toward understanding the historical past. By this view, to suppose that the methods of history can be gradually improved and perfected, like the internal combustion engine, is to ignore the essentially imaginative and intuitive character of historical thought. This position may be regarded as a special case of the plea for an intuitive approach to history which was discussed in the third section, and much of what I have to say in reply has been presented there. I wish to add, however, a few special points relating to questions of technique.

I take as my example statistical procedures, since these are what I know about. This is admittedly a limited subject because elaborate statistics are not appropriate for many, perhaps the great majority, of historical problems, and it is a mistake to force the use of the method when the data will not sustain it. Also, the method, even in cases where it can be applied, is laborious: the problems of gathering, classifying, manipulating, and interpreting the materials for statistical work are more formidable than will probably be appreciated by anyone who has not attempted this kind of research. Despite these difficulties statistics can perhaps offer certain advantages in subjects where they can properly be used, and I do not think that their value for historical purposes has been sufficiently explored or that enough attention has been given to the possibility of making verifiable generalizations through the formal arrangement of evidence. The bearing of quantification on generalization is too large a topic to be adequately discussed here—it would require a separate essay—but I should like to raise a few general points.

Quantitative procedures, which are now so much used for a variety of purposes, seem particularly to raise the hackles of a large section of the history profession, and the objections to new and unfamiliar methods have been directed with a special virulence against statistics. Protests have come from outside the history profession as well—for example, from C. Wright Mills in *The Sociological Imagination*—and the value of some of the monumental quantitative studies that have been conducted in the United States over the last two decades is still energetically disputed in certain quarters. There have in general been two lines of attack upon statistical enterprises: that their findings are trivial or unimportant, and that their conclusions are unproved or incorrect. It is argued that such studies have been too limited in outlook, that they have dealt with insignificant problems merely because they could be investigated instead of considering more important ones, and that the broader questions which really matter are apparently not amenable to this kind of treatment. It is also argued that the precision of techniques cannot compensate for the inexactitude of the raw data, that the crudeness of our observations and the vagueness of our fundamental categories will not be cured by manipulation of the paraphernalia of statistical methods, and that any significant conclusions reached by such means must depend on a chain of shaky reasoning that is too long and too vulnerable for the conclusions to be accepted with any degree of assurance.[49]

Richard Hofstadter has formulated what he calls the "paradox of quantification" arising from the apparent inconclusiveness of quantitative studies:

> The essence of this paradox is that the recent use of quantitative methods to test historical generalization has resulted in the wholesale destruction of categories that previously held sway in the historian's vocabulary without supplanting them with new generalizations of comparable significance.... It is, of course, quite conceivable that the uprooted generalizations will be replaced

---

[49] C. Wright Mills, *The Sociological Imagination* (New York: Oxford University Press, 1959), chap. 3; Nathan Glazer, " 'The American Soldier' as Science: Can Sociology Fulfill Its Ambitions?" *Commentary*, VIII (1949), 487–96; Cohen, pp. 663–65.

by interpretations having a more social-psychological cast. But in such case it is unlikely that the historian can, with the type of evidence available to him, put these interpretations on any better footing than that of intelligent and partially verified guesses. Should this be true, we might find ourselves in possession of more sophisticated and seemingly more satisfactory explanations which would have to stand largely upon a speculative foundation.[50]

It must be confessed that quantitative research can be discouraging. One finds trends that contribute so far as they go to confirm or refute certain hypotheses, but the very investigations that reveal the trends also reveal important exceptions to them that must be explained as well. It is also well understood that statistics prove nothing and that the results of a statistical investigation may be undependable for reasons unrelated to the quality of the mathematics in it. Every statistical presentation includes two non-statistical steps: (1) the assumptions, and the collection of data based on these assumptions, at the beginning; and (2) the inferences at the end. Both steps contain pitfalls. The detailed data available for any large historical project will almost certainly be incomplete and partly inaccurate, and this fact imposes an inevitable limitation on the conclusions ultimately drawn from them. Furthermore, the inferences at the end are not "proved" by the statistics, they are in fact not statistical statements at all, they are logically inferred, and their reliability is determined not by arithmetic but by whether we can make a persuasive case for them. This is not to say that they are nonsense, but they are matters of logic and judgment, not of figures, and for this reason no statistical treatment of a problem can ever be entirely objective. These points are, of course, no news. They are commonplaces, to be found in all the standard manuals of statistics. Statisticians are as alert to them as non-statisticians, more so, indeed, since the formal structure of their argument necessitates a more explicit formulation. Such objections are generally regarded, and correctly, as serving to mark the boundaries of what statistics can do rather than to discredit the method. After all these points have been allowed for, much is still feasible.

The significance or reliability of statistical results are, of course, relative matters. I have already given my reasons for believing that attempts to deal with questions that we are not yet in a position to answer may be self-defeating. Nor can I concede that a statistical demonstration is of necessity less convincing than some other kind,

[50] "History and the Social Sciences," in Fritz Stern (ed.), *Varieties of History: From Voltaire to the Present* (New York: Meridian, 1956), p. 415, n. 14.

though, of course, statistics can be mishandled as can any other method.

I should argue, on the contrary, that an orderly arrangement of the evidence is a major step toward coming to terms with it, as anyone knows who has had to do desk work of any kind, scholarly or administrative. A systematic arrangement of this kind can sometimes carry further than appeared possible at the outset of the investigation for, as we work into a problem, we sometimes find that certain information proves usable in ways not expected when we first encountered it. A formal arrangement also helps to achieve a greater degree of objectivity. Setting up categories for classifying the evidence necessitates some careful thought about their meaning and relevance and in this way imposes on the investigator the burden of clarifying his ideas and defining his assumptions more explicitly. Most important, a formal quantitative arrangement of the evidence forces upon the investigator's attention the discrepancies between theories and observation, the points at which they do not correspond, in a particularly obtrusive fashion. As Robert K. Merton says, the quantitative anomaly, unlike many qualitative ones, cannot be easily evaded.[51] The very nakedness of the results, the intolerable character of a discrepancy of this kind, acts as a stimulant to reformulation and may also give a good indication of the direction in which it can best be attempted.

Hofstadter's insistence that statistics are destructive rather than constructive, that they do not replace the generalizations they overturn with new formulations of comparable significance, suggests the implication, though this may not have been intended, that generalizations are useful only when they are absolute or invariant. If this were true, statistics, since they generally show exceptions to every rule, could scarcely provide adequate support for generalizations. The usual experience of historians, however, seems to be that absolute or invariant hypotheses are almost never confirmed and that few general statements of any significance are completely true. What is most useful is not to establish the truth or the falsity of a particular general statement but to determine the extent to which it holds, the exact degree of the trend. Historians deal with a universe not of absolutes but of probabilities, and for a world conceived in these terms statistics are the appropriate tool.

It is essential to make a distinction between a sweeping general

---

[51] "The History of Quantification in the Sciences: Report on a Conference," *Items*, XIV (1960), 3.

statement to which no limits are set and a generalization that is based on a measurable comparison. The comment by Proust, quoted earlier (p. 157), regarding the unwillingness of men to alter their beliefs in the light of the facts may serve as an illustration. Proust's statement at once commends itself for it seems amply confirmed by other observations we have made: most readers would be able to cite illustrations of it from their own experience. Yet it is obvious on a moment's thought that the proposition does not invariably hold and that the degree of illusion is not the same in all cases. One begins to wonder, on further thought, how frequently this kind of thing happens, to what sorts of people, in what sorts of circumstances, and how far the degree of self-deception varies in different cases. These are questions of a different kind, and they require an answer stated in comparative and, if possible, measurable terms. I should argue that general or sweeping statements that include no qualification are actually less informative than statements based on a comparison and that once we stop asking whether a given statement is true and inquire instead how far it is true the argument reaches a new level not only of reliability but also of significance.

A final point should be made in regard to the proposition that statistics are destructive rather than constructive, that they tear down generalizations instead of building them up. I cannot accept the view that to test a hypothesis and find it does not work simply leads to a dead end. Negative results, the exclusion of unacceptable hypotheses, are always useful; and in some contexts they can be as significant as positive results. Nor have the results of statistical inquiries always been purely negative.[52] For example, the statistical studies of voting behavior over the last generation have enormously deepened and improved our understanding of the nature of political choice and the mechanism of a political system. Though much still remains to be elucidated, the discussion of these questions now takes place on a level

[52] Hofstadter, when he speaks of the failure of statistics to supplant old categories with new generalizations of comparable significance, cites as one of his sources an article which I published some years ago in which I laid a good deal of emphasis on the point that the complexity of the evidence worked against simple formulations. The results of my research since then have proved more encouraging, and I have shifted my position to one of somewhat greater, though still guarded, optimism. See, for example, two recent articles of mine, the first dealing with problems of stratification and the second dealing with problems of political behavior: "The Business Interests of the Gentry in the Parliament of 1841–47," published as an appendix in G. Kitson Clark, *The Making of Victorian England* (London: Methuen, 1962), pp. 290–305, and "Voting Patterns in the British House of Commons in the 1840's," to be published in the January, 1963, issue of *Comparative Studies in Society and History*.

of knowledge and understanding, based on the patient accumulation of evidence, that would have been impossible thirty years ago. Beyond this, a refinement of the evidence and of the techniques of measuring evidence has often proved highly rewarding in terms of new discoveries.

Of course, no presentation is final, all measurements and descriptions are accurate to only a limited degree, all investigations are incomplete, and in any formulation of the results of research there will always be what P. W. Bridgman has happily termed a "penumbra of uncertainty." As Bridgman goes on to say, however, it is exactly within this penumbra of uncertainty that the important new advances are often made.[53] Something like this may be true for the study of history and of political behavior. Certainly I have had some pleasant confirmations of this in my own experience, to an extent altogether beyond what I had originally anticipated. The statistical method, though it is not in general regarded as an empirical one, can in this sense have a heuristic value. In an area where one has already given a good deal of thought to the evidence and to the assumptions involved in handling it, material gathered to test a particular thesis may not merely refute the thesis but also point the way to a new and more appropriate formulation. Exact measurements may sometimes provide new insights and new perspectives that one could gain in no other way. It may be granted that our present knowledge is relative and imperfect and our present measurements are inexact, but it does not follow from this that nothing will be gained by more exhaustive study and more accurate measurements. The arbitrary rejection of techniques for refining the evidence and making our grasp of it more precise not only fails to cure the disease but aggravates it; it works directly against our best hope for a further understanding of our problems.

[53] *The Logic of Modern Physics* (1927; new ed.; New York: Macmillan, 1960), pp. 33–34.

XI. *Explicit Data and Implicit Assumptions in Historical Study*

BY DAVID M. POTTER

It is characteristic of priesthoods that, although claiming to know the truth, they modestly disavow any personal function in determining it. Instead, they profess to have special access to the sources of truth and to be mere passive channels for communicating it from the repositories where it lies awaiting discovery—in the entrails of birds or in the cryptic phrases of Holy Writ or, if they are a legal priesthood, in natural law or in precedent and *stare decisis*.

In this practice the priesthood of historians has been no exception. During the era when "scientific history" was in the ascendancy, historians disclaimed any initiative in interpreting the past or ascribing meaning to it. Their only role, they insisted, was to gather the data of the past and arrange it in chronological sequence, whereupon its meaning—or, in other words, the truth—would reveal itself.

This faith of the devotees of scientific history that some embodiment of truth lay buried in the sources, waiting only to be unearthed and exposed to the light, has now been pretty effectively shattered. It is at least thirty years since the oracles of this faith spoke with undisputed authority. But though scientific history has almost passed from the scene, it still casts a long shadow. For during the era of its ascendancy, it shaped what we call "historical method," and this method has survived, more or less unchanged, long after the historical philosophy which gave rise to it was swept away.

Orthodox or formal historical method was shaped at a time when men believed that a body of data would reveal its own meaning and would interpret itself, if only it were valid or authentic and were arranged in time sequence. The central problem of method, therefore, was to validate the data rather than to interpret them. Hence the problem of historical interpretation was neglected; indeed, its very existence as a problem was denied at the theoretical level, and the principal questions which the problem of interpretation ought to have posed were left to non-historians. Thus, the problem of causation has been left to the philosophers; the problem of human motivation has been left to the psychologists; the problem of social organization has been left to the sociologists. Historians dealt every day with questions involving causation, motivation, and social organization, and often by virtue of their qualities of personal sagacity they handled these topics extremely well. But the anomalous fact remained that the chief problem which historians recognized in their method was the validation of data, while the chief problem which they actually encountered in their daily work was the interpretation of the data. Thus, the most important achievements of historians were attained in spite of their method rather than by means of it.

After living for a long period under the dominion of scientific history, historians at last threw off this creed and embraced historical relativism. As they did so, they passed from the belief that they could attain truth without troubling themselves about theory to the belief that they could not attain truth even if they invoked theory. The result was a sharp reaction, in which historians atoned for their previous pride by professions of self-abasement. They not only repudiated all their former claims to objectivity and to absolute knowledge but also insisted on making repeated confession of their subjectivism and even renounced their right to talk about the ultimate questions of history. If truth could not be attained and if the belief that it could was now in disrepute, the best way for a historian to avoid the imputation of harboring such a discredited belief was for him to abstain from even discussing what might be regarded as the ultimate questions.

This reaction showed up in an especially diagnostic way in the attitude of historians toward what had previously been called "causes." Causes, it was now agreed, did not reveal themselves. The historian still might try to hunt them down, and, of course, in practice historians did continue to seek them, but since they could not be attained in an absolute sense, a prudent man might avoid needless exposure to criticism if he would refrain from speaking of causes as such. Accordingly, one eminent American historian, in the preface to an important and intensive book which cannot be overlooked by anyone who is studying the causes of the Civil War, said that his work "is not intended to be a discussion of the causes of the Civil War." It was "only an attempt to state a few general impressions as to how events got into such shape that they could not be handled by the democratic process." He went on to complain that "some people cannot see the difference between such an effort and attempting to state causes."[1]

[1] Avery O. Craven, *The Growth of Southern Nationalism, 1848–1861* (Baton Rouge: Louisiana State University Press, 1953), p. x.

One of the people who apparently cannot see this difference is J. H. Hexter, who in his essay "Personal Retrospect and Postscript" writes:

In the nineteenth century, the word "cause" in either its noun form or its verb form would have done the work done by "factor." . . . But somehow, "cause" got into trouble with the philosophers and the scientists and was dropped by all the best and some of the less good intellectual clubs. The work the word had been doing had to go on being done, however, since everyone found it necessary to go on talking about the species of relation which "cause" had formerly designated. So "factor" was slid into the slot which "cause" had once filled in the vocabulary of rational discourse, and this made everybody very happy. Thus the human mind progresses—sideways.[2]

But the historians' scrupulous avoidance of the word *cause* did not arise merely from the fact that the word got into trouble with the philosophers. Rather their avoidance was symptomatic of what had happened to historians after they gave up their faith that objectivity was attainable. If they could not attain it, they must not even make overt use of the concepts that had pertained to it.

Thus both the cult of scientific history and the reaction against the cult placed a barrier between the historian's practice and his theory. The cult told him he could find what he sought without theory, and the reaction told him he could not find it even with theory. Hence, the development of theory has been inhibited in history as much as in any branch of learning. This neglect of theory did not mean, of course, that the historian really confined himself, as he often professed to do, to the mere compilation of data. In practice, he was constantly attempting to work out answers to the questions of causation, motivation, etc., but the assumptions of scientific history told him that he found these answers in the data and therefore did not need analytical tools—other than those for validating data—to assist him in working them out. After the decline of scientific history, he usually went right on, just as before, trying in practice to work out the answers to interpretative questions. But his belief that it was impossible to work them out in an absolute sense stifled his impulses to formulate any systematic theory. Consequently, for the better part of a century now, the historian's assumptions concerning the nature of his own work have prevented him from attempting a systematic consideration of the concepts which he uses constantly in the course of his work.

This gap between theory and practice has created a situation which

[2] J. H. Hexter, *Reappraisals in History* (Evanston, Ill.: Northwestern University Press, 1961), p. 200.

Explicit Data and Implicit Assumptions

might seem quite extraordinary—indeed, almost incredible—if we were not so accustomed to it. Here, in the field of history, is a profession which has several thousand members in the United States alone. These people produce one of the largest bodies of published literature issuing from any branch of academic study. They are represented in every university in the country, and they are constantly engaged in the training of new historians. This training process, leading to the doctoral degree, requires a minimum of three years of intensive work after the baccalaureate. Historians do not agree on whether their subject is a science, but they do virtually all agree that it has a discipline, and they are, on the whole, as proud of their discipline and as jealous of it as any other group of scholars.

Essentially, what all of these people are engaged in doing is converting the raw data which pertain to history, to past human experience, into statements, which we also call "history," about this experience. In the process of formulating these statements historians constantly work with the relationships between separate items of data—relationships which pertain to the effect of one thing in leading to another (what we call "cause") or to the effect of a given condition or event in inducing a particular impulse or purpose (what we call "motivation") or to the degree of similarity or dissimilarity between given units of time in a chronological sequence or given individuals in an aggregate (what we call, respectively, "periods" or "groups") or to many other kinds of relationships. In a certain sense this consideration of relationships is the chief part of their work. Yet the literature of their method and the procedures of their training give so little attention to the systematic analysis of such relationships that a majority of those trained in history have never confronted the general question of the nature of causation or of motivation or of group identity. This may seem singular, but what is really singular is that many who are being trained are not even aware that they have not confronted these questions, and many of the men who train them are not aware of it either.

Such historians, when asked why they have not concerned themselves with such questions, will reply with a double-barreled answer. They do not need to become entangled in theory, they will first assert, because they are not engaged in interpretation; they confine themselves to facts. And then they will add that theirs is a pragmatic approach—that is, one free from a priori generalizations—rather than a theoretical one. In a battle between pragmatists and theoreticians they will fight to the end, they announce, against the warping of facts to fit ideological formulas. They intend to keep on chopping away at the facts and to let the chips fall where they may. They make these assertions with great sincerity and in a way that sounds most convincing.

But is it really the function of the historian to confine himself to mere compilation? And can he so limit himself, even if he would? It is by no means agreed that he should accept any such narrow and limited role. Indeed, we have had two brilliant recent statements—by E. H. Carr[3] and J. H. Hexter[4]—which, if they are symptomatic, indicate a trend toward reasserting the larger responsibilities of the historian. Carr makes a refreshingly dogmatic reaffirmation of an old axiom when he states, without qualification: "The study of history is a study of causes." Hexter shows how heretical an old belief can be made to sound when he says:

> In fact, truth about history is not only attainable but is regularly attained. It is true, for example, that at Waterloo on 18 June 1815 Napoleon I and his army were decisively defeated by a coalition army commanded by the Duke of Wellington. This is true in the simple sense that it is an *accurate* description of something that happened in the past, and the accurate description of things that happened in the past is one of the ends of history writing. But is it an adequate description? The answer to that question is another question: "Adequate for what?" The statement as it appears is quite adequate for a dictionary of dates. It is not adequate for a historical study of the era of Napoleon; and if by "adequate" is meant a narration of everything thought and said and done at Waterloo that June day, no historical account of any event can ever be adequate. The whole issue has been confused by a failure to make some rudimentary distinctions, the most important being that between knowing something and knowing everything. To prove that there is nothing about which a finite mind can know everything, is not to prove that there is nothing about which a finite mind can know something; and to demonstrate that all human knowledge is incomplete and all human truth partial is not to demonstrate that all human knowledge is ignorance and all human truth false or some ambiguous thing between true and false. That this is the working conviction of historians as contrasted with their inept excursions into theory is easy to demonstrate.

Still, many historians will deny the goals which Carr and Hexter set for them and will continue to assert that theirs is a pragmatic consideration of facts, happily remote from the pitfalls of theory. If this assertion were true, their position would be a difficult one to assail, and the need for theory would indeed be doubtful. But the vital question in

[3] Edward Hallett Carr, *What Is History?* (New York: Knopf, 1962), p. 113.
[4] *Op. cit.*, p. 189.

Explicit Data and Implicit Assumptions

historical study is whether this choice between a pragmatic approach and a theoretic approach really exists. Or is the actual situation one in which the historian inescapably applies theoretical assumptions to his data, as the only possible alternative to leaving them in chaos? If such is the situation, then the real choice is between the conscious applications of reasoned and stated assumptions and the unconscious application of unreasoned and unrecognized assumptions.

The historian, in his compulsive wish to be pragmatic, has been very arbitrary in his readiness to recognize the role of theory in the forms in which he can abstain from it, while refusing to recognize its existence when it appears in the implicit forms in which he cannot avoid using it. Thus, historians have always agreed that (to state in other words a point that Hans Meyerhoff makes above)[5] an investigator who seeks to find the principles which apply as universal laws throughout history must resort to theory. If a historian is going to look for the cycles which regularly recur or for the basic sequences which always repeat themselves or for the parallels between various civilizations, of course he must reckon with theory. In other words, historians do not deny that the class of generalizations which Gottschalk defines above in his fourth, fifth, and sixth categories[6] inescapably involves a use of theory. But also, most historians make it a matter almost of pride to avoid generalizations at this high level of analogy, abstraction, or universality, and to confine themselves to more limited statements. Often such statements merely set forth two or more items of "fact," with, of course, an implied relation between them. Many historians fondly believe that such statements are factually pure and free of any infection of theory.

Yet even statements which appear to be most "factual" and most limited are often based upon assumptions so broad and ridden with implications so extensive that when one recognizes these aspects the whole distinction between high-level generalization and low-level generalization, or even between factual statements and theoretical statements, tends to break down. Two or three examples may serve to illustrate this point.

Take the statement "The pro-slavery wing of the Democratic Party blocked Van Buren's nomination in 1844, and in 1848 he ran for

[5] Pp. vi, n. 2 and 129, n. 17.

[6] Pp. 113–14 above.

the presidency on the Free Soil ticket."[7] The facts that are stated here are relatively solid; no one is likely to deny their correctness. But there is implied a relationship between them: what the proslavery Democrats did to Van Buren in 1844 had a bearing on his attitude toward Free Soil in 1848. Indeed, a motive is implied: perhaps because they defeated him, he turned against them. But to ascribe this motive alone is to minimize other possible motives, including especially his sincere ideological commitment to the antislavery cause. In broader terms, a theory of motivation is involved and is applied to the data—a theory which stresses the importance of considerations of self-interest rather than the power of ideals. Yet the historian who writes such a statement may never have formulated in his own mind a coherent attitude toward the problem of human motivation. The questions must arise, therefore, whether it would be possible in his training to make him more aware of the kinds of unconscious assumptions which he and his fellows are most likely to use and, if this could be done, whether the quality of his historical statements would be improved.

Let us look at another statement: "The Radical Republicans defeated Lincoln's mild program and inaugurated the era of drastic reconstruction." This relatively simple sentence, though apparently devoid of theory, contains at least three very broad generalizations, each one treacherous in the extreme. First is a generalization which ascribes to an unstated number of individuals a common identity strong enough to justify classifying them as a group—namely, the Radical Republicans—and ascribes to this group a crucial role in defeating one policy and implementing another. Yet, in terms of analysis historians have had great difficulty either in defining what constituted a Radical or in proving that any given aggregate of individuals formed a truly cohesive Radical bloc. Second is a chronological generalization—that a certain time span was pre-eminently significant for the process of what is called "Reconstruction"—setting up new regimes in the Southern states and restoring them to the Union—rather than for other developments, such as industrialization. Yet, that process lasted for very diverse intervals of time in various states, and the long-range problem of the relationship of Negroes and Whites continued to be important long after the so-called Reconstruction was "ended." Third is a generalization about the degree of severity of Reconstruction, which involves not only a

---

[7] This statement and the two which follow on pp. 184–85 are invented by the writer but are believed to be fairly illustrative of well-known types of historical affirmation.

verdict on the over-all effect of a whole series of acts of Congress but also an opinion on what kind of settlement can be regarded as drastic in the case of a defeated belligerent. Many of the measures adopted during Reconstruction are now regarded as salutary—for instance, the establishment of public education in some states—and other measures, such as the Amnesty Acts, do not conform to the generalization that Reconstruction was drastic.

May I offer one more example of a seemingly "factual" statement with little apparent infusion of theory? Suppose it is said that "John Wilkes Booth shot Lincoln at 10:30 P.M. with a derringer, at point blank range, behind the left ear, the bullet moving through his brain toward the right eye; and Lincoln died at 7:22 A.M. the next day." In formal terms this is a recital of a series of facts, but it is, in its implications, almost inescapably also an explanation of cause—the cause of Lincoln's death. In this statement there are several assorted items, all assumed to be part of the causative complex but unanalyzed concerning their relative part in the total result. These factors include an assassin (Booth), a ballistic weapon (the derringer), and a physical injury (Lincoln's wound). A physician would explain Lincoln's death in terms of the wound, and a ballistics expert would explain it in terms of the weapon; the historian in our culture would probably take the wound and the weapon for granted and would explain it in terms of the assassin. But this choice is culturally conditioned, for if the death had been caused by a special, previously unknown weapon or if Lincoln's assassin were being described by a writer in a culture which did not possess firearms, probably the derringer would receive primary attention. This observation is not meant to suggest that the historian ought to discard his cultural assumptions and to spell out every one of the infinitude of circumstances, from gravitation on, which are taken for granted in any situation. But it is to suggest that he might well have a more carefully reasoned basis for selecting as significant the factor which he does decide to emphasize.

Probably the historian would place the focus upon Booth individually not because Booth pulled the fatal trigger but because Booth planned the killing and without Booth it would not have happened. Without the derringer, presumably, it would have happened anyway, with some other weapon. If the killing had been planned by the Confederates and Booth had been a mere instrument for them, as his derringer was for him, he too would be de-emphasized by the historian. Implicitly, it would seem that to the historian, faced with a multiplicity of factors, the significant ones are the ones without which the event would not have occurred. But this is by no means a firm criterion, for usually a multiplicity of circumstances are necessary to the event (for instance, Lincoln's presence at the theater, the negligence of his guards, the physical layout of the presidential box and the anteroom beyond it),[8] but the historian is likely to treat most of these as being either understood or insignificant, without ever defining, either for himself or for others, the bases of his selection.

The point here, however, is not to settle upon the cause of Lincoln's death but rather to recognize that it is almost impossible to make a simple "factual" statement about the circumstances of his death without basing it upon assumptions about the nature of causation and what makes particular facts significant or insignificant.

If the above statements about Van Buren, the Radical Republicans, and Lincoln should be taken together, the striking thing about them is that in form they all resemble one another to a considerable degree. All appear to be mere narrative statements about what occurred. In terms of Gottschalk's six categories of historical generalization, all fall into either the first or second, the lowest levels of generalization,[9] for there is no broad comparison or analogy or abstraction or universalizing about them. At first glance, they would hardly be regarded as involving generalization at all. But though they seem alike in their factuality and in their avoidance of overt or explicit generalization, actually they are all suffused with implicit generalizations. These generalizations, although similar in level, are extremely diverse in kind, for one involves assumptions about motivation, another about classification, and the third about causation. Even in a pure narrative, therefore, where interpretative or explanatory or analytical discussion is most rigorously suppressed, the mere inclusion of items of "fact" in a particular sequence will suggest one relationship rather than another for the individuals involved in the events, one motivation rather than another for their acts, one cause rather than another for the course of events, and even one criterion rather than another for making an evaluation of what happened.

But if these simple statements are indeed enmeshed with assumptions of the broadest theoretical kind, we must then conclude that the

---

[8] These are, it may be argued, merely conducive factors, while Booth was an active factor, but this argument raises the questions: Can one systematically use this criterion to distinguish what is significant, and do historians do so?

[9] Pp. 113–14 above.

historian really cannot abstain from generalization and cannot escape theory. The choice before him is not between a "factual" and a "theoretical" approach but between, on the one hand, theoretical assumptions which have been recognized and, so far as possible, made rational and explicit and, on the other hand, unrecognized, half-hidden assumptions which remain unordered and chaotic.

If the true choice lies between the latter pair, it would seem to follow that one of the most important questions for historians today is: Can their common, working assumptions be systematized and refined to some degree and raised above the threshold of the subconscious? If there is to be a method for the practices which historians actually engage in and not merely for those which they imagine that they engage in, such an ordering of the historian's interpretative procedures would seem to be of the essence.

When I state this problem as a question, I intend it as a question—one to which the answer is really in doubt, for there are immense difficulties in the way of reducing the almost infinite range of operative historical assumptions to a system.

At one stage in the work of the Committee on Historical Analysis, I attempted to draw up an abstract statement of what historians write about, with the thought that if one could state in comprehensive terms what themes they deal with, it might then be possible to make at least a tentative inventory of what kinds of generalizations they use in connection with these themes. My effort resulted in the following statement, which I set down here not because I believe it to be adequate but because it may serve to illustrate the problem of identifying various kinds of generalizations:

Historical writing, in all its various forms, deals with people, as individuals or as aggregates, acting in relation to other individuals or aggregates, responding, with more or less freedom of response, to forces in the primary or secondary environment and motivated to follow a course of thought or action, often in preference to alternative courses of thought or action—with the result that certain developments become manifest. These manifestations, taking place in a context of specific culture and institutions, modify and are modified by the context, and historical change occurs. Historical writing also frequently offers conclusions, if not on the virtue and wisdom, at least on the effectiveness and suitability of given courses of thought or action.

In this statement, what kinds of generalizations may one identify? The term *aggregate* certainly points to the frequency of the classificatory generalizations which are discussed above in Finley's[10] and Wright's[11] articles and which involve the tricky question of deciding when a pattern of associations shows the existence of an organic group such as a faction, a school of thought, or a nationality—entities whose existence is commonly assumed without analysis. The concept that "historical writing . . . deals with . . . individuals . . . responding, with more or less freedom of response, to forces in the . . . environment" would place a focus upon examination of the generalizations about the extent to which events are deterministically controlled, without real choice on the part of the participants, and would also involve a scrutiny of concepts about the nature of the impact of environment. Historians who stress environmental forces frequently describe these forces in detail and then simply make assumptions about their impact, without real analysis of the data pertaining to the impact and without much attention to the character of the society upon which the forces impinge. It is sometimes asserted, for instance, that Frederick Jackson Turner's frontier had upon people with an Anglo-American, nineteenth-century culture a certain impact which it has not had upon other peoples with other cultures.

To continue: If my statement regarding the content of history is at all valid, historians are constantly concerned with the motivation of people in past situations, as such people follow one course of action or another. Historians constantly ascribe or at least imply motive in specific situations but without any general theory of the nature of motivation and without adequate recognition of what the behavioral scientists know about motivation. When Alexander George explains the conduct of Woodrow Wilson in terms of psychological compulsions arising from his childhood relations with his father;[12] when William Allen White explains the same conduct in terms of Wilson's fiercely Calvinistic principles;[13] and when someone else explains it in terms of the fact that Wilson found that he gained success by appealing to the people over the heads of the legislators when he was governor of New Jersey and during the days of the New Freedom and that he simply continued to use, with ultimately disastrous results, a tactic which for

[10] P. 21 above.

[11] P. 36 above.

[12] Alexander L. and Juliette L. George, *Woodrow Wilson and Colonel House: A Personality Study* (New York: John Day, 1956).

[13] *Woodrow Wilson* (Boston: Houghton Mifflin, 1924).

Explicit Data and Implicit Assumptions

a long while had served him well[14]—when such writers give their various interpretations, they are in part disagreeing about their immediate subject, but perhaps to a greater degree they are merely applying to it their disagreement about the nature of human motivations.

If I may use my definition still further, the practice of historians in treating certain developments as resulting from prior circumstances or events means that, as Carr has said, the study of history is inescapably the study of causes. Here again, when historians offer alternative explanations of what caused a given event, the nature of causation rather than of the specific event may be the issue on which they disagree. Yet usually, if they debate the point, they will couch their argument in terms of the event and not in terms of a philosophy of causation

Without attempting to wring all the other possible themes of generalization from my trial definition above, I might point out two other frequent forms of generalization which are suggested. One of these is generalization about the nature of the interplay between, on the one hand, developments and, on the other, the context of culture and institutions within which developments occur. Almost every historian has had occasion to apply assumptions about this interplay. For instance, the character of a culture clearly influences the character of government as an institution, but does the institutional character of the public authority also influence the character of the culture or the personality structure of individuals in the culture? Should a development such as the desegregation of the schools be explained primarily in terms of institutional change—that is, the reversal of judicial rulings between *Plessy* v. *Ferguson* and *Brown* v. *Board of Education*—or should it be explained in cultural terms, such as the changes in the educational and economic status of the Negro and the changes in popular attitudes toward race? The historian's assumptions concerning questions like these are likely to shape his treatment of events fully as much as his scrutiny of the specific data will shape it.

To mention one more class, there are also the evaluative generalizations. Historians sometimes conceal from themselves the fact that they use such generalizations, and they say that they abstain from moral judgments of good or evil. Some of them may indeed succeed in this act of abnegation. But it is hardly possible to explain why a given program did not accomplish its objectives, why a given policy did or did not have beneficial results, without in fact making assumptions about

[14] H. C. F. Bell, *Woodrow Wilson and the People* (Garden City, N.Y.: Doubleday, Doran, 1945).

the wisdom of given political tactics or the needs of a given society. The historian may avoid what Carr calls the "Good Queen Bess" and the "Bad King John" school of generalization, but he can hardly make an assertion that a given policy "succeeded" or "failed," that a given leader was "realistic" or "unrealistic," that a given decision was "effective" or "ineffective" without applying evaluative criteria of what is beneficial for society. Evaluative generalizations, solemnly exorcised at the front door, will inevitably creep in at the side entrance, and the historian will be their victim less often if he fixes them with a steady eye than if he insists they are not there.

The urgency of the need for a systematic awareness of the latent generalizations which pervade most of our explicit historical statements is all the greater in view of the ambiguous relationship between the historian's ideas and his data. He always writes as if he were deriving the ideas from the data rather than selecting the data in the light of his ideas (which would be "unhistorical"). But in actual practice, does not the historian often derive his view of history from his personal philosophy rather than from his analysis of the evidence? If he and another historian disagree, is their disagreement always inherent in the evidence or is it often a disagreement about the generalization which is to be applied to the evidence? Every historian will recognize, no doubt, that subjective factors are certain to influence his colleagues, and conceivably even himself. But what we do not always recognize perhaps is that what appears to be argumentation about a specific historical problem may really be controversy about the nature of the forces that operate in human society. Insofar as it is the latter, it could not possibly be solved in the terms in which it is being discussed— which is one reason why historical controversies are so seldom resolved.

Two examples will, I believe, reinforce this point. One is that tired bromide: Did the slavery issue cause the Civil War? Historians customarily discuss this in the context of a time-honored sequence of data: the abolition movement, the Compromise of 1850, *Uncle Tom's Cabin*, the Kansas-Nebraska Act, Bleeding Kansas, the Dred Scott Decision, the Lincoln-Douglas debates, etc. But after they have done this, historian A will then conclude that the power of antislavery ideals caused the war, historian B will conclude that the rivalry between agrarian and industrial interests caused a clash that was deterministically inescapable, and historian C will conclude that irrational emotions, springing from unrealistic mental images, were at the bottom of things. The questions arise, therefore, to what extent is any one of these historians deriving his generalizations from the familiar litany of events which he ceremonially recites or to what extent is he bringing them in from some unstated locus of origin—from philosophy, from his unconscious, from his culture, from his daily observation of how human affairs work, or from elsewhere?

Again, in the current historical literature on Populism one historian will explain the Populist impulse in terms of an idealistic reaction against exploitation and gross economic injustices; another will explain it in terms of simple self-interest—the desire of debtors and farmers to gain a better economic position vis-à-vis creditors and industrialists; still another will explain it in terms of the reactions of a social class which felt itself psychologically threatened. Here again, the incongruities lead one to face a question. Is the documented material on Populism the source from which these writers draw their generalizations or is it rather the medium in which they argue their generalizations?

If these examples are valid, their implication is drastic indeed. For they come painfully close to suggesting that until historians recognize their own generalizations they will frequently not even understand what it is intrinsically that they are discussing. This would be even worse than not being aware of the assumptions which they have employed.

In sum, what all this amounts to is that generalization in history is inescapable and that the historian cannot avoid it by making limited statements about limited data. For a microcosm is just as cosmic as a macrocosm. Moreover, relationships between the factors in a microcosm are just as subtle and the generalizations involved in stating these relationships are just as broad as the generalizations concerning the relation between factors in a situation of larger scale.

There is another aspect which makes the conscious recognition of implicit assumptions more urgent than it has been in the past. This is the fact that we now have from the behavioral sciences a far better body of learning with which to criticize historical assumptions than we had in the past. A half-century ago, if a writer made assumptions about the nature of the relationships between the collectivity of individuals who formed a nationality, he would have found very little research by means of which to criticize these assumptions, even if he spelled them out. But today studies by Karl Deutsch of the nature of the relationships involved in the forging of nationality would offer

DAVID M. POTTER

valuable critical tests against which any assumptions could be tried.[15] Similarly, if in the past a writer unconsciously attributed motive to irrational impulses, it would have done him no good to formulate his unconscious assumption, for scholarly knowledge of the workings of the human mind ended at the limits of rationality, but today we know enough about the nature of the unconscious to be able to some degree to evaluate our hunches about unconscious motivation. Similarly, an improved knowledge of social structure offers us guide lines for judging the worth of assumptions about the relationships between social classes—if these assumptions are overt and can be examined. In short, the more knowledge we have from any quarter concerning the nature of man and of society, the more imperative it becomes to put our ideas about man and society into a form such that they can be corrected in the light of this knowledge. But only when assumptions are made explicit and are consciously recognized is it possible to refine them, criticize them, and bring related knowledge to bear on them.

While this statement of the need for a better approach to the problem of historical assumptions and generalizations is a personal expression and not a statement from the Committee on Historical Analysis, it is true, nonetheless, that considerations along the same line as these influenced the Committee to settle upon the question of generalization as the most crucial problem to which they could turn their attention. If historical writing is not really a statement of a series of items of data in isolation from one another but is rather a statement of a series of relationships, specified or implied, between the items of data, then formal historical method does not effectively deal with what historical writing deals with, and there is an acute need to bring the two within hailing distance of each other.* Therefore, to state again a personal opinion which is shared to a considerable extent by members of the Committee, nothing is more urgent for historians than for them to analyze their practice of generalization, to define the principal kinds of generalization which they engage in, to subject these to critical study, and to seek an organized, conscious view of elements which have

[15] Karl W. Deutsch, *Nationalism and Social Communication* (New York: John Wiley and Technology Press of Massachusetts Institute of Technology, 1953); Deutsch *et al.*, *Political Community and the North Atlantic Area* (Princeton: Princeton University Press, 1957).

* [See the essay by Starr (pp. 15–18 above) for a similar recommendation.—EDITOR.]

remained unorganized and unrecognized though ubiquitous in historical writing.

Obviously, this is more easily said than done; in the span of six years the Committee has not been able to accomplish much more than to reconnoiter the problem and take findings on the present use of generalization and the present views of specialists in various fields concerning the question. Any attempt to make a systematic analysis of particular kinds of generalization—as, for instance, about causation or motivation or of an evaluative nature—was precluded by the fact that practicing historians do not specialize in one kind of generalization or another. They use all kinds in their daily work, and, therefore, no panel of working historians could have been found who were prepared to divide the various kinds of generalization among them and to deal seriatim with each in turn.

This is a difficulty at the practical level. At the theoretical level there is an even more formidable difficulty. For it is perhaps more than conceivable that the process of historical interpretation is simply too intricate to be reduced to any kind of rules or formulas. In the selection of data, it has now come to be accepted as a truism that the historian—or, at least, the Modern historian—has an infinity of data from which to select and that his criteria of selection must be sensitive indeed. Yet if the responsibility of selecting from an infinity of data seems forbidding, E. H. Carr has suggested an even more awesome responsibility.[16] As he argues, the historian, in explaining the causes of an event, is faced with an infinity of antecedent circumstances, both remote and immediate, which contributed in some degree to shaping that event. He must also select, therefore, among an infinity of relationships as well as among an infinity of data. This analysis of relationships is considerably more complex than the analysis of data, for in circumstances where the historian is dealing with alternative statements of fact, one alternative is likely to be invalid if the other is valid. Thus, if we are told both that Sergeant Boston Corbett shot John Wilkes Booth dead as he ran out of a barn in Maryland and that Booth escaped and fled to Texas, the acceptance of one statement as valid will automatically dispose of the other as false. But if we say that Booth was able to shoot Lincoln because of his special familiarity with Ford's Theater and that Booth was able to shoot Lincoln because of negligence by Lincoln's guard, both statements have a basic validity,

[16] *Op. cit.*, pp. 138–39.

and tests of validity are, therefore, of no value in deciding which statement is more significant.

If the historian has a responsibility not only to work in a context of infinite items of data but also of an infinity of attendant circumstances for each item of data, his only criterion of selection, as Carr observes, must be the significance of the points which he chooses to emphasize. But we have no yardsticks for measuring significance. The evaluation of significance may be a matter of sagacity and applied experience which cannot be taught as method. When we encounter this sagacity in politics, we call it statesmanship, and we do not for a moment suppose that students can be trained in school to be statesmen. When we encounter it in historical studies, we are likely to call it "an awareness of the historical process" (akin to what Finley[17] calls "professionalism"), and we are justified in a skepticism about whether this awareness can be reduced to rules any more than statesmanship can. It is by no means a presumption, therefore, that the use of generalization can be reduced to a science merely by shifting the spotlight of method away from the questions of the validity of data, with which historians are only occasionally concerned, to an analysis of the nature of historical relationships, with which they are constantly concerned.

Whether a systematic analysis and a systematic approach to this problem can ever be developed or not, it would seem that the mere effort to develop them might have therapeutic value. Surely it would temper the recklessness of many historians who are scrupulously objective about their data but subjective about the relationships within the data. It would help to define what is really at issue in many historical controversies where the ostensible point of dispute is only the hook on which the real disagreements are hung. And it would serve the purpose which is served by many other unattainable goals, such as the goal to "know thyself." For even a failing attempt to get there would take the historian far along a road which he needs to travel.

[17] Pp. 33–34 above.

XII. *Summary*

BY LOUIS GOTTSCHALK

As indicated in the Foreword, the essays in this volume are divided into two parts. Some of them were designed to deal with historical generalization in relation to specific periods, areas, or problems, while others were the consequence of speculation on the generic problem of historical generalization. It will not have escaped notice that Part I falls into three subdivisions. One deals with a field of history remote in time, another with an area remote in space to the Western historian, and a third with specified problems of Modern history.

Starr and Finley work in a field of history chronologically distant from its modern historians. Without being averse to limited and tentative abstractions in historical writing, Starr is one of the more nominalistic of the essayists in this volume. After suggesting that whether or not specific statements can be called true is itself a basic philosophical problem, he raises the question: Are general statements provable at all? He points out that while his field (Greece of the Classical period) has long been intensively cultivated, the experts "share to an amazing degree a common outlook on the problems." On the other hand, he indicates, the information available on many of them is extremely inadequate. Statistical inferences are possible only for limited numbers within limited categories; parallels to other societies are intuitive and, though more common, also more dubious. Generalizations inherited from a long tradition of Classical scholarship have been thoroughly analyzed and debated and remain debatable, while the steady flux of newly discovered sources makes any new ones tentative and induces the timid to eschew generalization altogether. Hence, Starr thinks that while "Ancient historians . . . are more inclined to draw universal laws of human nature . . . than are students of more modern eras," others among them "dissent strongly from any but the most limited generalization, on the grounds that historical development is a series of unique events which can only be chronicled" (pp. 4 and 8).

About half of Starr's essay is devoted to an examination of examples of two kinds of generalization. One kind—the quantitative—is illustrated by the labeling generalization termed *n Achievement*. According to those who have devised the term, the *n* Achievement of a given civilization at a given epoch is proportional to the number of men in it who are energetic risk-takers; their number can be roughly estimated by scoring the achievement imagery in that civilization's imaginative stories; and from mathematical tables produced by that method, it can be inferred that rises in *n* Achievement presumably caused rather than were caused by Greek economic growth (and falls in *n* Achievement presumably caused rather than were caused by economic decline). Starr criticizes this method not because he considers the generalization in question false but in part because insofar as it is correct, "it is already known through other, more subjective, means," making elaborate quantitative proof unnecessary. Moreover, Berlew's units of measurement of *n* Achievement seem to Starr to be themselves posited upon subjective assumptions: "Whenever I have analyzed scientific efforts to reduce historical phenomena to measurable quantities," Starr says, "I have found that the basic periodizations and hidden values which determine the grouping and selection of statistical data have been those already given by the historical discipline itself" (p. 12).

The second kind of generalization with which Starr deals is illustrated by a more qualitative approach. The example selected holds that, contrary to the general view, the Greek citizen felt no strong sense of political identification with an ideal community but rather considered himself an individual in a rural, personal situation. The method used, as Starr describes it, is: (1) relying heavily on the Homeric poems, to investigate the occurrence or absence and the meaning of terms relevant to this proposition, and (2) to portray Alcibiades as an outstanding (and presumably representative) example of the conscious individualist. Though the two theses under examination may overlap, for *n* Achievement and individualism in a personal situation may well have a high correlation, Starr believes that the one based upon the qualitative method, though open to question, is more likely to convince historians than the one based upon the quantitative method.

Starr then makes some generalizations about the use of generalizations. The unsatisfactoriness of those already risked has produced a tendency among students of Classical history to frown upon generalizations altogether—a skepticism which Starr himself treats with a decent respect. Nevertheless, he concludes that "in far too many essays and volumes on Ancient history the process of generalization is unduly limited" (p. 18); and he argues: "Generalization is not to be condemned if it is personally based. As inheritors of the rational tradition of Western civilization we need to apply firmly logical principles to our specific facts." The interpretations of a sound scholar "will persuade some of his confreres and will stimulate those who disagree into a deeper, wider investigation of the subject" (p. 15). Starr suspects, besides, that even those historians who "seek security of mind" in an unstable world "by working on the level of the specific . . . will generalize unconsciously" (p. 21).

Finley, while no less unhappy than Starr about some of the generalizations that have been ventured by writers of Ancient history, starts out vigorously with the thesis that the historian cannot avoid generalization. If, Finley argues, a historian in fact refused to construe words by means of concepts and to translate concepts from one context into another, "he could safely say no more than that individual X performed action Y in a given place on a given day" (p. 23). (Cf. the comments on *who, doing what, where, and when* on p. 125.) But historians do say more, and, according to Finley, the expected result follows: "Every historian is plunged into all-pervading causes the moment he goes beyond mere naming or counting or dating" (pp. 28–29). The first question, therefore, becomes for this author "not how much or how little generalization" the historian may permit himself "but what kinds and levels of generalization" (p. 20).

In Finley's view several kinds of historical generalization are "indispensable" (p. 21). He first considers the *classificatory*—compare Wright's *labeling* generalization (p. 36)—which he illustrates by a number of examples, foremost of which is the classification *slave*. His argument runs that, whatever misconceptions the modern label may convey because it inexactly translates Hellenic concepts—or betrays, to use Starr's phrase, "*modern* states of mind" (p. 13)—any more Hellenic term would still have to be translated into some concept or other freighted with the connotations and denotations that the later historian would bring to it. Finley then takes up the problem of periodization or, as he calls it, "classification by period" (p. 23). Analyzing some recent work on Roman law, he indicates that assumptions about periodization in political history may impose an unexplained or unjustified organization of the subject matter to be presented and may bring in their wake other unexamined assumptions or generalizations. Next, Finley takes up the kinds of generalizations that come under the headings of *interrelations* of events and *causes* (p. 26). The historian who deals with a theme like *war*, he contends, does not avoid causal generalization because he chooses to deal with a particular war and to shun "all-pervading factors." Generalizations that are unexpressed (such as: War is a natural fact like life and death) may be less defensible, more likely to reflect the "objective" historian's role in his own society, than the avowed generalizations that he sedulously tries to avoid as subjective and unverifiable (p. 28).

Finley then goes on to consider the relation of generalization to *extrapolation*, or inferences to fill the gaps between one known but isolated episode and another. (Compare Gottschalk's remarks [p. 118] on imagination in historical writing.) While Finley distinguishes extrapolations from generalizations, he holds that the former may rest on the latter. Gaps in historical knowledge may sometimes be filled by examining comparable developments in other societies or periods. But, the author warns, Ancient historians when using comparative social analysis are under a particular burden to make certain that the labels and assumptions borrowed from outside are indeed analogous, and he thinks that *professionalism* ("among other things, the habit of mind which comes from experience with historical study and reflection" [pp. 33–34]) will tell the historian the right questions to ask, though without necessarily providing the right answers, for verification of historical generalizations may not be attainable beyond the establishment of a greater or lesser probability.

Analysis of the problem, Finley concludes, perhaps can be done least effectively in Ancient history, where the sources are limited and the dependence on Classicists and other non-historians is great. Nevertheless, "the issues in one historical period are not essentially different from those in another" (p. 35) (and, presumably, solutions in one period will have their bearing upon others).

Wright and Bodde deal with the history of an area, China, some of whose history is remote in time and all of whose culture normally is remote in experience to the Western historian. Wright feels that because of a paucity of verified data, the historian of China is tempted to employ inferences, assumptions, and generalizations freely, although the paucity in his field—unlike that in Ancient history—is due not to lack of sources but to lack of scholarly exploitation of them.

Wright first indicates that there are at least two different kinds of generalizations—general terms that form categories (e.g., "time of troubles") and general statements which take the form of laws (e.g., "ideas generally proceed along the trade routes"). He calls the first kind "labeling generalizations" and the second "regularity generalizations" (pp. 36–37). He devotes his initial attention to generalizations derived during ages of earnest study of history from the self-image of the Chinese literati. Among these he places the labeling generalization "the Central Kingdom." This label, he points out, has led Chinese historians to think of China not only as the center of the civilized world but also as a country with a high but common set of cultural values. Interrelated with this labeling generalization is "the dynastic cycle," which is a regularity generalization implying that politics go through the same life-cycle as man. Hence it leads not only to the drawing of doubtful parallels in the organization of Chinese dynastic histories (the birth, growth, maturity, senescence, and death of the successive dynasties) but also to ascribing parallel cyclical phases to many other areas of culture (e.g., painting and prices); it even provides related regularity generalizations (e.g., a symptomatology of political life, causing men in power so to behave that "their actions tended to sustain the regularity" [p. 42]).

In the twentieth century, Chinese historians, faced with the "need to find new ways to locate themselves in time, space, and culture" (p. 45) pressed into service a ready-made series of labeling generalizations devised for the understanding of Western history—with the result, Wright feels, that "Chinese history was strained and warped by being suddenly forced into categories developed to explain a very different history" (p. 47). A small group sought to refine and adapt these categories, but the more impatient majority wanted a total theory of historical interpretation "that would equal in comprehensiveness the Confucian system of an earlier day" (*ibid*.). The Western historian of China, Wright continues (pp. 48–49), has had to face similar problems, but in reverse, and was "tempted to work his concepts and his theories to the limit" in order to translate Chinese history into Western idiom and to fill the gaps between the widely separated areas of detailed knowledge in the two and a half millenniums of Chinese history. Hence he also made hypotheses that ranged from cautious interpretative concepts to bold theories.

Wright then goes on to show how some Western and Chinese historians have recently attempted to portray Chinese history through a mixture of Chinese and Western concepts. The regularity generalization of the dynastic cycle persists, he finds, but at times combined with a Western concept of continuous and cumulative changes that seeks to explain dynastic transitions in terms of a broader historical process. Meanwhile, traditional labeling generalizations have lost their force in the modern Chinese language, appearing now only as clichés in analytic "social-science" sentences. The labeling generalization "the Central Kingdom" has been modified by a new, largely Western view of world history, while the dubious identification of the Chinese institution *feng-chien* with Western feudalism "has involved historians and ideologues alike in the tortured effort to explain how great centralized bureaucratic empires can be 'feudal' " (p. 54). Western historians are especially prone to characterize Chinese subject matter by assimilating it to well-known Western subject matter (e.g., "The Chinese Caesar," "Chinese baroque," "Chinese gentry").

Among Wright's examples of tailoring Chinese history to fit Western concepts the final one is that of the "oriental" or "hydraulic" society. This concept, in his opinion, was not developed out of the study of Chinese history but was formulated, rather, to illustrate a generalization already assumed to be true. For Chinese history, Wright concludes, "the lack of a formidable body of monographic studies . . . meant that a universalistic theory rushed into an interpretative vacuum," and generalizations that command a considerable following "have spawned a variety of grotesque popular summaries of Chinese history and society" (pp. 56–57). Yet, despite their defects, Wright considers the tentative generalizations he discusses "constructive as catalysts." Among other advantages that they offer, "generalizations used as hypotheses—not asserted as dogmas—offer the best hope for the eventual development of a mature Chinese historiography."

A few striking comparisons that emerge from the three papers so far discussed may well be underlined. Wright's strictures upon the transfer of labeling generalizations from one culture to another in space is reminiscent of Finley's upon the transfer of classificatory generalizations from one culture to another in time. Finley's contention that the Classicist's literary tradition acts as blinkers upon the Ancient historian, whose horizons should be wider (pp. 30–33), is confirmed by Wright's view of the impact of Sinology on the historian of China (p. 48 and n. 22). And what Wright says about the constructiveness of tentative generalizations as catalysts is akin to Starr's unwillingness to condemn generalization "if it is personally based."

In commenting on Wright's paper Bodde, removing himself from among "the purists" (p. 63), takes somewhat the same view as did

Summary

Finley in commenting on Starr's paper. Bodde is aware of the danger inherent in generalizations—that they may oversimplify complex and changing bodies of fact. Nevertheless, he holds that generalizations are inevitable and necessary: "Without the formulation and acceptance of countless generalizations, man could not create a stable society nor could he communicate ideas on more than a very rudimentary level" (p. 59). While admitting and even elaborating upon the strictures that Wright makes concerning the Chinese self-image, Bodde thinks that such a general abstraction may have its uses. A labeling generalization like "dynastic cycle" "*does* constitute a convenient and in many ways meaningful unit of time and should not be given up until we are reasonably certain that whatever system of periodization takes its place is really more meaningful" (p. 61). He admits the danger inherent in the application to Chinese history of Western labels but expresses the fear that overzealous avoidance of them may give impetus to the equally distorting generalization that Chinese civilization is *sui generis*. Hence he urges continuation of effort along the lines that Wright ascribes to the minority of Chinese historians of our day—"not the wholesale rejection of Western-derived generalizations as such but rather their testing and refinement in the light of what we actually know about China itself" (p. 62). In Bodde's opinion, having taken the proper safeguard against overdrawing the similarities a historian might validly correlate *feudalism* and *feng-chien*. However lamentably the Western self-image may distort views of non-Western history, "few of us can hope to remain wholly free from distortions." The cruder generalizations would not find acceptance, anyway, among top historians, and "we can at least make ourselves more keenly aware of their existence" (p. 65). This argument leads Bodde to a conclusion that Wright and others would doubtless accept: "What is needed . . . is the channeling of future research into topics that are concrete and manageable in scope, yet have a bearing on problems of broad general interest. From the resulting monographs it may eventually become possible to formulate generalizations that are factually secure as well as intellectually alluring" (*ibid.*).

In the wide sweeps of Classical and Chinese history the gaps in the historian's knowledge are notorious. A question immediately suggests itself: Is it likely that the more extensive a field of history proves to be in proportion to the quantity of known data relevant to it, the greater the tendency becomes to generalize—in other words, the fewer the concrete data, the more frequent the abstract theories? If that is so, would similar abstractions, whether or not inevitable or desirable, be less suspect in a less extensive and more fully documented field of history? The answer to the latter question seems to be given a cautious affirmative answer in the last set of papers of Part I.

Those papers deal not only with modern Western history but with particular labeling or classificatory generalizations that have contemporary as well as past applicability—*revolution, national character,* and *social role.* Palmer's paper presents the problem of generalization as he confronted it in writing his book *The Age of the Democratic Revolution, 1760–1800.* He seems to be even more skeptical than Starr or Wright of the historian's ability to make or to prove substantive generalizations, but he nevertheless believes that historians "should make use of concepts drawn from social science or any other useful source" (p. 66). He indicates that he has himself borrowed such concepts to provide his work with a thesis, to form a basis for its structure and to suggest relevancy and significance, and he specifies a number at different levels of generality (pp. 67–74). Among them are several that might easily fit into the categories that Gottschalk (pp. 113–14) calls No. 3 (interpretative), No. 4 (comparative), and No. 5 (nomothetic)—that Western civilization presents a certain unity, that revolutionary activity is involved with both contemporary movements of a similar nature and subsequent theories of revolution, that "successful revolution occurred [in the eighteenth century] only where the agricultural population generally collaborated with middle-class leaders" (p. 72), and that the course of revolution is closely related to the course of concomitant warfare. These general concepts arose explicitly, he states (p. 74), in connection with the material he had to interpret; larger concepts of causality and influence were allowed to remain purely implicit.

Further correspondence between Palmer and the Committee confirmed that he doubted the ability of historians to test the validity of the generalizations they use. Whether derived from social science or an inspired source such as La Rochefoucauld's *Maxims,* Palmer believes, "they serve their purpose if they help us to understand a particular situation and enable us to communicate this understanding to others—that is, to persuade others that the view we favor is somehow more satisfactory, enlightening, or useful" (p. 75). As for the possibility of deriving generalizations bearing upon similar movements in several civilizations, Palmer takes for granted that "a kind of wisdom gained from the study of one [civilization] has some application to another (to deny this would condemn all history and social science to sterility)," but he does not know "how this applicability can be stated with . . . rigor and precision" or "whether propositions about human affairs can be 'proved' or not" (p. 76). Palmer's attitude, in fine, is that acceptable generalizations become available in several ways, but proving them is probably beyond the historian's capacity and their acceptability depends upon their general plausibility and their utility for his special purpose.

A totally different approach appears in Metzger's article, in which he undertakes to scrutinize closely the validity of a single labeling generalization, *national character*. He begins with the argument that objections to the term *national character* often arise not over the classification of character as *national* but over the definition of *character*. He indicates that *character* has been defined in numerous ways through "centuries of untidy usage," leading to what he calls "traditional confusions' (p. 78). One of the most confusing was the (usually implicit) definition of *national character* as a uniform national type. Definitions of that kind "shut off the possibility of comparison in terms of relative frequencies or in terms of the distribution of variants that admit of considerable overlap." They made character differences between nations appear "generic, not statistical" (p. 83).

Metzger then examines two kinds of group-psychology analysis—the Freudian model and "the dramaturgical model" (the theory of social-role behavior). In the Freudian scheme, character and culture interplay. "The *do*'s and *don't*'s of the parent . . . form an internal monitor which must vie with instinctual drives, powerfully operative from birth, and with the cognitive-intellectual functions, which arise through transactions with reality, for control of the character of the organism. . . . Character embodies culture but cannot fully be described in terms of it" (p. 86). Freudian psychology was adapted to group character when Freud's followers learned from cultural anthropologists to speak of specific cultures rather than of an abstract "Culture" (with a capital *C*) and when anthropologists began to study personality. Now, if applied with "care and subtlety," the Freudian model, Metzger believes (pp. 87–90), may shed light upon national character as a subtype of the common-character group.

The theory of social role, according to Metzger, centers in the idea that "every society, in order to achieve its goals, requires its members to play standardized roles"—for example, the roles that parent and child play in relation to each other. "A world full of interest beckons," Metzger finds, "when we start our quest [for national character] at the intersection of what society prescribes with what people do." The social roles that best exemplify character, he assumes, are generally those "in which the player invests a good deal of emotion"; one must not ignore "the vast amount of simulation that enters into social intercourse" (pp. 90, 92, and 94).

If the term *national character* is well defined by means of a conceptual model or a dramaturgical metaphor, Metzger thinks, "many objections to it dissolve" (p. 94). The emphasis passes then from the noun *character* to the adjective *national*, from the definition of the noun to classification by the adjective, from concern with the *components* of *character* to concern with the *influences* upon *character*. Metzger submits that the nation, for better or for worse, is a significant crucible of personality. Whatever else a nation may be, "it is also a community of peoples who are exposed to *common experiences*," and "growing up and living in one country rather than in another is a matter of characterological importance" (pp. 97 and 98).

But how important is such common experience in relation to other characterological factors? In attempting to answer this question, Metzger borrows the technique of "matched comparisons," particularly from Stouffer's investigation of American political tolerance. Comparing regions of the United States, Stouffer found that the West seemed more tolerant than the South. To examine further whether the difference was attributable to region rather than to other conceivable factors, he matched in turn four different types of Westerners with the same types of Southerners. This detailed comparison revealed that in each of the four matchings the Westerners were more tolerant than the Southerners, and "now [in Metzger's opinion] he [Stouffer] could say with greater confidence that the regional factor was important" (p. 100).

Stouffer's method may be used, Metzger argues, also to establish differences in national character. In comparing English with American character, for instance, we might match not Englishmen and Americans in gross but in more refined categories (e.g., English farmers with American farmers) or in still more refined categories; and if we find that despite matchings of "religion, occupation, education, and the rest," they still come out different in some character trait, we would be justified in assuming that the difference is due to differences in nationality—that is, to the differences in their experiences as English-

Summary

men and Americans respectively. Obviously, Metzger not only accepts the generalization that a people develops a national character because of experiences that it has had in common but holds in addition that some such group concepts are capable of being fairly tenably demonstrated and then applied to the understanding of history no less than of social behavior (pp. 100–102).

Cochran's paper arose out of discussion of a particular point raised by Metzger, the possible value to the historian of the concept of *social role*. Cochran's definition of *social role* is not essentially different from Metzger's, though his emphasis is more on *social* than on *role*. He defines it in its simplest form as the way in which an individual lives up to the expectations of the social group with which he is involved (p. 105). Since, however, every individual tends to be involved with more than one social group, a complete description of a social role may require considerable knowledge of the expectations of several groups. Cochran calls the complement of role-relationships a *role-set*, and those who exercise some influence in shaping the social role of an individual he calls that individual's *defining group* (*ibid.*). The individual is constrained, in addition, by inner drives like private aims and personal compulsions; these inner drives are called his *reference group* (pp. 107–8). The more successfully an individual plays his social role, the more fully the reference group coincides with the expectations of the defining group, for social expectations and individual aims tend to modify each other. Individual behavior thus appears to be a response to (1) the demands of a particular task, (2) the expectations of a defining group, and (3) personal motivation. It is often difficult but not impossible, Cochran concludes, for the historian to apply the concept of *social role*, but the concept is "useful for systematically examining situations involving well-defined status and group relationships" (p. 110).

Metzger and Cochran, without blinking the difficulty of applying to history heuristic concepts and methods that are abroad in the social sciences, are, on the whole, more convinced than Starr or Palmer of the fruitfulness of applying selected ones to historical research. Nor is any of the writers of the articles in Part I wholly unconvinced that some potential good may accrue to the historian from the use of general terms or statements, whether derived from social science or elsewhere —not even those who are the most skeptical of generalizations as being subjective and of only tentative and limited validity.

Part II of this report, being made up exclusively of articles by members of the Committee, does not deal with special fields or concrete problems of history but with the abstract problem of generalization in the writing of history. Gottschalk's article (pp. 113–29) maintains that historians can be classified into six schools if the extent to which they are willing to use generalization is the criterion. These six are (1) the school of the unique, consisting of editors and compilers who make generalizations only if they are unaware that they do so and try to eliminate those of which they are aware; (2) the school of the strictly limited generalization, consisting of narrative-descriptive historians who rest content to chronicle indiscriminate and discrete events with a studied effort to avoid committing themselves regarding interrelations among the events they chronicle or their relative importance; (3) the interpretative school, consisting of historians who strive for some connecting thread or trend through history that will permit a synthesis of interrelated historical events, (4) the comparative school, consisting of historians who look for parallel or analogous though not necessarily causally interrelated episodes or regularities; (5) the nomothetic school, consisting of historians who deliberately seek to confirm or to derive anew generalizations that have held true for past conditions, may hold true for the future under similar conditions, and thus may have value for prediction or control; and (6) philosophers of history who propound cosmic and panoramic ideologies or historical determinisms.

The remaining essays in Part II more or less deliberately deal only or primarily with Gottschalk's categories 3, 4, and 5—the theoretical historians; their authors consider the compiler-editors of the school of the unique (no. 1), the narrative-descriptive historians of the school of the strictly limited generalization (no. 2) and the cosmic philosophers (no. 6) outside the area of their main concern. Two members of the Committee—Nichols and Aydelotte—address themselves (as did Metzger also) to the question whether any tests of the relative validity of historical generalizations can be suggested.

Nichols examines at considerably greater length a question raised by Starr (p. 6) and others—the descent of inherited generalizations. He delves (pp. 131–41) into the genealogy of the general statements that have been made by way of interpretation of the American Civil War—and it may be noted that Metzger did somewhat the same for *national character* (pp. 80–83)—and finds four generations of them, each on the whole more acceptable than its predecessors. He is led to conclude that "one of the few means which the historian has of judging the probable degree of validity of a generalization is to examine its age and the degree to which it has stood the scrutiny of succeeding generations." He recognizes that "long life may indicate only respectability —that is, that the generalization is acceptable to a particular culture." Nevertheless, he feels, such respectability, while not necessarily insuring truth, "may supply a presumption" (p. 142). Nichols' article closes with a plea that the writer of history study not merely the sources of his historical theme but also "give attention to previous formulations and their reception," lest he "miss implications which occurred to others nearer in time to the events in question but which he, because of his chronological distance, might not perceive" (p. 144).

After a critical examination of some of the arguments made both by other essays in this book and elsewhere against generalization by historians, Aydelotte's article comes to the conclusion that carefully formulated, tentative generalizations of "middle range" (pp. 162–63) are, in our present state of knowledge, the most sensible. "The choice," he contends, "is not between making proved statements or unproved ones but between making unproved statements or keeping silent" (p. 159). The darkness is relative: "To say that all statements are uncertain is not to say that they are equally uncertain" (pp. 159–60). One must cast one's nets as wide as possible for ideas and ask not *whether* they are true but rather *how far* they are true (pp. 167 and 175). Aydelotte thinks that "the means by which we derive generalizations are irregular and unpredictable," though the results, if "based on significant accumulations of detailed knowledge" and "directed to problems sufficiently restricted in scope" (pp. 169–70) may show great insight and profoundly influence future study. The verification of such insights is another matter: his impression is that "on the whole historians have paid too little rather than too much attention to the problem of verification of statements of any complexity" (p. 170), and (in contrast to Starr) he makes a strong plea for, among other tests, the heuristic value of quantitative, statistical procedures in cases where they can be applied: "In an area where one has already given a good deal of thought to the evidence and to the assumptions involved in handling it, material gathered to test a particular thesis may not merely refute the thesis but also point the way to a new and more appropriate formulation" (p. 177).

Potter's essay, the final one before this "Summary," like several of the others but more fully than they, deals with the general assumptions that are implicit in single words or the arrangement of words. Potter holds (pp. 178-92) that when a historian talks, as every historian must, of groups or aggregates, periods of time, change or cause and effect, even if that historian tries to avoid making theoretical statements, he is actually engaged in doing so, though perhaps at a low, latent level of generalization. For the mere formulation of data in particular groupings and sequences suggests one relationship rather than another and thus involves a choice among theoretical constructs. Hence, according to Potter, commitment to some kind of generalization is inescapable in the writing of history and is universal among historians. Kinds as well as levels of generalization may differ, Potter points out, kinds being distinguishable by the *nature of the action* or the *grouping of the actors* rather than by the *degree of abstraction* or theory involved (p. 186). Illustrating this point by examples, sometimes invented *ad hoc* and sometimes derived from others' works, Potter shows that generalizations at the same latent level may involve, if only implicitly, differing problems of motivation, causation, and classification. Each kind, however, may require its own criteria for testing validity, and the historian, trained in methods that are inadequate if not obsolete, is seldom properly prepared to test any of them (pp. 180-83). Many disputes about specific historical problems are not, therefore, about items of the data that appear in the evidence but rather about the nature of the forces that operate in human society (pp. 188-91). Potter concludes (pp. 192-94)—as did Starr, but less emphatically, and some others, but less explicitly—by urging that the training of historians pay more attention to the systematic development of criteria for the interpretation and explanation of historical data, taking generalization out of its *sub rosa* status in historiographical circles and lifting it to an organized and recognized level of scholarly endeavor.

In sum, the historians who have written articles for this volume all agree that the historian willy-nilly uses generalizations at different levels and of different kinds. They all agree, too, that some good purpose is served when he does so, if only to present a thesis for debate. They do not all agree that the generalizations he uses need be merely borrowed ones; he might, in the opinion of some of the authors, be independently able to construct modest ones. A few maintain even that, whether borrowed or independently derived, historical generalizations can in some persuasive manner be tested.

The Committee shares the attitude of those authors who are more friendly to generalization in historical research. Its line of reasoning runs somewhat as follows: Historians borrow ready-made generalizations, whether they know it or not. If they were to borrow them knowingly, they might be in a stronger intellectual position. They might then undertake to assay and refine their borrowed generalizations by whatever means—definition, qualification, reservation, conformity to known facts, logic, psychology, statistics, matched comparisons, genealogical endurance, or other tests—might be most appropriate and, avoiding the more untried and unverifiable ones, make good use of those found valid. Perhaps in the process, if sufficiently motivated and properly trained, they might originate and advance some restricted, tentatively acceptable generalizations of their own. At the very least, the professional training of historians ought to include systematic instruction in how to deal with the otherwise stultifying ubiquity of generalization in the writing of history.

PART III

Bibliography of Writings on Historiography and the Philosophy of History

BY MARTIN KLEIN

Contents

Abbreviations/213
I. Historical Method/214
II. History of History/215
III. Philosophy of History/224
    A. Some Recent Editions of Early Writings/224
    B. Some Philosophical Discussions/225
    C. History and the Social Sciences/237
IV. The Pattern of the Past and Historical Interpretation/239
V. Supplement to the Bibliography of Bulletin 54: Books Published before 1946 and Not Listed There/245

This bibliography is a supplement to that in Social Science Research Council Bulletin 54 (published in 1946) and does not contain any titles listed there. It is based in part on a bibliography of works on the philosophy of history compiled by David Nivison (see p. xi, n. 4 above). The *Bibliography of Works in the Philosophy of History, 1945–1957*, compiled by John C. Rule for *History and Theory* (The Hague: Mouton, 1961), was also helpful, but it is less selective and is organized on different principles.

Abbreviations

JOURNALS

AHR	American Historical Review
BJPS	British Journal for the Philosophy of Science
CSSH	Comparative Studies in Society and History
DVLG	Deutsche Vierteljahrschrift für Literaturwissenschaft und Geistesgeschichte
HSANZ	Historical Studies: Australia and New Zealand
HT	History and Theory
HZ	Historische Zeitschrift
JHI	Journal of the History of Ideas
JMH	Journal of Modern History

JP	Journal of Philosophy
JWH	Journal of World History
MVHR	Mississippi Valley Historical Review
PAS	Proceedings of the Aristotelian Society
PMLA	Publications of the Modern Language Association
PPR	Philosophy and Phenomenological Research
PQ	Philosophical Quarterly
PR	Philosophical Review
PS	Philosophy of Science
RH	Revue historique
RMM	Revue de metaphysique et de morale
WAG	Welt als Geschichte

PUBLISHERS

APC	Appleton-Century-Crofts
CUAP	Catholic University of America Press
CUP	Cambridge University Press
ColUP	Columbia University Press
CorUP	Cornell University Press
HUP	Harvard University Press
OUP	Oxford University Press
PUF	Presses Universitaires de France
PUP	Princeton University Press
UCP	University of Chicago Press
UCalP	University of California Press
UOP	University of Oklahoma Press
YUP	Yale University Press

I. *Historical Method*

BARZUN, JACQUES, and GRAFF, HENRY A. *The Modern Researcher*. New York: Harcourt, Brace, 1957.

BRYANT, ARTHUR. *The Art of Writing History*. New York: OUP, 1946.

CROCE, BENEDETTO. "Metodologia storica," *Quaderni della "Critica,"* II (1946). (4 articles.)

GARRAGHAN, GILBERT J. *A Guide to Historical Method*. New York: Fordham University Press, 1946.

GOTTSCHALK, LOUIS. *Understanding History*. New York: Knopf, 1950.

———. "The Historian's Use of Generalization," in *The State of the Social Sciences*. Edited by LEONARD D. WHITE. Chicago: UCP, 1956.

GRAY, WOOD, et al. *Historian's Handbook*. Boston: Houghton Mifflin, 1959.

GUSTAVSON, CARL G. *A Preface to History*. New York: McGraw-Hill, 1955.

HALKIN, LÉON-E. *Initiation à la critique historique*. Paris: Colin, 1951.

HALPHEN, LOUIS. *Introduction à l'histoire*. Paris: PUF, 1946.

L'histoire et ses méthodes. Published under the direction of CHARLES SAMARAN. Paris: Gallimard, 1961.

HOCKETT, HOMER C. *The Critical Method in Historical Research and Writing*. New York: Macmillan, 1955.

INTERNATIONAL COMMITTEE OF HISTORICAL SCIENCES (Tenth Congress, Rome, September 4–11, 1955). *Relazioni.* Vol. I: *Metodologia, Problemi generali. Scienze ausiliarie della storia.* Florence: Sansoni, 1955.
——— (Eleventh Congress, Stockholm, August 21–28, 1960). *Rapports.* Vol. I: *Méthodologie. Histoire des universités. Histoire des prix avant 1750.* Uppsala: Almqvist & Wiksell, 1960.
KIRN, PAUL. *Einführung in die Geschichtswissenschaft.* Berlin: deGruyter, 1947.
MARROU, HENRI-IRÉNÉE. *De la connaissance historique.* Paris: Seuil, 1955.
REINHARD, MARCEL. *L'enseignement de l'histoire et ses problèmes.* Paris: PUF, 1957.
RENIER, GUSTAF J. *History, Its Purpose and Method.* Boston: Beacon, 1950.

II. *History of History*

ANDERLE, OTHMAR. "Giambattista Vico als Vorläufer einer morphologischen Geschichtsbetrachtung," WAG, XVI (1956), 85–97.
ANGUS-BUTTERWORTH, L. M. *Ten Master Historians.* Aberdeen: University Press, 1961.
ANTONI, CARLO. *From History to Sociology: The Transition in German Historical Thought.* Translated from Italian by HAYDEN V. WHITE. Detroit: Wayne State University Press, 1959.
ARON, RAYMOND. *German Sociology.* Translated by M. and T. BOTTOMORE. Glencoe, Ill.: Free Press, 1957.
———. "Thucydide et le récit des événements," HT, I (1961), 103–28.
AUSUBEL, HERMAN. *Historians and Their Craft: A Study of the Presidential Addresses to the American Historical Association, 1884–1945.* New York: ColUP, 1952.
AUSUBEL, HERMAN; BREBNER, J. BARTLET; and HUNT, ERLING M. (eds.). *Some Modern Historians of Britain: Essays in Honor of R. L. Schuyler by Some of His Former Students at Columbia University.* New York: Dryden, 1951.
BARNES, SHERMAN B. "Historians in the Age of Enlightenment," *Kent State University Bulletin,* Research Series No. 1 (1952), 7–36.
BEALE, HOWARD K. (ed.). *Charles A. Beard: An Appraisal.* Lexington: University of Kentucky Press, 1954.
BEASLEY, W. G., and PULLEYBANK, EDWIN (eds.). *Historians of China and Japan.* New York: OUP, 1961.
BELLOT, H. HALE. *American History and American Historians: A Review of Recent Contributions to the Interpretation of the History of the United States.* Norman: UOP, 1952.
BENDIX, REINHARD. *Max Weber: An Intellectual Portrait.* Garden City, N.Y.: Doubleday, 1960.
BENSON, LEE. *Turner and Beard: American Historical Writing Reconsidered.* Glencoe, Ill.: Free Press, 1960.
BERG, ELIAS. *The Historical Thinking of Charles A. Beard.* Stockholm: Almqvist & Wiksell, 1957.
BERGSTRÄSSER, ARNOLD. "Wilhelm Dilthey and Max Weber: An Historical Approach to Historical Synthesis," *Ethics,* LVII (1947), 92–110.

BERINGAUSE, ARTHUR F. *Brooks Adams: A Biography*. New York: Knopf, 1955.
BERRY, T. M. *The Historical Theory of Giambattista Vico*. Washington: CUAP, 1949.
BOWMAN, FRANCIS J. *A Handbook of Historians and History Writing*. Dubuque, Iowa: Brown, 1951.
BRANDI, KARL. *Geschichte der Geschichtswissenschaft*. Bonn: Universitätsverlag, 1947.
BROWN, TRUESDELL S. "Herodotus and His Profession," AHR, LIX (1954), 829–43.
BRUMFITT, J. H. *Voltaire, Historian*. New York: OUP, 1958.
BUTTERFIELD, HERBERT. *Man on His Past: The Study of the History of Historical Scholarship*. Cambridge: CUP, 1954; Boston: Beacon, 1960.
CAPONIGRI, ROBERT. *Time and Idea: The Theory of History of Giambattista Vico*. Chicago: Regnery, 1953.
———. *History and Liberty: The Historical Writings of Benedetto Croce*. Chicago: Regnery, 1955.
CEPLECHA, CHRISTIAN. *The Historical Thought of José Ortega y Gasset*. Washington: CUAP, 1958.
CHABOD, FEDERICO. "Croce storico," *Rivista storica italiana*, LXIV (1952), 473–530.
CIARDO, MANLIO. *Le quattro epoche dello storicismo. Vico, Kant, Hegel, Croce*. Bari: Laterza, 1947.
CLARK, ROBERT T., JR. "Herder, Cesarotti, and Vico," *Studies in Philology*, XLIV (1947), 645–71.
———. *Herder: His Life and Thought*. Berkeley: UCalP, 1955.
CLIVE, JOHN. "Macaulay's Historical Imagination," *Review of English Literature*, I (1960), 20–27.
COLE, C. W. "The Heavy Hand of Hegel," in *Nationalism and Internationalism: Essays Inscribed to C. J. H. Hayes*. Edited by EDWARD MEAD EARLE. New York: ColUP, 1950.
COLLINGWOOD, R. G. *The Idea of History*. Oxford: Clarendon, 1946.
COMITÉ JAPONAIS DES SCIENCES HISTORIQUES. *L'état actuel et les tendances des études historiques au Japon*. Tokyo: Nippon Gakujutau Shinkôkai, 1960.
COOKE, JACOB E. *Frederic Bancroft, Historian*. Norman: UOP, 1957.
CORSI, MARIO. *Le origini del pensiero di Benedetto Croce*. Florence: Nuova Italia, 1951.
COWEL, F. R. *History, Civilization and Culture: An Introduction to the Historical and Social Philosophy of Pitirim A. Sorokin*. Boston: Beacon, 1952.
CROCE, BENEDETTO. *Storia della storiografia italiana nel secolo decimonono*. 3d ed. 2 vols. Bari: Laterza, 1947.
CROCKER, LESTER G. *An Age of Crisis: Man and World in Eighteenth Century French Thought*. Baltimore: Johns Hopkins Press, 1959.
CRUBELLIER, MAURICE. *Sens de l'histoire et religion: August Comte, Northrup, Sorokin, Arnold Toynbee*. Paris: Desclée de Brouwer, 1957.
CRUDEN, ROBERT. *James Ford Rhodes: The Man, the Historian, and His Work*. Cleveland: Press of Western Reserve University, 1961.
CURTI, MERLE. *Probing Our Past*. New York: Harper, 1955.

CURTIS, LEWIS P. "Gibbon's Paradise Lost" in *The Age of Johnson: Essays Presented to Chauncey Brewster Tinker*. Edited by F. W. HILLES. New Haven: YUP, 1949.

DEININGER, WHITAKER T. "The Skepticism and Historical Faith of Charles A. Beard," JHI, XV (1954), 573–89.

DELMAS, CLAUDE. "Men and Their History," *Diogenes*, No. 12 (1955), 100–117.

DENTAN, ROBERT C. (ed.). *The Idea of History in the Ancient Near East*. New Haven: YUP, 1955.

DIWALD, HELLMUT. *Das historische Erkennen: Untersuchungen zum Geschichtsrealismus im 19. Jahrhundert*. Leyden: Brill, 1955.

DOCKHORN, KLAUS. *Der deutsche Historismus in England: ein Beitrag zur englischen Geistesgeschichte des 19. Jahrhunderts*. Baltimore: Johns Hopkins Press, 1950.

DONOVAN, TIMOTHY PAUL. *Henry Adams and Brooks Adams: The Education of Two American Historians*. Norman: UOP, 1961.

DORPALEN, ANDREAS. *Heinrich von Treitschke*. New Haven: YUP, 1957.

———. "Historiography as History: The Work of Gerhard Ritter," JMH, XXXIV (1962), 1–18.

DUBS, HOMER H. "The Reliability of Chinese Histories," *Far Eastern Quarterly*, VI (1946), 23–43.

DUJOVNE, LEÓN. *La filosofía de la historia de Nietzsche a Toynbee*. Buenos Aires: Galatea–Nueva Visión, 1957.

DUNN, WALTER HILARY. *James Anthony Froude: A Biography*. Vol. I: *1818–1856*. Vol. II, *1857–1894*. Oxford: Clarendon, 1961 and 1963.

EISENSTADT, A. S. *Charles McLean Andrews: A Study in American Historical Writing*. New York: ColUP, 1955.

ENGEL, JOSEF. "Die deutschen Universitäten und die Geschichtswissenschaft," HZ, CLXXXIX (1959), 223–378.

ENGEL-JANOSI, FRIEDRICH. *Four Studies in French Romantic Historical Writing*. Baltimore: Johns Hopkins Press, 1955.

FINDLAY, J. N. *Hegel: A Re-examination*. New York: Macmillan, 1958.

FITZSIMONS, MATTHEW A.; PUNDT, ALFRED G.; and NOWELL, CHARLES E. (eds.). *The Development of Historiography*. Harrisburg, Pa.: Stackpole, 1954.

FLOWER, MILTON E. *James Parton: The Father of Modern Biography*. Durham, N.C.: Duke University Press, 1951.

FORBES, DUNCAN. "Historismus in England," *Cambridge Journal*, IV (1951), 387–400.

———. *The Liberal Anglican Idea of History*. New York: CUP, 1952.

FORT, WILLIAM E., JR. "Troeltsch's Theory of History," *Personalist*, XXVIII (1946), 59–71.

FÜLLING, ERICH. *Geschichte als Offenbarung: Studien zur Frage Historismus und Glaube von Herder bis Troeltsch*. Berlin: A. Töpelmann, 1956.

FUGLUM, PER. *Edward Gibbon: His View of Life and Conception of History*. Oxford: Blackwell, 1953.

GARDINER, PATRICK (ed.). *Theories of History. Readings from Classical and Contemporary Sources*. Glencoe, Ill.: Free Press, 1959.

GERSHOY, LEO. "Carl Becker on Progress and Power," AHR, LV (1949), 22–35.

———."Zagorin's Interpretation of Becker: Some Observations." AHR, LXII (1956), 12–17.

GILMORE, MYRON P. "Freedom and Determinism in Renaissance Historians," *Studies in the Renaissance*, III (1956), 49–60.

GÖRLITZ, WALTER. *Idee und Geschichte. Die Entwicklung des historischen Denkens*. Freiburg: Badischer, 1949.

GOETZ, WALTER. *Historiker in meiner Zeit: gesammelte Aufsätze*. Cologne: Böhlau Verlag, 1957.

GOOCH, G. P. *History and Historians in the Nineteenth Century*. 2d ed. New York: Longmans, Green, 1952.

GOUHIER, HENRI. "La philosophie de l'histoire d'Auguste Comte," JWH, II (1955), 503–20.

GRAMSCI, ANTONIO. *Il materialismo storico e la filosofia di Benedetto Croce*. 2d ed. Turin: Einaudi, 1952.

HAAC, OSCAR A. *Les principes inspirateurs de Michelet: sensibilité et philosophie de l'histoire*. New Haven: YUP, 1951.

HALL, D. G. E. (ed.). *Historians of South-East Asia*. New York: OUP, 1961.

HALL, JOHN W. "Historiography in Japan," in *Teachers of History. Essays in Honor of Laurence Bradford Packard*. Edited by H. S. HUGHES. Ithaca, N.Y.: CorUP, 1954.

HALPERIN, S. WILLIAM (ed.). *Some 20th Century Historians: Essays* [in honor of Bernadotte E. Schmitt] *on Eminent Europeans*. Chicago: UCP, 1961.

HAN, YU-SHAN. *Elements of Chinese Historiography*. Hollywood, Calif.: Hawley, 1955.

HANKE, LEWIS. *Bartolomé de Las Casas, Historian*. Gainesville: University of Florida Press, 1952.

HARDY, PETER. *Historians of Medieval India*. London: Luzac, 1960.

HARNACK, AXEL VON. "Ranke und Burckhardt," *Neue Rundschau*, LXII (1951), 73–88.

HATTON, RAGNHILD. "Some Notes on Swedish Historiography," *History*, XXXVII (1952), 97–113.

HELBLING, HANNO. *Leopold von Ranke und der historische Stil*. Zurich: J. Weiss, 1953.

———. *Saeculum humanum: Ansätze zu einem Versuch über spätmittelalterliches Geschichtsdenken*. Naples: Istituto Italiano per gli Studi Storici, 1958.

HELLER, ERICH. "Oswald Spengler and the Predicament of the Historical Imagination," *Cambridge Journal*, V (1952), 225–35.

HERR, RICHARD. *Tocqueville and the Old Regime*. Princeton, N.J.: PUP, 1962.

HERRICK, JANE. *The Historical Thought of Fustel de Coulanges*. Washington: CUAP, 1954.

HEUSS, ALFRED. *Theodor Mommsen und das 19. Jahrhundert*. Kiel: Ferdinand Hirt, 1956.

HIMMELFARB, GERTRUDE. *Lord Acton: A Study in Conscience and Politics*. Chicago: UCP, 1952.

HINRICHS, CARL. *Ranke und die Geschichtstheologie der Goethezeit*. Göttingen: Musterschmidt, 1954.

HODGES, H. A. *The Philosophy of Wilhelm Dilthey*. London: Routledge, 1952.
HOFER, WALTHER. *Geschichtsschreibung und Weltanschauung: Betrachtungen zum Werk Friedrich Meineckes*. Munich: R. Oldenbourg, 1950.
HOLBORN, HAJO. "Greek and Modern Conceptions of History," JHI, X (1949), 3–13.
HUGHES, H. STUART. *Oswald Spengler: A Critical Estimate*. New York: Scribner's, 1952.
———. *Consciousness and Society*. New York: Knopf, 1958.
———. (ed.). *Teachers of History: Essays in Honor of Laurence Bradford Packard*. Ithaca, N.Y.: CorUP, 1954.
HYPPOLITE, JEAN. *Introduction à la philosophie de l'histoire de Hegel*. Paris: Rivière, 1948.
JOHNSON, A. H. "Whitehead's Philosophy of History," JHI, VII (1946), 234–57.
JOLLES, MATTHIJS. "Lessing's Conception of History," *Modern Philology*, XLIII (1946), 175–91.
JORDY, WILLIAM H. *Henry Adams: Scientific Historian*. New Haven: YUP, 1952.
KAEGI, WERNER. *Jacob Burckhardt: eine Biographie*. 3 vols. Basel: Benno Schwabe, 1947–56.
KESSEL, EBERHARD. "Rankes Idee der Universalhistorie," HZ, CLXXVIII (1954), 269–308.
KESTING, HANNO. *Geschichtsphilosophie und Weltbürgerkrieg: Deutungen der Geschichte von der französischen Revolution bis zum ost-west Konflikt*. Heidelberg: Carl Winter Universitätsverlag, 1959.
KIRN, PAUL. *Das Bild des Menschen in der Geschichtsschreibung von Polybios bis Ranke*. Göttingen: Vendenhoeck & Ruprecht, 1955.
KLUBACK, WILLIAM. *Wilhelm Dilthey's Philosophy of History*. New York: ColUP, 1956.
KOCHAN, LIONEL. *Acton on History*. London: Deutsch, 1954.
KOLKO, GABRIEL. "A Critique of Max Weber's Philosophy of History," *Ethics*, LXX (1959), 21–36.
KRAUS, MICHAEL. *The Writing of American History*. Norman: UOP, 1953.
KRIEGER, LEONARD. "Marx and Engels as Historians," JHI, XIV (1953), 381–403.
———. "History and Law in the Seventeenth Century: Pufendorf," JHI, XXI (1960), 198–210.
KUHN, HELMUT. "Ernst Cassirer's Philosophy of Culture," in *The Philosophy of Ernst Cassirer*. Edited by PAUL SCHILPP. New York: Tudor, 1949.
LAISTNER, M. L. W. *The Greater Roman Historians*. Berkeley: UCalP, 1947.
LAMBIE, JOSEPH T. (ed.). *Architects and Craftsmen: Festschrift für Abbot Payson Usher*. Tübingen: Mohr, 1956.
LEVENSON, J. C. *The Mind and Art of Henry Adams*. Boston: Houghton Mifflin, 1957.
LEVENSON, JOSEPH R. "Redefinition of Ideas in Time: The Chinese Classics and History," *Far Eastern Quarterly*, XV (1956), 399–404.
LEVIN, DAVID. *History as Romantic Art: Bancroft, Prescott, Motley, and Parkman*. Stanford, Calif.: Stanford University Press, 1959.

LEVY, FRITZ. "The Elizabethan Revolution in Historiography," *History*, (New York: Meridian Books), No. 4 (1961), pp. 27–52.
LEYDEN, WILLIAM VON. "Antiquity and Authority: A Paradox in Renaissance Theory of History," *JHI*, XIX (1958), 473–92.
LOUBÈRE, LEO A. "Louis Blanc's Philosophy of History," *JHI*, XVII (1956), 70–88.
LOVEJOY, ARTHUR O. "Herder and the Enlightenment Philosophy of History," in his *Essays in the History of Ideas*. Baltimore: Johns Hopkins Press, 1948.
MAHDI, MUHSIN. *Ibn Kaldun's Philosophy of History*. New York: Macmillan, 1957.
MAJUMDAR, A. K. "Sanskrit Historical Literature and Historians," *JWH*, VI (1960), 283–302.
MALIN, JAMES C. *Essays on Historiography*. Lawrence, Kans.: the author, 1946.
MANDELBAUM, MAURICE. "Lovejoy and the Theory of Historiography," *JHI*, IX (1948), 412–23.
MARCUS, JOHN T. "Time and the Sense of History: East and West," *CSSH*, III (1961), 123–39.
MARKS, HARRY J. "Ground under Our Feet: Beard's Relativism," *JHI*, XIV (1953), 628–33.
MARROU, HENRI-IRÉNÉE. "La méthodologie historique: orientations actuelles à propos d'ouvrages récents," *RH*, CCIX (1953), 256–70.
———. "L'histoire et les historiens. Seconde chronique de méthodologie historique," *RH*, CCXVII (1957), 270–89.
MARTIN, A. W. O. VON. *Burckhardt und Nietzsche philosophieren über Geschichte*. Krefeld: Scherpe-Verlag, 1948.
MASUR, GERHARD. "Wilhelm Dilthey and the History of Ideas," *JHI*, XIV (1952), 94–107.
———. "Distinctive Traits of Western Civilization through the Eyes of Western Historians," *AHR*, LXVII (1962), 591–608.
MAZOUR, ANATOLE. *Russian Historiography*. 2d ed. Princeton, N.J.: Van Nostrand, 1958.
MEINECKE, FRIEDRICH. "Ranke and Burckhardt," translated from German by HANS KOHN in *German History: Some New German Views*. Edited by HANS KOHN. Boston: Beacon, 1954.
MENDELL, CLARENCE W. *Tacitus: The Man and His Work*. New Haven: YUP, 1957.
MILBURN, ROBERT L. P. *Early Christian Interpretations of History*. New York: Harper, 1954.
MOMIGLIANO, ARNALDO. "Gibbon's Contribution to Historical Method," *Historia*, II (1954), 450–63.
———. "A Hundred Years after Ranke," *Diogenes*, No. 7 (1954), 52–58.
———. *Contributo alla storia degli studi classici*. Rome: Edizioni di Storia e Letteratura, 1955.
———. "The Place of Herodotus in the History of Historiography," *History*, XLIII (1958), 1–13.

———. *Secondo contributo alla storia degli studi classici*. Rome: Edizioni di Storia e Letteratura, 1960.
MURRAY, GILBERT. "Lessons from History," *Diogenes*, No. 1 (1953), 43–48.
MYRES, JOHN N. L. *Herodotus, Father of History*. Oxford: Clarendon, 1953.
NEFF, EMERY. *The Poetry of History*. New York: ColUP, 1947.
NORTH, C. R. *The Old Testament Interpretation of History*. London: Epworth Press, 1946.
O'CONNOR, SISTER MARY CONSOLATA. *The Historical Thought of François Guizot*. Washington: CUAP, 1955.
ORTEGA Y GASSET, JOSÉ. "A Chapter from the History of Ideas: Wilhelm Dilthey and the Idea of Life," in his *Concord and Liberty*. Translated by H. WEYL. New York: Norton, 1946.
PAPAIOANNOU, KOSTAS. "Nature and History in the Greek Conception of the Cosmos," *Diogenes*, No 25 (1959), 1–27.
———. "The Consecration of History: An Essay on the Genealogy of the Historical Consciousness," *Diogenes*, No. 31 (1960), 29–55.
PEARSON, LIONEL. *The Lost Histories of Alexander the Great*. New York: American Philological Association, 1960.
PEASE, OTIS A. *Parkman's History: The Historian as a Literary Artist*. New Haven: YUP, 1953.
PERKINS, DEXTER, and SNELL, JOHN. *The Education of Historians in the United States*. New York: McGraw-Hill, 1961.
PFLUG, GUNTHER. "Die Entwicklung der historischen Methode in 18. Jahrhundert," DVLG, XXVIII (1954), 447–71.
PHILIPS, C. H. (ed.). *Historians of India, Pakistan and Ceylon*. London: OUP, 1961.
POCOCK, J. G. A. *The Ancient Constitution and the Feudal Law: A Study of English Historical Thought in the Seventeenth Century*. Cambridge: CUP, 1957.
———. "The Origins of the Study of the Past: A Comparative Approach," CSSH, IV (1962), 209–46.
POWICKE, F. M. *Modern Historians and the Study of History*. London: Odhams Press, 1955.
PRAKASH, BUDDHA. "The Hindu Philosophy of History," JHI, XVI (1955), 494–505.
PREYER, ROBERT. *Bentham, Coleridge, and the Science of History*. Bochum-Langendreer, Germany: Pöppinghaus, 1958.
RANDALL, J. H. "Cassirer's Theory of History as Illustrated in His Treatment of Renaissance Thought," in *The Philosophy of Ernst Cassirer*. Edited by PAUL SCHILPP. New York: Tudor, 1949.
RICOEUR, PAUL. "Husserl et le sens de l'histoire," RMM, LIV (1949), 280–316.
RODRIGUES, JOSÉ HONÓRIO. *Teoria da história do Brasil*. São Paulo: Instituto Progresso Editorial, 1949.
———. *Noticia de varia historia*. Rio de Janeiro: Livraria São José, 1951.
ROSENTHAL, FRANZ. *A History of Muslim Historiography*. Leiden: Brill, 1952.
ROSENTHAL, JEROME. "Voltaire's Philosophy of History," JHI, XVI (1955), 151–78.

Rossi, Pietro. *Lo storicismo tedesco contemporaneo*. Turin: Einaudi, 1956.
Sampson, Ronald V. *Progress in the Age of Reason: The Seventeenth Century to the Present Day*. London: Heinemann, 1956.
Sanchez Alonso, Benito. *Historia de la historiografía española*. 3 vols. Madrid: Consejo Superior de Investigaciones Científicas, 1941–50.
Sanctis, Gaetano de. *Studi di storia della storiografia greca*. Florence: Nuova Italia, 1951.
Saveth, Edward N. "Science of American History," *Diogenes*, No. 26 (1959), 107–22.
Schaaf, Julius Jakob. *Geschichte und Begriff. Eine kritische Studie zur Geschichtsmethodologie von Ernst Troeltsch und Max Weber*. Tübingen: Mohr, 1946.
Schargo, Nelly. *History in the* Encyclopédie. New York: ColUP, 1947.
Schelting, Alexander von. *Russland und Europa im russischen Geschichtsdenken*. Bern: A. Francke, 1948.
Schevill, Ferdinand. *Six Historians*. Chicago: UCP, 1956.
Schieder, Theodor. "Die deutsche Geschichtswissenschaft im Spiegel der *Historischen Zeitschrift*," HZ, CLXXXIX (1959), 1–104.
———. "Grundfragen der neueren deutschen Geschichte: zum Problem der historischen Urteilsbildung," HZ, CXCII (1961), 1–16.
Schoeps, Hans Joachim. *Vorläufer Spenglers: Studien zum Geschichtspessimismus im 19. Jahrhundert*. Leyden: Brill, 1955.
Schuyler, Robert Livingston. "The Historical Spirit Incarnate: Frederic William Maitland," AHR, LVII (1952), 303–22.
Sinor, Denis (ed.). *Orientalism and History*. Cambridge: Heffer, 1954.
Skerpan, Alfred A. "Modern Russian Historiography," *Kent State University Bulletin*, Research Series No. 1 (1952), 37–60.
Smith, Charlotte Watkins. *Carl Becker: On History and the Climate of Opinion*. Ithaca, N.Y.: CorUP, 1956.
Sorenson, Lloyd. "Charles A. Beard and German Historiographical Thought," MVHR, XLII (1955), 274–87.
———. "Historical Currents in America," *American Quarterly*, VII (1955), 234–46.
Speiser, Ephraim A. "The Ancient Near East and Modern Philosophies of History," *Proceedings of the American Philosophical Society*, XCV (1951), 583–88.
Spitz, Lewis W. "Leibniz's Significance for Historiography," JHI, XIII (1952), 333–48.
———. "Natural Law and the Theory of History in Herder," JHI, XIII (1955), 453–75.
Spranger, Eduard. "Die Geburt des geschichtsphilosophischen Denkens aus Kulturkrisen," *Schweizer Monatschrift*, XXXIV (1954), 11–27.
Sprigge, J. S. *Benedetto Croce, Man and Thinker*. New Haven: YUP, 1952.
Srbik, Heinrich von. *Geist und Geschichte vom deutschen Humanismus bis zur Gegenwart*. 2 vols. Munich: Bruckmann, 1950–51.
Stadelmann, R. (ed.). *Grosse Geschichtsdenker*. Tübingen: R. Wunderlich, 1949.

———. "Jacob Burckhardts weltgeschichtliche Betrachtungen," HZ, CLXIX (1949), 31–72.
STENGERS, J. "Marc Bloch et l'histoire," *Annales*, VIII (1953), 329–38.
STERN, FRITZ (ed.). *Varieties of History*. New York: Meridian, 1956.
STROMBERG, R. N. "History in the Eighteenth Century," JHI, XII (1951), 295–305.
STROUT, CUSHING. "Historical Thought in America," *Virginia Quarterly Review*, XXVIII (1952), 242–57.
———. *The Pragmatic Revolt in American History: Carl Becker and Charles Beard*. New Haven: YUP, 1958.
SYME, RONALD. *Tacitus*. 2 vols. New York: OUP, 1958.
THOLFSEN, TRYGVE. "What Is Living in Croce's Theory of History?" *Historian*, XXIII (1961), 283–302.
TONSOR, STEPHEN J. "Lord Acton on Döllinger's Historical Theology," JHI, XX (1959), 329–52.
ULLMAN, B. L. "Leonardo Bruni and Humanistic Historiography," *Medievalia et Humanistica*, IV (1946), 45–61.
VAN TASSEL, DAVID. *Recording America's Past: An Interpretation of the Development of Historical Studies in America, 1607–1884*. Chicago: UCP, 1960.
VIERHAUS, RUDOLF. *Ranke und die soziale Welt*. Münster: Aschendorff, 1957.
VOGT, JOSEPH. *Wege zum historischen Universum*. Stuttgart: W. Kohlhammer, 1961.
VON LAUE, THEODORE H. *Leopold Ranke: The Formative Years*. Princeton: PUP, 1950.
VYVERBERG, HENRY. *Historical Pessimism in the French Enlightenment*. Cambridge, Mass.: HUP, 1958.
WAGNER, FRITZ. *Geschichtswissenschaft*. Freiburg: Alber, 1951.
———. *Modern Geschichtsschreibung: Ausblick auf eine Philosophie der Geschichtswissenschaft*. Berlin: Duncker & Humblot, 1960.
WALLACE, ELISABETH. "Goldwin Smith on History," JMH, XXVI (1954), 220–32.
WALSH, P. G. *Livy: His Historical Aims and Methods*. New York: CUP, 1961.
WARTH, ROBERT D. "Leon Trotsky, Writer and Historian," JMH, XX (1948), 27–41.
WATSON, BURTON. *Ssu-ma Ch'ien: Grand Historian of China*. New York: ColUP, 1958.
WEIS, EBERHARD. *Geschichtsschreibung und Staatsauffassung in der französischen Enzyklopedie*. Wiesbaden: Steiner, 1956.
WELLS, G. A. "Herder's and Coleridge's Evaluation of the Historical Approach," *Modern Language Review*, XLVIII (1953), 167–75.
———. "The Critics of Buckle," *Past and Present*, No. 9 (1956), 75–89.
———. "Herder's Determinism," JHI, XIX (1958), 105–13.
———. *Herder and After: A Study in the Development of Sociology*. The Hague: Mouton, 1959.
———. "Herder's Two Philosophies of History," JHI, XXI (1960), 527–37.
WESTERGAARD, WALDEMAR. "Danish History and Danish Historians," JMH, XXIV (1952), 167–80.

WETTER, GUSTAVO A. *Dialectical Materialism*. Translated by PETER HEATH. New York: Praeger, 1959.

WICKERT, LOTHAR. *Theodor Mommsen: eine Biographie*. Vol. I. Frankfurt am Main: Klostermann, 1959.

WIDGERY, ALBAN G. *Interpretations of History*. London: Allen & Unwin, 1961.

WILKINS, BURLEIGH TAYLOR. *Carl Becker*. Cambridge, Mass.: HUP, 1961.

WILLIAMS, WILLIAM A. "A Note on Charles Austin Beard's Search for a General Theory of Causation," AHR, LXII (1956), 59–80.

WISH, HARVEY. *The American Historian: A Social-Intellectual History of the Writing of the American Past*. New York: OUP, 1960.

WOLFSON, PHILIP J. "Friedrich Meinecke (1862–1954)," JHI, XVII (1956), 511–25.

WRIGHT, ARTHUR F., and HALL, JOHN W., "Historians of China and Japan," AHR, LXVII (1962), 978–85.

ZAGORIN, PEREZ. "Carl Becker on History. Professor Becker's Two Histories: A Skeptical Fallacy," AHR, LXII (1956), 1–11.

ZIFFER, BERNARD. *Poland, History and Historians: Three Bibliographical Essays*. New York: Mid-European Studies Center, 1952.

III. *Philosophy of History*

A. SOME RECENT EDITIONS OF EARLY WRITINGS

ACTON, JOHN E. E. D. *Essays on Freedom and Power*. Selected by GERTRUDE HIMMELFARB. Boston: Beacon, 1948.

BURY, J. B. "Cleopatra's Nose," in *Selected Essays of J. B. Bury*. Edited by H. TEMPERLEY. Cambridge: CUP, 1930.

———. "The Place of Modern History in the Perspective of Knowledge," *ibid*.

DILTHEY, WILHELM. *The Essence of Philosophy*. Translated by S. A. and W. T. EMERY. Chapel Hill: University of North Carolina Press, 1954.

———. *Dilthey's Philosophy of Existence*. Translated with an Introduction by WILLIAM KLUBACK and MARTIN WEINBAUM. New York: Bookman, 1957.

———. *Meaning in History*. Edited with an Introduction by H. P. RICKMAN. London: Allen & Unwin, 1961.

HEGEL, G. W. F. *Reason in History: A General Introduction to the Philosophy of History*. Translated by R. S. HARTMAN. New York: Liberal Arts Press, 1953.

IBN KHALDUN. *The Muqaddimah: An Introduction to History*. 3 vols. Translated by FRANZ ROSENTHAL. New York: Pantheon, 1958.

KANT, IMMANUEL. "Idea for a Universal History with Cosmopolitan Intent," in *The Philosophy of Kant*. Edited by CARL FRIEDRICH. New York: Random House, 1949.

LENIN, VLADIMIR. *Imperialism*. New York: International Publishers, 1939.

PLEKHANOV, G. V. *The Role of the Individual in History*. Moscow: Foreign Languages Publishing House, 1946.

———. *In Defense of Materialism: The Development of the Monist View of History*. Translated by ANDREW ROTHSTEIN. London: Lawrence & Wishart, 1947.

STEPHEN, JAMES FITZJAMES. "The Study of History," HT, I (1961), 186–201.
TREVELYAN, G. M. *The Life and Letters of Lord Macaulay*. 2 vols. New York: OUP, 1961.
VICO, GIAMBATTISTA. *The Autobiography of Giambattista Vico*. Translated by T. G. BERGIN and M. H. FISCH. Ithaca, N.Y.: CorUP, 1944.
——. *The New Science of Giambattista Vico*. Translated by T. G. BERGIN and M. H. FISCH. Ithaca, N.Y.: CorUP, 1948.
WINDELBAND, WILHELM. *Introduction to Philosophy*. Translated by Joseph McCabe. London: Unwin, 1921.

B. SOME PHILOSOPHICAL DISCUSSIONS

ABEL, THEODORE. "The Operation Called *Verstehen*," in *Readings in the Philosophy of Science*. Edited by H. FEIGL and M. BRODBECK. New York: APC, 1953.
ALBERT, ETHEL M. "Causality in the Social Sciences," JP, LI (1954), 695–706.
ALTAMIRA Y CREVEA, RAFAEL. *Proceso histórico de la historiografía humana*. Mexico City: Porrúa, 1948.
ANDERLE, OTHMAR. "The Revolution in the World-View of History," *Diogenes*, No. 9 (1955), 43–54.
——. "Theoretische Geschichte," HZ, CLXXXV (1958), 1–54.
ANGERMEIER, HEINZ. "Historisches Denken in der Geschichtsphilosophie und in der Geschichtswissenschaft," HZ, CXC (1960), 497–516.
ANSCOMBE, G. E. M. "The Reality of the Past," in *Philosophical Analysis*. Edited by MAX BLACK. Ithaca, N.Y.: CorUP, 1950.
ARON, RAYMOND. "The Philosophy of History," in *Philosophical Thought in France and the United States*. Edited by MARVIN FARBER. Buffalo: University of Buffalo Publications in Philosophy, 1950.
——. "Evidence and Inference in History," in *Evidence and Inference*. Edited by DANIEL LERNER. Glencoe, Ill.: Free Press, 1959.
——. *Dimensions de la conscience historique*. Paris: Plon, 1961.
——. *Introduction to the Philosophy of History*. Translated by GEORGE IRWIN. Boston: Beacon, 1961.
——. *The Opium of the Intellectuals*. Translated by TERENCE KILMARTIN with a new Foreword by the author. New York: Norton, 1962.
—— (ed.). *L'histoire et ses interprétations: Entretiens autour de Arnold Toynbee*. Paris: Mouton, 1961.
AYER, A. J. *The Problem of Knowledge*. London: Macmillan, 1956.
BARKER, SIR ERNEST. *Change and Continuity*. Oxford: OUP, 1949.
BARRACLOUGH, GEOFFREY. *History in a Changing World*. Oxford: Blackwell, 1955.
BEALE, HOWARD. "The Professional Historian: His Theory and His Practice," *Pacific Historical Review*, XXII (1953), 227–53.
BECK, LEWIS WHITE. "The Limits of Skepticism in History," *South Atlantic Quarterly*, XLIX (1950), 461–68.
BECKER, CARL. *Detachment and the Writing of History*. Edited by PHIL SNYDER. Ithaca, N.Y.: CorUP, 1958.

BECKER, CARL. "What Are Historical Facts?" *Western Political Quarterly*, VIII (1955), 327–40. Reprinted in *The Philosophy of History in Our Time*. Edited by HANS MEYERHOFF. Garden City, N.Y.: Doubleday, 1959.

BERGMANN, GUSTAV. "Ideology," *Ethics*, LXI (1951), 205–18.

———. "Process and History," in his *Philosophy of Science*. Madison: University of Wisconsin Press, 1957.

BERLIN, ISAIAH. *The Hedgehog and the Fox*. New York: Simon & Schuster, 1953.

———. *Historical Inevitability*. New York: OUP, 1954.

———. "History and Theory: The Concept of Scientific History," HT, I (1960), 1–31.

BLAKE, CHRISTOPHER. "Can History Be Objective?" *Mind*, LXIV (1955), 61–78.

BLOCH, MARC L. B. *The Historian's Craft*. Introduction by JOSEPH R. STRAYER. Translated from the French by PETER PUTNAM. New York: Knopf, 1953.

BOAS, GEORGE. "Aristotle's Presuppositions about Change," *American Journal of Philology*, LXVIII (1947), 404–13.

———. "Instrumentalism and the Philosophy of History," in *John Dewey: Philosopher of Science and Freedom*. Edited by SIDNEY HOOK. New York: Dial, 1950.

———. "Some Problems in Intellectual History," in his *Studies in Intellectual History*. Baltimore: Johns Hopkins Press, 1953.

BOWEN, CATHERINE DRINKER. *Adventures of a Biographer*. Boston: Atlantic–Little, Brown, 1959.

BRODBECK, MAY. "On the Philosophy of the Social Sciences," PS, XXI (1954), 140–56.

BROWN, ROBERT. "Explanation by Laws in the Social Sciences," PS, XXI (1954), 125–32.

BRUNNER, AUGUST. *Geschichtlichkeit*. Bern: Francke Verlag, 1961.

BRYANT, ARTHUR. *Literature and the Historian*. London: CUP, 1952.

BUNGE, MARIO. *Causality: The Place of the Causal Principle in Modern Science*. Cambridge, Mass.: HUP, 1959.

BURKS, RICHARD V. "Conception of Ideology for Historians," JHI, X (1949), 183–98.

BURNS, ARTHUR L. "Ascertainment, Probability, and Evidence in History," HSANZ, IV (1951), 327–39.

———. "International Theory and Historical Explanation," HT, I (1960), 55–75.

BUTLER, JAMES R. M. *The Present Need for History*. New York: CUP, 1949.

BUTTERFIELD, HERBERT. *History and Human Relations*. London: Collins, 1951.

———. "The Role of the Individual in History," *History*, XL (1955), 1–17.

———. "The History of Science and the Study of History," *Harvard Library Bulletin*, XIII (1959), 329–47.

ČAPEK, MILIČ. "Toward a Widening of the Notion of Causality," *Diogenes*, No. 28 (1959), 63–90.

CARR, EDWARD HALLETT. *What Is History?* New York: Knopf, 1962.

CASSIRER, ERNST. *The Problem of Knowledge: Philosophy, Science, and History since Hegel*. New Haven: YUP, 1950.

———. *The Logic of the Humanities*. Translated by CLARENCE SMITH HOWE. New Haven: YUP, 1961.
CHILD, ARTHUR. "Moral Judgment in History," *Ethics*, LXI (1951), 297–308.
———. "History as Imitation," PQ, II (1952), 193–207.
CHILDE, V. GORDON. *What Is History?* New York: H. Schuman, 1953.
CHOULGUINE, ALEXANDER. *L'histoire et la vie, les lois, le hasard, la volonté humaine*. Paris: Rivière, 1957.
CLAGETT, MARSHALL (ed.). *Critical Problems in the History of Science*. Proceedings of the Institute for the History of Science at the University of Wisconsin. Madison: University of Wisconsin Press, 1959.
COHEN, J. "Teleological Explanation," PAS, LI (1950), 255–92.
COHEN, MORRIS R. *The Meaning of Human History*. La Salle, Ill.: Open Court, 1947.
———. "Reason in Social Science," in *Readings in the Philosophy of Science*. Edited by H. FEIGL and MAY BRODBECK. New York: APC, 1953.
CONGRÈS DES SOCIETÉS DE PHILOSOPHIE DE LANGUE FRANÇAISE (Sixth Congress, Strasbourg, September 10–14, 1952). *L'homme et l'histoire*. Paris: PUF, 1952.
COWAN, THOMAS A. "The Historian and the Philosophy of Science," *Isis*, XXXIII (1947), 11–17.
CRAWFORD, R. M. "History as a Science," HSANZ, III (1947), 153–75.
CROCE, BENEDETTO. *Il concetto moderno della storia*. Bari: Laterza, 1947.
———. *Filosofia e storiografia*. Bari: Laterza, 1949.
———. *My Philosophy and Other Essays*. Translated by E. T. CARRITT. London: Allen & Unwin, 1949.
———. *Scritti di storia letteraria e politica*. Bari: Laterza, 1954.
DANIÉLOU, JEAN. *Essai sur le mystère de l'histoire*. Paris: Seuil, 1953.
DANTO, ARTHUR C. "Mere Chronicle and History Proper?" JP, L (1953), 173–82.
———. "On Historical Questioning," JP, LI (1954), 89–99.
———. "On Explanations in History," PS, XXIII (1956), 15–30.
D'ARCY, MARTIN C. *The Sense of History*. London: Faber, 1959.
DARDEL, ERIC. *L'histoire, science du concret*. Paris: PUF, 1946.
DEININGER, WHITAKER. "Some Reflections on Epistemology and Historical Inquiry," JP, LIII (1956), 429–42.
DEL VECCHIO, GIORGIO. "Historical Materialism and Psychologism," *Scienza Nuova*, No. 2 (1955), 5–14.
DEMPF, ALOIS. *Kritik der historischen Vernunft*. Munich: R. Oldenbourg, 1957.
DESTLER, CHESTER M. "Some Observations on Contemporary Historical Theory," AHR, LV (1950), 503–29.
DONAGAN, ALAN. "The Verification of Historical Theses," PQ, VI (1956), 193–208.
———. "Explanation in History," *Mind*, LXIV (1957), 146–64.
DOVRING, FOLKE. *History as a Social Science: An Essay on the Nature and Purpose of Historical Studies*. The Hague: Martinus Nijhoff, 1960.
DRAY, WILLIAM H. *Laws and Explanation in History*. New York: OUP, 1957.
———. "Historical Understanding as Rethinking," *Toronto Quarterly*, XXVII (1958), 200–215.

EDEL, ABRAHAM. "Levels of Meaning and the History of Ideas," JHI, VII (1946), 355–60.
ELIOT, T. S. *Notes toward the Definition of Culture.* New York: Harcourt, Brace, 1949.
ELLIS, ELMER. "The Profession of Historian," MVHR, XXXVIII (1951), 3–20.
ENGEL, JOSEF. "Analogie und Geschichte," *Studium Generale,* IX (1956), 96–107.
ERDMANN, KARL DIETRICH. "Das Problem des Historismus in der neueren englischen Geschichtswissenschaft," HZ, CLXX (1950), 73–88.
ERNST, FRITZ. "Zeitgeschehen und Geschichtschreibung," WAG, XVII (1957), 137–89.
Eventail de l'histoire vivante: hommage à Lucien Febvre offert par l'amitié d'historiens, linguistes, géographes, économistes, sociologues, ethnologues. 2 vols. Paris: Colin, 1953.
FALES, WALTER. "Historical Facts," JP, XLVIII (1951), 85–94.
FALLS, CYRIL. *The Place of War in History.* Oxford: Clarendon, 1946.
FAY, SIDNEY B. "The Idea of Progress," AHR, LII (1947), 231–46.
FEBVRE, LUCIEN. "Vers un autre histoire," RMM, LIV (1949), 225–47.
———. *Combats pour l'histoire.* Paris: Colin, 1953.
FEUER, LEWIS S. "What Is Philosophy of History?" JP, XLIX (1952), 329–40.
———. "Causality in the Social Sciences," JP, LI (1954), 681–95.
FIFE, ROBERT. "The Basis of Literary History," PMLA, LXVI (1951), 11–20.
FORDE, DARYLL. "The Human Record," *Diogenes,* No. 9 (1955), 8–27.
FRANKEL, CHARLES. "Explanation and Interpretation in History," PS, XXIV (1957), 137–55.
———. "Philosophy and History," *Political Science Quarterly,* LXXII (1957), 350–69.
FRIESS, HORACE L. "Historical Interpretation and Culture Analysis," JP, XLIX (1952), 340–50.
GAISER, KONRAD. "Der Mensch und die Geschichtlichkeit," WAG, XVIII (1958), 157–76.
GALBRAITH, V. H. *Historical Study and the State.* Oxford: Clarendon, 1948.
GALLIE, W. B. "Explanations in History and the Genetic Sciences," *Mind,* LXIV (1955), 160–80.
———. "In Reply to Mr. Montefiore," *Mind,* LXVII (1958), 192–96.
GARDINER, MARTIN. "Beyond Cultural Relativism," *Ethics,* LXI (1950), 38–45.
GARDINER, PATRICK. *The Nature of Historical Explanation.* New York: OUP, 1952.
———. "The 'Objects' of Historical Knowledge." *Philosophy,* XXVII (1952), 211–20.
———. "Metaphysics and History," in *The Nature of Metaphysics.* Edited by D. F. PEARS. London: Macmillan, 1957.
GARRATY, JOHN A. *The Nature of Biography.* New York: Knopf, 1957.

GASKING, D. "The Historian's Craft and Scientific History," HSANZ, IV (1950), 112–24.
GEIGER, L. B. "Métaphysique et relativité historique," RMM, LVII (1952), 381–414.
GEWIRTH, ALAN. "Subjectivism and Objectivism in the Social Sciences," PS, XXI (1954), 157–63.
GEYL, PIETER. *From Ranke to Toynbee*. Northampton, Mass.: Smith College, 1952.
———. *Debates with Historians*. London: Batsford, 1955.
———. *Use and Abuse of History*. New Haven: YUP, 1955.
GIBELIN, J. *Leçons sur la philosophie de l'histoire*. Paris: Vrin, 1946.
GIBSON, QUENTIN. *The Logic of Social Enquiry*. London: Routledge, 1960.
GOTTSCHALK, LOUIS. "A Professor of History in a Quandary," AHR, LIX (1954), 273–86.
GOUHIER, HENRI. " 'Evolution' ou 'création' dans l'histoire des idées," *Psyché*, III (1948), 15–48.
———. *L'histoire et sa philosophie*. Paris: Vrin, 1952.
GREGORY, T. S. "The Meaning of History," *Dublin Review*, No. 440 (1947), 74–87.
GROOT, EMILE DE. "Is There a Metaphysic of History?" *Hibbert Journal*, LI (1953), 217–25.
GRÜNBAUM, A. "Causality and the Science of Human Behavior," *American Scientist*, XL (1952), 665–76. Reprinted in *Philosophic Problems*. Edited by M. MANDELBAUM, F. W. GRAMLICH, and A. R. ANDERSON. New York: Macmillan, 1957.
GRUNBERG, EMILE. "Notes on Historical Events and General Laws," *Canadian Journal of Economics and Political Science*, XIX (1953), 510–19.
HALPERN, BEN. " 'Myth' and 'Ideology' in Modern Usage," HT, I (1961), 129–50.
HARRIS, ERROL E. "Collingwood's Theory of History," PQ, VII (1957), 35–49.
HARTT, JULIAN N. "Metaphysics, History, and Civilization: Collingwood's Account of Their Interrelationship," *Journal of Religion*, XXXIII (1953), 198–211.
HARTUNG, F. E. "Cultural Relativity and Moral Judgments," PS, XXI (1954), 118–26.
HATTO, ARTHUR. " 'Revolution': An Inquiry into the Usefulness of an Historical Term," *Mind*, LVIII (1949), 495–517.
HAYEK, F. A. VON. *The Counter-Revolution of Science: Studies on the Abuse of Reason*. Glencoe, Ill.: Free Press, 1952.
HEIMPEL, HERMANN. "Geschichte und Geschichtswissenschaft," *Vierteljahrbücher für Zeitgeschichte*, V (1957), 1–17.
HEINEMANN, F. H. "Reply to Historicism," *Philosophy*, XXI (1946), 245–57.
HELMER, O., and RESCHER, N. "On the Epistemology of the Inexact Sciences," *Management Science*, VI (1959), 25–52.
HEMPEL, CARL G. "The Function of General Laws in History," JP, XXXIX (1942), 35–48.
———. "Typological Procedures in the Natural and Social Sciences," in

"Symposium: Problems of Concept and Theory Formation in the Social Sciences," *Science, Language, and Human Rights*. Philadelphia: University of Pennsylvania for the American Philosophical Association, 1952.

HEMPEL, CARL G., and OPPENHEIM, P. "Studies in the Logic of Explanation," PS, XV (1948), 135–75.

HEXTER, J. H. "The Historian and His Day," *Political Science Quarterly*, LXIX (1954), 219–33.

———. *Reappraisals in History*. London: Longmans, 1961; Evanston, Ill.: Northwestern University Press, 1962.

HINSHAW, VIRGIL, JR. "The Objectivity of History," PS, XXV (1958), 51–58.

HOCKING, W. E. "Fact and Destiny," *Review of Metaphysics*, IV (1951), 319–42.

HOFER, WALTHER. *Geschichte zwischen Philosophie und Politik*. Basel: Verlag für Recht und Gesellschaft, 1956.

HOLT, W. S. "An Evaluation of the *Report on Theory and Practice in Historical Study*," *Pacific Historical Review*, XVIII (1949), 239–43.

HOOK, SIDNEY. "Intelligence and Evil in Human History," in *Freedom and Experience: Essays Presented to Horace M. Kallen*. Edited by S. HOOK and M. R. KONVITZ. Ithaca, N.Y.: CorUP, 1947.

———. *The Quest for Being and Other Studies in Naturalism and Humanism*. New York: St Martin's Press, 1961.

HOSPERS, J. "On Explanation," JP, XLIII (1946), 337–56. Reprinted in *Essays in Conceptual Analysis*. Edited by A. FLEW. London: Macmillan, 1956.

HOURS, JOSEPH. *Valeur de l'histoire*. Paris: PUF, 1954.

HUIZINGA, JOHANN. *Geschichte und Kultur: gesammelte Aufsätze*. Edited by KURT KÖSTER. Stuttgart: A. Kroner, 1954.

INGARDEN, ROMAN. "Reflections on the Subject Matter of History of Philosophy," *Diogenes*, No. 29 (1960), 11–21.

JAMESON, J. FRANKLIN. "The Future Uses of History," AHR, LXV (1959), 61–72.

JASPERS, KARL. "Freedom and Authority," *Diogenes*, No. 1 (1953), 25–42.

JONES, HOWARD MUMFORD. "Ideas, History, Technology," *Technology and Culture*, I (1959), 20–27.

JOYNT, C. B., and RESCHER, N. "Evidence in History and in the Law," JP, LVI (1959), 561–77.

———. "On Explanation in History," *Mind*, LXVIII (1959), 383–88.

———. "The Problem of Uniqueness in History," HT, I (1961), 150–63.

KAEGI, WERNER. *Historische Meditationen*. 2 vols. Zurich: Fritz & Washmuth, 1946.

KAUFMANN, WALTER A. "The Hegel Myth and Its Method," PR, LX (1951), 459–86.

KENNAN, GEORGE F. "The Experience of Writing History," *Virginia Quarterly Review*, XXXVI (1960), 205–14.

KERN, FRITZ. *Geschichte und Entwicklung*. Bern: Francke, 1952.

KNOWLES, DAVID. *The Historian and Character*. New York: CUP, 1955.

KÖHLER, O. "Idealismus und Geschichtlichkeit: über Neuerscheinungen auf dem Gebiete der Geschichtsphilosophie," *Saeculum*, II (1951), 122–56.

KREY, AUGUST C. *History and the Social Web: A Collection of Essays*. Minneapolis: University of Minnesota Press, 1955.
KRIEGER, LEONARD. "The Horizons of History," AHR, LXIII (1957), 62–74.
KRISTELLER, PAUL O. "The Philosophical Significance of the History of Thought," JHI, VII (1946), 360–66.
KRÜGER, GERHARD. *Die Geschichte im Denken der Gegenwart*. Frankfurt: Klostermann, 1947.
———. *Geschichte und Tradition*. Stuttgart: Kreuz-Verlag, 1948.
———. *Freiheit und Weltverwaltung*. Freiburg: Alber, 1958.
LAMM, HERBERT. "The Problem of Cultural Synthesis in History," *Journal of General Education*, VI (1951), 64–73.
LAMPRECHT, STERLING. *Nature and History*. New York: ColUP, 1950.
LANDMANN, MICHAEL. *Das Zeitalter als Schicksal: die geistesgeschichtliche Kategorie der Epoche*. Basel: Verlag für Recht und Gesellschaft, 1956.
LANGER, WILLIAM L. "The Next Assignment," AHR, LXIII (1958), 283–304.
LEE, DWIGHT E., and BECK, ROBERT N. "The Meaning of 'Historicism,' " AHR, LIX (1954), 568–78.
LEE, HAROLD, "The Hypothetical Nature of Historical Knowledge," JP, LI (1954), 213–20.
LEFEBVRE, GEORGES. "Avenir de l'histoire," RH, CXCVII (1947), 55–61.
LEVENSON, JOSEPH. "Historical Significance," *Diogenes*, No. 32 (1960), 17–27.
LITT, THEODOR. *Mensch und Welt; Grundlinien einer Philosophie des Geistes*. Munich: Piper, 1948.
———. *Wege und Irrwege geschichtlichen Denkens*. Munich: Piper, 1948.
———. *Mensch vor der Geschichte*. Bremen: Schünemann, 1950.
———. *Die Wiederweckung des geschichtlichen Bewusstseins*. Heidelberg: Duelle & Meyer, 1956.
LOEWENBERG, B. J. "Some Problems Raised by Historical Relativism," JMH, XXI (1949), 17–23.
LÖWITH, KARL. *Meaning in History: The Theological Implications of the Philosophy of History*. Chicago: UCP, 1949.
———. "Skepsis und Glaube in der Weltgeschichte," WAG, X (1950), 143–55.
LOVEJOY, ARTHUR O. "The Historiography of Ideas," in his *Essays in the History of Ideas*. Baltimore: Johns Hopkins Press, 1948.
LYND, HELEN M. "The Nature of Historical Objectivity," JP, XLVII (1950), 29–43.
MACIVER, A. M. "Historical Explanation," in *Logic and Language*. 2d series. Edited by ANTHONY FLEW. New York: Philosophical Library, 1953.
MACIVER, A. M.; WALSH, W. H.; and GINSBERG, M. "Explanation in History and Philosophy," Supplement to PAS, XXI (1947).
MCKEON, RICHARD. "Philosophy and the Diversity of Cultures," *Ethics*, LX (1950), 233–60.
MACKINNON, D. M. *On the Notion of a Philosophy of History*. London: OUP, 1954.
MALIN, JAMES. *On the Nature of History: Essays about History and Dissidence*. Lawrence, Kans.: the author, 1954.

MALIN, JAMES. *The Contriving Brain and the Skillful Hand in the United States: Something about History and the Philosophy of History*. Lawrence, Kans.: the author, 1955.

———. *Confounded Rot about Napoleon, Reflections upon Science and Technology, Nationalism, World Depression of the Eighteen-nineties and Afterward*. Lawrence, Kans.: the author, 1961.

MANDELBAUM, MAURICE. "Critique of Philosophies of History," JP, XLV (1948), 365-78.

———. "Historical Determinism and the Gospel of Freedom," *Journal of General Education*, VI (1951), 7-16.

———. "Some Neglected Philosophical Problems Regarding History," JP, XLIX (1952), 317-29.

———. "Societal Laws," BJPS, VIII (1957), 211-24.

———. "Historical Explanation: The Problem of 'Covering Laws,' " HT, I (1961), 229-42.

MARGENAU, HENRY. *Open Vistas: Philosophical Perspectives of Modern Science*. New Haven: YUP, 1961.

MARITAIN, JACQUES. *On the Philosophy of History*. New York: Scribner's, 1957.

MARROU, HENRI-IRÉNÉE. "De la logique de l'histoire à une éthique de l'historien," RMM, LIV (1949), 248-72.

MASI, EVELYN. "A Note on Lewis's Analysis of the Meaning of Historical Statements," JP, XLVI (1949), 670-74.

MASSON-OURSEL, PAUL. *La morale et l'histoire*. Paris: PUF, 1955.

MAYER, ANTON. *Probleme, Ziele, und Grenzen der Geschichtsrevision*. Nuremberg: Glocke & Lutz, 1947.

MAZLISH, BRUCE. "History and Morality," JP, LV (1958), 230-40.

MEINECKE, FRIEDRICH. *Aphorismen und Skizzen zur Geschichte*. 2d rev. ed. Stuttgart: K. F. Koehler, 1953.

MELDEN, A. I. "Historical Objectivity, a 'Noble Dream,' " *Journal of General Education*, VII (1952), 17-24.

MEYERHOFF, HANS (ed.). *The Philosophy of History in Our Time*. Garden City, N.Y.: Doubleday, 1959.

MILLER, HUGH. *The Community of Man*. New York: Macmillan, 1949.

MONTEFIORE, ALAN. "Professor Gallie on 'Necessary and Sufficient Conditions,' " *Mind*, LXV (1956), 534-41.

MOORE, O. K. "Nominal Definitions of Culture," PS, XIX (1952), 245-56.

MORAZÉ, CHARLES. *Trois essais sur histoire et culture*. Paris: Colin, 1948.

MORISON, SAMUEL ELIOT. *By Land and by Sea: Essays and Addresses*. New York: Knopf, 1953.

NAGEL, ERNEST. "The Logic of Historical Analysis," *Scientific Monthly*, LXXIV (1952), 162-69.

———. *Logic without Metaphysics*. Glencoe, Ill.: Free Press, 1956.

———. "Determinism in History," PPR, XX (1960), 291-317.

NAGEL, ERNEST, and HEMPEL, CARL. "Symposium: Problems of Concept and Theory Formation in the Social Sciences" in *Science, Language, and Human Rights*. Philadelphia: University of Pennsylvania for the American Philosophical Association, 1952.

NAMIER, L. B. *Avenues of History*. London: Hamish Hamilton, 1952.

NATANSON, MAURICE. "George H. Mead's Metaphysics of Time," JP, L (1953), 770–82.
NEILSON, FRANCES. "Time and the Pattern of History," *American Journal of Economics and Sociology*, XIII (1953), 27–37.
NEVINS, ALLAN. "Not Capulets, Not Montagus," AHR, LXV (1960), 253–71.
NILSON, S. S. "Mechanics and Historical Laws," JP, XLVIII (1951), 201–11.
NORTHROP, F. S. C. *Logic of the Sciences and the Humanities.* New York: Macmillan, 1947.
———. "The Philosophy of Culture and Its Bearing on the Philosophy of History," PPR, IX (1949), 568–74.
NOWELL, CHARLES E. "Has the Past a Place in History?" JMH, XXIV (1952), 331–40.
OAKESHOTT, MICHAEL. "The Activity of Being an Historian," in *Historical Studies: Papers Read before the Second Irish Conference of Historians.* Edited by T. DESMOND WILLIAMS. London: Bowes & Bowes, 1958.
O'GORMAN, EDMUNDO. *Crisis y porvenir de la ciencia histórica.* Mexico City: Imprenta Universitaria, 1947.
OLAFSON, F. A. "Existentialism, Marxism, and Historical Justification," *Ethics*, LXV (1955), 126–34.
OLAGÜE, IGNACIO. "Contemporary Geopolitics and the Geographical Framework," *Diogenes*, No. 27 (1959), 22–38.
OMODEO, ADOLFO. *Il senso della storia.* Turin: Einaudi, 1948.
OPPENHEIM, FELIX. "In Defense of Relativism," *Western Political Quarterly*, VIII (1955), 411–17.
ORCEL, JEAN, and LEFEBVRE, GEORGES. "Réflexions sur l'histoire," *La Pensée*, No. 61 (1955), 25–34.
ORTEGA Y GASSET, JOSÉ. *Man and Crisis.* Translated from Spanish by MILDRED ADAMS. New York: Norton, 1958.
———. "The Difficulty of Reading," *Diogenes*, No. 28 (1959), 1–17.
———. *History as a System, and Other Essays toward a Philosophy of History.* New York: Norton, 1961.
PARES, RICHARD. *The Historian's Business and Other Essays.* Edited by R. A. and ELISABETH HUMPHREYS. New York: OUP, 1961.
PASSMORE, J. A. "Can the Social Sciences Be Value-Free?" in *Readings in the Philosophy of Science.* Edited by H. FEIGL and M. BRODBECK. New York: APC, 1953.
———. "The Objectivity of History," *Philosophy*, XXXIII (1958), 97–110.
———. "History, the Individual and Inevitability," PR, LXVIII (1959), 93–102.
PICON, GAËTAN. "Aesthetics and History," *Diogenes*, No. 4 (1953), 31–51.
PIEPER, JOSEF. *The End of Time: A Meditation on the Philosophy of History.* Translated by M. BULLOCK. New York: Pantheon, 1954.
PIGANIOL, ANDRÉ. "Qu'est-ce que l'histoire?" RMM, LX (1955), 225–47.
PITT, J. "Generalizations in Historical Explanation," JP, LXI (1959), 578–86.
POPPER, KARL. *The Open Society and Its Enemies.* Rev. ed. Princeton: PUP, 1950.
———. *The Poverty of Historicism.* Boston: Beacon, 1957.

PRIBRAM, KARL. *Conflicting Patterns of Thought.* Washington: Public Affairs Press, 1949.
RANDALL, J. G. "Historianship," AHR, LVIII (1953), 249–64.
RANDALL, JOHN H. *Nature and Historical Experience.* New York: ColUP, 1958.
READ, CONYERS. "The Social Responsibilities of the Historian," AHR, LV (1950), 275–85.
REISNER, ERWIN. "Progressive und regressive Geschichte," *Zeitschrift für philosophische Forschung,* VI (1952), 222–34.
RENOUARD, YVES. "La notion de génération en histoire," RH, CCIX(1953), 1–23.
RICOEUR, PAUL. *Histoire et verité.* Paris: Seuil, 1955.
RIEZLER, K. "The Historian and the Truth," JP, XLV (1948), 378–88.
RIKER, WILLIAM H. "Events and Situations," JP, LIV (1957), 57–70.
RITTER, GERHARD. *Geschichte als Bildungsmacht: ein Beitrag zur historisch-politischen Neubesinnung.* Stuttgart: Deutsche Verlags-Anstalt, 1946.
———. "Zum Begriff der 'Kulturgeschichte': ein Diskussionsbeitrag," HZ, CLXXI (1951), 293–302.
———. "Scientific History, Contemporary History, and Political Science," HT, I (1961), 261–79.
ROMEIN, JAN. "Theoretical History," JHI, IX (1948), 56–64.
———. "Common World Pattern," JWH, IV (1958), 449–63.
ROSEN, S. "Order and History," *Review of Metaphysics,* XII (1958), 257–76.
ROSENSTOCK-HUESSY, EUGEN F. M. *The Christian Future; or The Modern Mind Outrun.* New York: Scribner's, 1946.
ROSHWALD, M. "Value-Judgements in the Social Sciences," BJPS, VII (1955), 186–208.
ROSSI, MARIO. *A Plea for Man.* Edinburgh: Thomas Nelson, 1956.
ROSTOW, WALT W. "The Interrelation of Theory and Economic History," *Journal of Economic History,* XVII (1957), 509–23.
ROTENSTREICH, NATHAN. *Between Past and Present: An Essay on History.* New Haven: YUP, 1958.
———. "From Facts to Thought: Collingwood's Views on the Nature of History," *Philosophy,* XXXV (1960), 122–36.
ROTHACKER, ERICH. *Die dogmatische Denkform in den Geisteswissenschaften und das Problem des Historismus.* Wiesbaden: F. Steiner, 1954.
ROWSE, A. L. *The Use of History.* New York: Macmillan, 1947.
RUDNER, RICHARD S. "Philosophy and Social Science," PS, XXI (1954), 104–68.
RÜDINGER, KARL. *Unser Geschichtsbild. Der Sinn in der Geschichte.* Munich: Bayerischer Schulbuch, 1950.
RUSSELL, BERTRAND. "History as Art," in *Portraits from Memory and Other Essays.* New York: Simon & Schuster, 1956.
———. *Understanding History and Other Essays.* New York: Philosophical Library, 1957.
RYLE, GILBERT. *The Concept of Mind.* London: Hutchinson, 1949.
SALOMON, A. *The Tyranny of Progress.* New York: Noonday, 1955.
SAUNDERS, R. M. "Some Thoughts on the Study of History," *Canadian Historical Review,* XXXVII (1956), 109–18.

SAVELLE, MAX. "Historian's Progress; or The Quest for Sancta Sophia," *Pacific Historical Review*, XXVII (1958), 1–27.
———. "The Functions of History in the Age of Science," *Historian*, XXII (1960), 347–60.
SAVETH, EDWARD. "Scientific History in America: Eclipse of an Idea," in *Essays in American Historiography: Papers Presented in Honor of Allan Nevins*. Edited by DONALD SHEEHAN and HAROLD C. SYRETT. New York: ColUP, 1960.
SCHAFF, ADAM. "Why History Is Constantly Rewritten," *Diogenes*, No. 30 (1960), 62–74.
SCHEFFLER, ISRAEL. "Verifiability in History: A Reply to Miss Masi," JP XLVII (1950), 158–66.
SCHELER, MAX. "Man and History," in his *Philosophical Perspectives*. Translated by OSCAR HAAC. Boston: Beacon, 1958.
SCHLEGEL, WOLFGANG. "Geschichtsbild und Geschichtliche Bildung," WAG, XVII (1957), 280–90.
SCHMITT, BERNADOTTE. *The Fashion and Future of History: Historical Studies and Addresses*. Cleveland: Western Reserve University Press, 1960.
SCHNEIDER, FREDERICK D. "Collingwood and the Idea of History," *University of Toronto Quarterly*, XXII (1953), 172–83.
SCHOEPS, HANS-JOACHIM. *Was ist und was will die Geistesgeschichte: über Theorie und Praxis der Zeitgeistforschung*. Göttingen: Musterschmidt, 1959.
SCHULZ, ROBERT (ed.). *Beiträge zur Kritik der gegenwärtigen bürgerlichen Geschichtsphilosophie*. Berlin: Deutscher Verlag der Wissenschaften, 1958.
SCHUTZ, ALFRED. "Concept and Theory Formation in the Social Sciences," JP, LI (1954), 257–73.
SEIDENBERG, RODERICK. *Posthistoric Man: An Inquiry*. Chapel Hill: University of North Carolina Press, 1950.
SIMPSON, LESLIE BYRD. *The Writing of History: A Dialogue*. Berkeley: UCalP, 1947.
SMART, J. J. C. "The River of Time," *Mind*, LVIII (1949), 483–94.
SNELL, BRUNO. "Tradition und Geistesgeschichte," *Studium Generale*, IV (1951), 339–45.
SPRANGER, EDUARD. "Aufgaben des Geschichtsschreibers," HZ, CLXXIV (1952), 251–68.
STERN, ALFRED. "Fact and Understanding in History," JP, XLIV (1947), 617–25.
STEWARD, JULIAN. "Cultural Causality and Law," *American Anthropologist*, LI (1949), 1–27.
STRAUSS, LEO. "Political Philosophy and History," JHI, X (1949), 30–50.
———. "On Collingwood's Philosophy of History," *Review of Metaphysics*, II (1952), 559–86.
———. *Natural Right and History*. Chicago: UCP, 1953.
STRONG, E. W. "How Is Practice of History Tied to Theory?" JP, XLVI (1949), 637–44.
———. "Criteria of Explanation in History," JP, XLIX (1952), 57–67.
———. "The Irreversibility of History," *Diogenes*, No. 29 (1960), 1–15.

STÜRMANN, JOSEF. *Der Mensch in der Geschichte, philosophisch-anthropologische Geschichtsbetrachtung.* Munich: Kurt Desch, 1949.
SWABEY, MARIE COLLINS. *The Judgment of History.* New York: Philosophical Library, 1954.
TAPP, E. J. "Some Aspects of Causation in History," JP, XLIX (1952), 67–79.
Theory and Practice in Historical Study: A Report of the Committee on Historiography. Social Science Research Council Bulletin 54. New York, 1946.
THORNDIKE, LYNN. "Whatever Was, *Was Right*," AHR, LXI (1956), 265–83.
THORPE, EARL E. *The Desertion of Man: A Critique of Philosophy of History.* Baton Rouge, La.: Harrington, 1958.
TREVELYAN, GEORGE M. *An Autobiography and Other Essays.* London: Longmans, Green, 1949.
TREVOR-ROPER, H. R. *Men and Events: Historical Essays.* New York: Harper, 1957.
USHER, ABBOT PAYSON. "The Significance of Modern Empiricism for History and Economics," *Journal of Economic History*, IX (1949), 137–55.
VENDRYES, PIERRE. *De la probabilité en histoire.* Paris: Michel, 1952.
VOSSLER, OTTO. "Objektivität in der Geschichte," WAG, X (1950), 71–85.
WALSH, W. H. "R. G. Collingwood's Philosophy of History," *Philosophy*, XXII (1947), 153–60.
―――. *An Introduction to Philosophy of History.* London: Hutchinson, 1951.
WATERS, BRUCE. "The Past and the Historical Past," JP, LII (1955), 253–69.
WATKINS, J. W. N. "Ideal Types and Historical Explanation," in *Readings in the Philosophy of Science.* Edited by H. FEIGL and M. BRODBECK. New York: APC, 1953.
―――. "Historical Explanation in the Social Sciences," BJPS, VIII (1957), 104–17.
WEBB, WALTER PRESCOTT. "History as High Adventure," AHR, LXIV (1959), 265–81.
WEDGWOOD, C. V. *The Sense of the Past.* New York: CUP, 1957.
―――. *Truth and Opinion: Historical Essays.* New York: Macmillan, 1960.
WELTE, BERNHARD. "Wahrheit und Geschichtlichtkeit," *Saeculum*, III (1952), 177–91.
WHITE, MORTON. *Social Thought in America: The Revolt against Formalism.* New York: Viking, 1949.
―――. "Towards an Analytic Philosophy of History," in *Philosophic Thought in France and the United States.* Edited by M. FARBER. New York: University of Buffalo Publications in Philosophy, 1950.
―――. "A Plea for an Analytic Philosophy of History," in his *Religion, Politics, and the Higher Learning.* Cambridge, Mass.: HUP, 1959.
WIEMAN, HENRY N. *The Directive in History.* Boston: Beacon, 1949.
WIENER, PHILIP P. "The Logical Significance of the History of Thought," JHI, VII (1946), 366–73.
WILKINS, BURLEIGH TAYLOR. "Pragmatism as a Theory of Historical Knowledge: John Dewey on the Nature of Historical Inquiry," AHR, LXIV (1959), 878–90.

WILLIAMS, DONALD C. "More on the Ordinariness of History," JP, LII (1955), 269–77.
WITTRAM, REINHARD. "Geschichtsauffassung und Wahrheitsfrage," *Sammlung*, II (1946–47), 89–104.
———. "Das Faktum und der Mensch," HZ, CLXXXV (1958), 55–87.
———. *Das Interesse an der Geschichte: zwölf Vorlesungen über Fragen des zeitgenössischen Geschichtsverständnisses*. Göttingen: Vandenhoeck & Ruprecht, 1958.
WOLLHEIM, R. "Historicism Reconsidered," *Sociological Review*, N.S., II (1954), 76–97.
WOOD, H. G. *Freedom and Necessity in History*. Riddell Memorial Lecture. London: OUP, 1957.
WOODWARD, C. VANN. *The Age of Reinterpretation*. Washington: Service Center for Teachers of History, 1961.
YOLTON, J. W. "Criticism and Historic Understanding," *Ethics*, LXV (1955), 206–12.
———. "History and Metahistory," PPR, XV (1955), 477–92.
ZAGORIN, PEREZ. "Historical Knowledge: A Review Article on the Philosophy of History," JMH, XXXI (1959), 243–55.
ZITTEL, BERNHARD. "Der Typus in der Geschichtswissenschaft," *Studium Generale*, V (1952), 378–84.

C. HISTORY AND THE SOCIAL SCIENCES

AITKEN, HUGH G. J. (ed.). *The Social Sciences in Historical Study: A Report of the Committee on Historiography*. Social Science Research Council Bulletin 64. New York, 1954.
BARBU, ZEVEDEI. *Problems of Historical Psychology*. New York: Grove, 1961.
BARNETT, H. G. *Innovation: The Basis of Cultural Change*. New York: McGraw-Hill, 1953.
BECKER, HOWARD P. *Through Values to Social Interpretation*. Durham, N.C.: Duke University Press, 1950.
———. "Science, Culture and Society," PS, XIX (1952), 273–87.
BOCK, KENNETH E., "Evolution and Historical Process," *American Anthropologist*, LIV (1952) 486–96.
———. *The Acceptance of Histories: Toward a Perspective for Social Science*. Berkeley: UCalP, 1956.
BRAUDEL, FERNAND. "Histoire et sciences sociales: la longue durée," *Annales*, XIII (1958), 725–53.
———. "Sur une conception de l'histoire sociale," *Annales*, XIV (1959), 308–19.
CHALLENER, RICHARD, and LEE, MAURICE, JR. "History and the Social Sciences: The Problem of Communication," AHR, LXI (1956), 331–38.
CHASE, STUART. *The Proper Study of Mankind: An Inquiry into the Science of Human Relations*. New York: Harper, 1948.
COBBAN, ALFRED. "The Vocabulary of Social History," *Political Science Quarterly*, LXXI (1956), 1–17.
DAVY, GEORGES. "L'explication sociologique et le recours à l'histoire, d'après Comte, Mill, et Durkheim," RMM, LIV (1949), 330–62.

DUPRONT, ALPHONSE. "Problèmes et méthodes d'une histoire de la psychologie collective," *Annales*, XVI (1961), 3–11.
EINSTEIN, LEWIS. *Historical Change.* New York: CUP, 1946.
FRANCIS, E. K. "History and the Social Sciences: Some Reflections on the Reintegration of Social Science," *Review of Politics*, XIII (1951), 354–74.
FREYER, HANS. "Soziologie und Geschichtsphilosophie," *Jahrbuch für Sozialwissenschaft*, IV (1959), 115–25.
GINSBURG, MORRIS. *Essays: Sociology and Social Philosophy.* 2 vols. London: Heinemann, 1956.
———. "Factors in Social Change," in *Transactions of the Third World Congress of Sociology.* Vol. I. London, 1956.
GRUHLE, HANS W. *Geschichtschreibung und Psychologie.* Bonn: Bouvier, 1953.
GURVITCH, GEORGES. "Continuité et discontinuité en histoire et en sociologie," *Annales*, XII (1957), 73–84.
GUSDORF, GEORGES. "The Ambiguity of the Sciences of Man," *Diogenes*, No. 26 (1959), 48–70.
HALPERN, BEN. "The Dynamic Elements of Culture," *Ethics*, LXV (1955), 235–49.
HINSHAW, V. G. "Epistemological Relativism and the Sociology of Knowledge," *PS*, XVI (1948), 4–10.
HUGHES, H. STUART. "The Historian and the Social Scientist," *AHR*, LXVI (1960), 20–46.
KOMAROVSKY, MIRRA (ed.). *Common Frontiers of the Social Sciences.* Glencoe, Ill.: Free Press, 1957.
KOPPERS, WILHELM. "Der historische Grundcharakter der Völkerkunde," *Studium Generale*, VII (1954), 135–43.
KROEBER, A. L. *The Nature of Culture.* Chicago: UCP, 1952.
———. "An Anthropologist Looks at History," *Pacific Historical Review*, XXVI (1957), 281–87.
KUZNETS, SIMON. "Statistical Trends and Historical Changes," *Economic History Review*, III (1951), 265–78.
LASSWELL, HAROLD D. "Impact of Psychoanalytic Thinking on the Social Sciences," in *The State of the Social Sciences.* Edited by LEONARD D. WHITE. Chicago: UCP, 1956.
LÉVI-STRAUSS, CLAUDE. "Histoire et ethnologie," *RMM*, LIV (1949), 363–91.
———. "L'Anthropologie sociale devant l'histoire," *Annales*, XV (1960), 625–37.
LEVY, MARION. "Some Basic Methodological Difficulties in the Social Sciences," *PS*, XVII (1950), 287–301.
MANNHEIM, KARL. *Essays on the Sociology of Knowledge.* Edited by PAUL KECSKEMETI. London: Routledge & Kegan Paul, 1952.
MAQUET, J. J. *The Sociology of Knowledge.* Translated by JOHN LOCKE. Boston: Beacon, 1951.
MEAD, MARGARET. "Anthropologist and Historian: Their Common Problems," *American Quarterly*, III (1951), 3–13.
MERTON, ROBERT K. *Social Theory and Social Structure.* Glencoe, Ill.: Free Press, 1957.

MONTAGU, M. F. ASHLEY. *Man in Process*. New York: World, 1961.
PARSONS, TALCOTT. *The Social System*. Glencoe, Ill.: Free Press, 1951.
PARSONS, TALCOTT, and SHILS, EDWARD. *Toward a General Theory of Action*. Cambridge, Mass.: HUP, 1951.
REINHARD, MARCEL. "Histoire et démographie," RH, CCIV (1950), 193–205.
RIEFF, PHILIP. "History, Psychoanalysis, and the Social Sciences," *Ethics*, LXIII (1953), 107–20.
RÓHEIM, GÉZA (ed.). *Psychoanalysis and the Social Sciences*. 3 vols. New York: International Universities Press, 1947–51.
SCHOECK, HELMUT, and WIGGINS, JAMES W. (eds.). *Relativism and the Study of Man*. Princeton, N.J.: Van Nostrand, 1961.
SCHOENWALD, RICHARD L. "Historians and the Challenge of Freud," *Western Humanities Review*, X (1956), 99–108.
SWARTZ, MARC J. "History and Science in Anthropology," PS, XXV (1958), 59–70.
WAGNER, HELMUT. "Mannheim's Historicism," *Social Research*, XIX (1952), 300–321.
WEBER, MAX. *From Max Weber: Essays in Sociology*. Edited and translated by H. H. GERTH and C. WRIGHT MILLS. New York: OUP, 1946.
———. *The Theory of Social and Economic Organization*. Translated by TALCOTT PARSONS. New York: OUP, 1947.
———. *Max Weber on the Methodology of the Social Sciences*. Translated and edited by EDWARD SHILS and HENRY FINCH. Glencoe, Ill.: Free Press, 1949.
WINCH, PETER. *The Idea of a Social Science*. London: Routledge, 1958.
WHITE, LESLIE. *The Science of Culture: A Study of Man and Civilization*. New York: Farrar, Straus, 1949.

IV. *The Pattern of the Past and Historical Interpretation*

ACCAME, SILVIO. "De l'histoire universelle," JWH, IV (1958), 464–70.
ACHMINOW, HERMAN. "Mythos und Wahrheit in der Geschichtslehre von Marx," *Saeculum*, XI (1960), 266–94.
ACTON, H. B. *The Illusion of the Epoch: Marxism-Leninism as a Philosophical Creed*. London: Cohen & West, 1955.
ANDERLE, OTHMAR. *Das universalhistorische System A. J. Toynbees*. Frankfurt: Humboldt, 1955.
ANDERSEN, PER SVEAS. *Westward Is the Course of the Empire. A Study in the Shaping of an American Idea: Turner's Frontier*. Oslo: Oslo University Press, 1956.
ARENDT, HANNAH. *The Origins of Totalitarianism*. New York: Harcourt, Brace, 1951.
———. *The Human Condition*. Chicago: UCP, 1958.
———. *Between Past and Future*. New York: Viking, 1961.
ARON, RAYMOND. *The Century of Total War*. Translated by E. W. DICKES and O. S. GRIFFITHS. Garden City, N.Y.: Doubleday, 1954.

ARON, RAYMOND. "Workers, Proletarians, and Intellectuals," *Diogenes*, No. 10 (1955), 31–46.

———. *The Dawn of Universal History*. Translated by DOROTHY PICKLES. New York: Praeger, 1961.

BAGBY, PHILIP. *Culture and History: Prolegomena to the Comparative Study of Civilizations*. Berkeley: UCalP, 1959.

BECK, ROLAND H. *Die Frontiertheorie von Frederick Jackson Turner*. Zurich: Europa, 1955.

BLACK, C. E. (ed.). *Rewriting Russian History: Soviet Interpretations of Russia's Past*. New York: Praeger, 1956.

BRINTON, CRANE. "Toynbee's City of God," *Virginia Quarterly Review*, XXXII (1956), 361–75.

BROWN, ROBERT E. *Charles Beard and the Constitution*. Princeton, N.J.: PUP, 1956.

BULTMANN, RUDOLF. *History and Eschatology*. Edinburgh: Edinburgh University Press, 1957.

BURRELL, SIDNEY. "Calvinism, Capitalism and the Middle Classes: Some Afterthoughts on an Old Problem," JMH, XXXII (1960), 129–41.

CARELESS, J. M. S. "Frontierism, Metropolitanism, and Canadian History," *Canadian Historical Review*, XXXV (1954), 1–21.

CASTRO, AMERICO. *The Structure of Spanish History*. Translated by EDMUND L. KING. Princeton, N.J.: PUP, 1954.

CLOUGH, SHEPARD B. *The Rise and Fall of Civilization: An Inquiry into the Relationship between Economic Development and Civilization*. New York: McGraw-Hill, 1951.

CORNFORTH, M. *Historical Materialism*. London: Lawrence, 1953.

COULBORN, RUSHTON. *The Origin of Civilized Societies*. Princeton, N.J.: PUP, 1959.

——— (ed.). *Feudalism in History*. Princeton, N.J.: PUP, 1956.

CROCE, BENEDETTO. "La monotonia e la vacuità della storiografia communistica," *Quaderni della "Critica,"* V (1949), 34–45.

DANIELS, ROBERT V. "Fate and Will in Marx," JHI, XXI (1960), 538–52.

DAWSON, CHRISTOPHER. *The Dynamics of World History*. New York: Sheed & Ward, 1957.

———. *The Historic Reality of Christian Culture: A Way to the Renewal of Human Life*. New York: Harper, 1960.

DOBB, MAURICE. "Historical Materialism and the Role of the Economic Factor," *History*, XXXVI (1951), 1–11.

DRAY, WILLIAM. "Toynbee's Search for Historical Laws," HT, I (1960), 32–55.

EASTON, LLOYD. "Alienation and History in Early Marx," PPR, XXII (1961), 193–205.

ELKINS, STANLEY, and MCKITRICK, ERIC. "A Meaning for Turner's Frontier," *Political Science Quarterly*, LXIX (1954), 321–53 and 565–602.

FAIRBANK, JOHN K. "East Asian Views of Modern European History," AHR, LXII (1957), 527–36.

FERGUSON, WALLACE K. *The Renaissance in Historical Thought: Five Centuries of Interpretation*. Boston: Houghton Mifflin, 1948.

FEUERWERKER, ALBERT. "China's History in Marxian Dress," AHR, LXVI (1961), 323–54.
FEUERWERKER, ALBERT, and CHENG, S. *Chinese Communist Studies of Modern Chinese History*. Cambridge, Mass.: HUP, 1961.
FITZGERALD, C. P. "Continuity in Chinese History," HSANZ, VII (1956), 136–48.
FRIEDRICH, CARL J., and BRZEZINSKI, ZBIGNIEW K. *Totalitarian Dictatorship and Autocracy*. Cambridge, Mass.: HUP, 1956.
GARGAN, EDWARD T. (ed.). *The Intent of Toynbee's History*. Chicago: Loyola University Press, 1961.
GAY, PETER. "Carl Becker's Heavenly City," *Political Science Quarterly*, LXXII (1957), 182–99.
GEYL, PIETER. "Toynbee's Answer," *Mededelingen der Koninklijke Nederlandse Akademie van Wetenschappen, afd. Letterkunde*, XXIV (1961), 181–204.
GINSBURG, MORRIS. *The Idea of Progress: A Revaluation*. Boston: Beacon, 1953.
GREEN, ROBERT W. (ed.). *Protestantism and Capitalism: The Weber Thesis and Its Critics*. Boston: Heath, 1959.
GREENE, THEODORE M. "A Philosophical Appraisal of the Christian Interpretation of History," *Pacific Historical Review*, XXVI (1957), 123–30.
GROUSSET, RENÉ. *The Sum of History*. Translated by A. and H. TEMPLE PATTERSON. Hadleigh, Essex: Tower Hill Publications, 1951.
GRUMAN, GERALD J. " 'Balance' and 'Excess' as Gibbon's Explanation of the Decline and Fall," HT, I (1960), 75–86.
GRUSHIN, B. A. "Karl Marx und die modernen Methoden der Geschichtsforschung," *Sowjetwissenschaft. Gesellschaftwissenschaftliche Beiträge*, No. 10 (1958), 1155–72.
GUARDINI, ROMANO. *The End of the Modern World*. Translated by JOSEPH THEMAN and HERBERT BURKE. New York: Sheed & Ward, 1956.
HALECKI, OSCAR. *The Limits and Divisions of European History*. New York: Sheed & Ward, 1950.
HALÉVY, DANIEL. *Essai sur l'accélération de l'histoire*. Paris: Îles d'Or, 1948.
HARBISON, E. HARRIS. "The 'Meaning of History' and the Writing of History," *Church History*, XXI (1952), 97–107.
HAVIGHURST, ALFRED F. (ed.). *The Pirenne Thesis: Analysis, Criticism and Revision*. Boston: Heath, 1958.
HAYEK, FRIEDRICH VON (ed.). *Capitalism and the Historians*. Chicago: UCP, 1954.
HEILBRONER, ROBERT L. *The Future as History: The Historic Currents of Our Time and the Direction in Which They Are Taking America*. New York: Harper, 1960.
HELLPACH, WILLY HUGO. *Beitrage zur Individual- und Sozialpsychologie der historischen Dialektik*. Heidelberg: Carl Winter, 1952.
HELTON, TINSLEY (ed.). *The Renaissance: A Reconsideration of the Theories and Interpretations of the Age*. Madison: University of Wisconsin Press, 1961.
HEXTER, J. H. "Storm over the Gentry: The Tawney–Trevor-Roper Controversy," *Encounter*, No. 56 (May, 1958), 23–34.
HIGHAM, JOHN. "The Cult of American Consensus: Homogenizing Our History," *Commentary*, XXVII (1959), 93–101.

HIGHAM, JOHN. "Beyond Consensus: The Historian as Moral Critic," AHR, LXVII (1962), 609–25.
HODGSON, MARSHALL. "Hemispheric Interregional History as an Approach to World History," JWH, I (1953), 715–23.
HOFSTADTER, RICHARD. "Turner and the Frontier Myth," *American Scholar*, XVIII (1949), 433–43.
———. "Beard and the Constitution: The History of an Idea," *American Quarterly*, II (1950), 195–213.
HUIZINGA, JOHANN. *Homo Ludens: A Study of the Play-Element in Culture.* London: Routledge & Kegan Paul, 1949
IGGERS, GEORG G. "The Idea of Progress in Recent Philosophies of History," JMH, XXX (1958), 215–26.
JASPERS, KARL. *The Origin and Goal of History.* Translated by MICHAEL BULLOCK. London: Routledge & Kegan Paul, 1953.
JORDAN, PASCUAL. *Science and the Course of History: The Influence of Scientific Research on Human Events.* Translated by RALPH MANHEIM. New Haven: YUP, 1955.
JOUKOV, E. "Des principes d'une histoire universelle," JWH, III (1956), 527–35.
KALLEN, HORACE. *Patterns of Progress.* New York: ColUP, 1950.
KOHN, HANS (ed.). *German History: Some New German Views.* Boston: Beacon, 1954.
KRIEGER, LEONARD. "The Uses of Marx for History," *Political Science Quarterly*, LXXV (1960), 255–78.
KROEBER, A. L. "The Delimitation of Civilizations," JHI, XIV (1953), 264–75.
———. *Style and Civilization.* Ithaca, N.Y.: CorUP, 1957.
KRUSZEWSKI, CHARLES. "The Pivot of History," *Foreign Affairs*, XXXII (1954), 388–401.
KUHN, HELMUT. "Dialectic in History," JHI, X (1949), 14–31.
LADURIE, EMMANUEL LE ROY. "Histoire et Climat," *Annales*, XIV (1959), 3–34.
LATOURETTE, KENNETH SCOTT. "The Christian Understanding of History," AHR, LIV (1949), 259–77.
LEFEBVRE, GEORGES. "Quelques réflexions sur l'histoire des civilisations," *Annales historiques de la Révolution française*, XXVII (1955), 97–109.
MCCLELLAND, DAVID. *The Achieving Society.* Princeton, N.J.: Van Nostrand, 1961.
MACDONALD, FORREST. *We the People: The Economic Origins of the Constitution.* Chicago: UCP, 1958.
MACMASTER, ROBERT E. "Danilevsky and Spengler: A New Interpretation," JMH, XXVI (1954), 154–61.
MCNEILL, WILLIAM H. *Past and Future.* Chicago: UCP, 1954.
MASON, HENRY L. *Toynbee's Approach to World Politics.* New Orleans: Tulane University Press, 1958.
MASUR, GERHARD. "Arnold Toynbees Philosophie der Geschichte," HZ, CLXXIV (1952), 269–86.

MAYO, H. B. "Marxism as a Philosophy of History," *Canadian Historical Review*, XXXIV (1953), 1–17.
MAZOUR, ANATOLE G., and BATEMAN, HERMAN E. "Recent Conflicts in Soviet Historiography," JMH, XXIV (1952), 56–68.
MEHNERT, KLAUS. *Stalin versus Marx: The Stalinist Historical Doctrine*. London: Allen & Unwin, 1952.
MONTAGU, M. F. ASHLEY (ed.). *Toynbee and History: Critical Essays and Reviews*. Boston: Sargent, 1956.
MONTER, OTTO. "Die Philosophischen Grundlagen des historischen Materialismus," *Saeculum*, XI (1960), 1–26.
MOORE, BARRINGTON. "On Notions of Progress, Revolution, Freedom," *Ethics*, LXXII (1962), 106–19.
MORAZÉ, CHARLES. *Essai sur la civilisation d'occident: l'homme*. Paris: Colin, 1950.
MULLER, HERBERT J. *The Uses of the Past: Profiles of Former Societies*. New York: OUP, 1952.
MUNK, ARTHUR W. *History and God: Clues to His Purposes*. New York: Ronald, 1952.
MUNZER, EGBERT. "Solovyev and the Meaning of History," *Review of Politics*, XI (1949), 281–93.
NEF, JOHN U. *War and Human Progress: An Essay on the Rise of Industrial Civilization*. Cambridge, Mass.: HUP, 1950.
NIEBUHR, REINHOLD. *Faith and History: A Comparison of Christian and Modern Views of History*. New York: Scribner's, 1949.
———. *The Self and the Drama of History*. New York: Scribner's, 1955.
———. *The Structure of Nations and Empires: A Study of the Recurring Patterns and Problems of the Political Order in Relation to the Unique Problems of the Nuclear Age*. New York: Scribner's, 1959.
———. *Beyond Tragedy*. New York: Scribner's, 1961.
NORTHROP, F. S. C. *The Meeting of East and West: An Inquiry concerning World Understanding*. New York: Macmillan, 1949.
POTTER, DAVID M. "The Historian's Use of Nationalism and Vice Versa," AHR, LXVII (1962), 924–50.
QUIGLEY, CARROLL. *The Evolution of Civilizations: An Introduction to Historical Analysis*. New York: Macmillan, 1961.
RICHARDSON, DAVID B. "The Philosophy of History and the Stability of Civilizations," *Thomist*, XX (1957), 158–90.
RICOEUR, PAUL. "Christianity and the Meaning of History: Progress, Ambiguity, Hope," *Journal of Religion*, XXXII (1952), 242–53.
RIEGEL, ROBERT. "American Frontier Theory," JWH, III (1956), 356–80.
RITTER, GERHARD. *The Corrupting Influence of Power*. Hadleigh, Essex: Tower Bridge, 1952.
ROCKER, RUDOLPH. *Die Entscheidung des Abendlandes*. Hamburg: Friedrich Ötinger, 1948.
ROCKWOOD, RAYMOND O. (ed.). *Carl Becker's Heavenly City Revisited*. Ithaca, N.Y.: CorUP, 1958.
ROSTOW, WALT W. *The Stages of Economic Growth: A Non-Communist Manifesto*. New York: CUP, 1960.

Rüstow, Alexander. *Ortsbestimmung der Gegenwart.* Zurich: Eugen Rentsch 1957.
Sanchez-Albornoz, Claudio. *España, un enigma histórico.* 2 vols. Buenos Aires: Editorial Sudamericana, 1956.
Schaff, Adam. *Zu einigen Fragen der marxistische Theorie der Wahrheit.* Translated from Polish by Professor Klaus. Berlin: Dietz, 1954.
Schrecker, Paul. *Work and History: An Essay on the Structure of Civilization.* Princeton, N.J.: PUP, 1948.
Schroeter, M. *Metaphysik der Untergangs: eine kulturkritische Studie über Oswald Spengler.* Munich: Leibniz Verlag, 1949.
Schumpeter, Joseph A. *Capitalism, Socialism and Democracy.* 3d ed. New York: Harper, 1950.
Simon, Pierre-Henri. *L'esprit et l'histoire.* Paris: Colin, 1954.
Taylor, G. R. (ed.). *The Turner Thesis.* Boston: Heath, 1949.
Toynbee, Arnold. *A Study of History.* 12 vols. New York and London: OUP, 1934–61.
———. *Civilization on Trial.* New York: OUP, 1948.
———. *The World and the West.* New York: OUP, 1953.
———. "Der Historiker, seine Vorstellungen und seine Probleme," *Ruperto-Carola*, No. 26 (1959), 17–24.
Toynbee, Arnold, et al. "The Contribution of Arnold Toynbee," *Diogenes*, No. 13 (1956), 6–99.
Tran-Duc-Thao. "Existentialisme et materialisme dialectique," RMM, LIV (1949), 317–29.
Treadgold, Donald W. "Russian Expansion in the Light of Turner's Study of American Frontier," *Agricultural History*, XXVI (1952), 147–52.
Turner, Ralph, et al. "Plan of a History of the Scientific and Cultural Development of Mankind," JWH, I (1953), 223–38.
Van Zandt, Roland. *The Metaphysical Foundations of American History.* The Hague: Mouton, 1959.
Voegelin, Eric. *Order and History.* 3 vols. Baton Rouge: Louisiana State University Press, 1956–57.
Walz, Hans H. *Sinn und Ziel der Geschichte.* Bonn: Universitäts-Verlag, 1947.
Webb, Walter P. *The Great Frontier.* Boston: Houghton Mifflin, 1952.
Weber, Alfred. *Farewell to European History; or The Conquest of Nihilism.* Translated by R. F. C. Hull. New Haven: YUP, 1948.
———. *Der dritte oder der vierte Mensch. Vom Sinn des geschichtlichen Daseins.* Munich: R. Piper, 1953.
White, Leslie A. *The Evolution of Culture: The Development of Civilization to the Fall of Rome.* New York: McGraw-Hill, 1959.
Whittlesey, Derwent. *Environmental Foundations of European History.* New York: APC, 1949.
Wilson, Colin. *The Outsider.* Boston: Houghton Mifflin, 1950.
Wittfogel, Karl A. *Oriental Despotism: A Comparative Study of Total Power.* New Haven: YUP, 1957.
Wright, Arthur F. "The Study of Chinese Civilization," JHI, XI (1960), 233–55.

WYMAN, WALKER D., and KROEBER, CLIFTON B. (eds.). *The Frontier in Perspective.* Madison: University of Wisconsin Press, 1957.

YANG, LIEN-SHENG. "Toward a Study of Dynastic Configurations in Chinese History," *Harvard Journal of Asiatic Studies,* XVII (1954), 329–45.

ZAHN, ERNST F. J. *Toynbee und das Problem der Geschichte: eine Auseinandersetzung mit dem Evolutionismus.* Cologne: Westdeutscher Verlag, 1954.

V. *Supplement to the Bibliography of Bulletin 54: Books Published before 1946 and Not Listed There*

ALEXANDER, S. "The Historicity of Things," in *Philosophy and History: Essays Presented to Ernst Cassirer.* Oxford: OUP, 1936.

BALZ, ALBERT G. "Evolution and Time," in *Essays in Honor of John Dewey.* New York: Holt, 1929.

BECKER, CARL. *Progress and Power.* Stanford, Calif.: Stanford University Press, 1936.

BERGMANN, GUSTAV. "Holism, Historicism, and Emergence," PS, XI (1944), 209–21.

BOAS, GEORGE. "The History of Philosophy," in *Naturalism and the Human Spirit.* Edited by Y. KRIKORIAN. New York: ColUP, 1944.

BRIGHTMAN, E. S., et al. "The Problem of an Objective Basis for Value Judgments," in *Science, Philosophy and Religion: Third Symposium.* Edited by LYMAN BRYSON and LOUIS FINKELSTEIN. New York: Harper, 1943.

BURNHAM, JAMES. *The Managerial Revolution: What Is Happening in the World.* New York: John Day, 1941.

CARBONELL, DIEGO. *Escuelas de historia en America.* Buenos Aires: Imprenta López, 1943.

CASSIRER, ERNST. *An Essay on Man.* New Haven: YUP, 1944.

COHEN, MORRIS R. "History versus Value," in his *Reason and Nature.* New York: Harcourt, Brace, 1923.

COLLINGWOOD, R. G. "Are History and Science Different Kinds of Knowledge?" *Mind,* XXXI (1922), 443–66.

———. *Speculum Mentis.* Oxford: Clarendon, 1924.

———. *An Essay in Philosophical Method.* Oxford: Clarendon, 1934.

———. "On the So-called Idea of Causation," PAS, XXXVIII (1937–38), 85–112.

———. *An Autobiography.* Oxford: Clarendon, 1939.

CREEGAN, R. F. "Radical Empiricism and Radical Historicism," JP, XLI (1944), 126–31.

CROCE, BENEDETTO. *The Philosophy of Giambattista Vico.* Translated from Italian by R. G. COLLINGWOOD. London: Latimer, 1913.

ENGEL-JANOSI, FRIEDRICH. *The Growth of German Historicism.* Johns Hopkins University Studies in History and Political Science, Series 62, No. 2. Baltimore: Johns Hopkins Press, 1944.

FORD, GUY STANTON. "Some Suggestions to American Historians," AHR, XLIII (1938), 253–69.

FRANK, PHILIPP, et al. "The Relativity of Truth and the Objectivity of Values," in *Science, Philosophy and Religion: Third Symposium*. Edited by LYMAN BRYSON and LOUIS FINKELSTEIN. New York: Harper, 1943.

FREUD, SIGMUND. *Civilization and Its Discontents*. Translated by JOAN RIVIERE. London: Hogarth, 1930.

FURNAS, C. C. and S. M. *Man, Bread and Destiny*. New York: Reynal & Hitchcock, 1937.

GHOSHAL, U. N. *The Beginnings of Indian Historiography and Other Essays*. Calcutta: R. Ghoshal, 1944.

HARVEY, J. W. "Knowledge of the Past," PAS, XLI (1940–41), 149–66.

HODGES, H. A. *Wilhelm Dilthey: An Introduction*. London: Kegan Paul, 1944.

HOFSTADTER, ALBERT. "Generality and Singularity in Historical Judgment," JP, XLII (1945), 57–65.

HUNTINGTON, ELLSWORTH. *Mainsprings of Civilization*. London: Chapman & Hall, 1945.

JASPERS, KARL. *Man and the Modern Age*. Translated by EDEN and CEDAR PAUL. London: Routledge, 1933.

KAUFMANN, FELIX. *Methodology of the Social Sciences*. New York: OUP, 1944.

KROEBER, A. L. *Configurations of Culture Growth*. Berkeley: UCalP, 1944.

KU CHIEH-KANG. *The Autobiography of a Chinese Historian: Being the Preface to a Symposium on Ancient Chinese History*. Translated by ARTHUR W. HUMMEL. Leyden: Brill, 1931.

LEBERGOTT, STANLEY. "Chance and Circumstance: Are Laws of History Possible?" JP, XLI (1944), 393–411.

LOVEJOY, A. O., and SPITZER, LEO. "Geistesgeschichte vs. History of Ideas as Applied to Hitlerism," JHI, V (1944), 191–219.

MARGOLIOUTH, DAVID S. *Lectures on Arabic Historians*. Calcutta: University of Calcutta, 1930.

MATTHEWS, DEAN W. R. "What Is an Historical Event?" PAS, XXXVIII (1937–38), 207–16.

MEAD, GEORGE H. "The Nature of the Past," in *Essays in Honor of John Dewey*. New York: Holt, 1929.

MERTON, ROBERT K. "The Sociology of Knowledge," in *Twentieth Century Sociology*. Edited by GEORGE GURVITCH and WILBERT MOORE. New York: Philosophical Library, 1945.

OAKESHOTT, MICHAEL. *Experience and Its Modes*. Cambridge: CUP, 1933.

OAKLEY, H. D. "The World as Memory and as History," PAS, XXVII (1926–27), 219–316.

———. "The Status of the Past," PAS, XXXII (1931–32), 227–50.

———. "Perception and Historicity," PAS, XXXVIII (1937–38), 21–46.

PARGITER, FREDERICK E. *Ancient Indian Historical Tradition*. London: OUP, 1922.

PARKHURST, HELEN H. "The Cult of Chronology," in *Essays in Honor of John Dewey*. New York: Holt, 1929.

POOLE, REGINALD (ed.). *Studies in Chronology and History*. Oxford: Clarendon, 1934.

PRENTICE, E. PARMALEE. *Hunger and History*. New York: Harper, 1939.

RANDALL, J. H. "Historical Naturalism," in *American Philosophy Today and*

Tomorrow. Edited by Sidney Hook and H. Kallen. New York: L. Furman, 1935.

———. "On Understanding the History of Philosophy," JP, XXVI (1939), 460–74.

———. "Dewey's Interpretation of the History of Philosophy," in *The Philosophy of John Dewey*. Edited by Paul Schilpp. Evanston: Northwestern University, 1940.

Rose, William J. "Polish Historical Writing," JMH, II (1930), 569–85.

Rothacker, Erich. *Geschichtsphilosophie*. Munich and Berlin: R. Oldenbourg, 1934.

Roupnel, Gaston. *Histoire et destin*. Paris: B. Grasset, 1943.

Ryle, Gilbert. "Unverifiability-by-me," *Analysis*, IV (1936), 1–11.

Sabine, George H. "Logic and Social Studies," PR, XLVIII (1939), 155–76.

Schumpeter, Joseph A. *Theory of Economic Development*. Cambridge, Mass.: HUP, 1934.

Sears, Lawrence. "The Meanings of History," JP, XXXIX (1942), 393–401.

Strong, E. W. "The Materials of Historical Knowledge," in *Naturalism and the Human Spirit*. Edited by Y. Krikorian. New York: ColUP, 1944.

Teggart, Frederick J. "The Humanistic Study of Change in Time," JP, XXIII (1926), 309–15.

———. *Theory and Processes of History*. Berkeley and Los Angeles: UCalP, 1941.

Turner, Frederick Jackson. *The Frontier in American History*. New York: Holt, 1920.

Zilsel, E. "Physics and the Problem of Historico-Sociological Laws," PS, VIII (1941), 567–79.

Index

Abraham, Karl, 85 n.
Acton, Lord, 121
Adams, John, 70, 73
Adams family, 115
Aggregates, 75, 77, 104, 107 n., 108, 114, 125, 184, 187–88, 208. *See also* Groups; Types
Agora excavations, 16
Alcibiades, 11, 14, 196
Alexandria, 7, 13
Allport, Gordon W., 78 n.
America, 70, 72, 74, 83, 91, 116, 137, 157. *See also* United States
American Civil War, viii, 125, 130, 131, 134–41, 179, 190, 206
Ancient history, xi n. *See also* Antiquity
Anglo-American colonies, 67, 69, 72
Anthropology, 9–10, 11, 32, 84, 87, 126, 137–38, 203. *See also* Culture
Antiquity, xii n., 21–23. *See also* Ancient history; Classical
Archeology, 5–7, 16 n., 19, 24, 29
Arendt, Hannah, 170
Aristocracy, 69
Aristocratic resurgence, 70, 72
Aristotle, 30, 80
Aron, Raymond, 150
Art, v–vi, 6, 24, 39–40, 43, 78, 126, 128; Chinese, 55; Western, 55
Asia, 39
Astronomy, 50 n.
Athens, 13 n., 14, 17, 22–23, 31, 33, 133
Atkinson, John W., 9 n.
Attica, 23, 30
Augustine, 124
Austro-Hungarian monarchy, 67, 68, 139

Bachhofer, Ludwig, 55
Bagehot, Walter, 152 n.
Barraclough, Geoffrey, 162
Bary, Wm. T. de, 42
Bassett, John Spencer, 135
Beadle, Erastus D., 131
Beale, Howard K., 130

Beard, Charles, 72, 121, 122, 136, 140, 166 n.
Beard, Mary, 136, 140
Beasley, W. G., 41 n.
Becker, Carl, 121, 122
Behavioral sciences. *See* Science(s), behavioral
Belgium, 67–69, 72, 74, 139
Bell, W. C. F., 189 n.
Beloch, Julius, 20
Benedict, Ruth, 92 n.
Benson, Lee, 166 n.
Berlew, David E., 8–15
Berlin, Sir Isaiah, 149, 150, 151, 155
Bernheim, Ernst, 7
Beveridge, W. I. B., 169 n.
Bidney, David, 83 n.
Bielenstein, Hans, 50 n.
Blackstone, Sir William, 71
Blaine, James G., 132
Bloch, Marc, 170
Blum, Jerome, 127 n.
Bohemia, 69
Booth, John Wilkes, 185, 193
Boyle, Robert, 119
Bradley, A. C., 166
Bridgman, P. W., 177
Brinton, Crane, 153 n., 156
British Commonwealth of Nations, 139
British Empire, 72, 139
Brodbeck, May, 157 n.
Broneer, Oscar, 16, 17
Brown, William Garrott, 135
Bruce, Robert, 108
Bryce, James, 81, 83 n.
Buchanan, James, 107
Buckle, Henry Thomas, 154
Buddhism, 40, 53
Burgess, John William, 134
Burke, Edmund, 70, 71, 73, 77, 115
Burton, Robert, 157
Bury, J. B., 20
Butler, Samuel, 157, 158

Caesar, Julius, 14 n., 55, 124
Caldwell, Joseph R., 16 n.

249

Index

Canada, 67
Cape Colony, 67
Capitalism, 10, 13, 21 n., 88, 122, 126, 136, 191
Carnegie, Andrew, 108
Carr, E. H., 182, 189, 190, 193, 194
Cassirer, Ernst, 154 n.
Cate, James L., 121 n., 154 n.
Catherine II, 67
Cause, vi–vii, vii n., 3, 15, 20, 21 n., 25–30, 37, 68, 74, 86, 89–90, 113, 125–26, 128, 130, 131, 134, 178–82, 185–86, 187, 189, 190–92, 193, 197–98, 202, 206, 208
Central Cultural Florescence, 39
Central Kingdom, 39, 43–45, 52, 125, 199–200. *See also* China
Chambers, Robert, 155 n.
Channing, Edward, 136, 140
Chao I, 38 n., 41 n.
Character, 78–81, 83–88, 90–92, 95–96, 98–100, 116, 203, 204. *See also* Personality
Cheng, S., 54 n.
Chi, Chao-ting, 57 n.
Ch'ien Mu, 53, 54 n., 57 n.
Ch'in Shih-huang-ti, 55
China, x, xii n., 36, 38–43, 45–49, 50 n., 52–54, 56–58, 61–65, 139, 198–201; T'ang, 51 n. *See also* Central Kingdom
Chinese classics, 38
Cicero, 6
City-state, 10
Civilization: Atlantic, 67, 75, 125; Greek, x; Western, 6–7, 14–15, 67, 197, 202
Clapham, Sir John, 165
Clark, Burton R., 92 n.
Clark, G. Kitson, 176 n.
Clark, R. A., 9 n.
Classical, xii n., 7, 7 n., 8, 10, 23, 25–26, 26 n., 125, 195, 196. *See also* Ancient history; Antiquity
Classicists, 31–33, 198, 200
Classification, v, 21–26, 30, 78, 94–102, 119, 124–25, 148, 178–79, 181, 186, 187–88, 197, 200, 202–4, 206, 208. *See also* Generalizations, labeling
Coates, Willson H., 160 n.
Cochran, Thomas C., 160 n.
Cohen, Morris R., 157 n., 173 n.
Cole, A. H., 104 n.

Collingwood, R. G., 12 n.
Columbus, Christopher, 116
Commager, Henry Steele, 80 n.
Communism, 68, 99
Community, ix, 10, 11, 14, 131, 196, 204
Comparison, v, 5, 11, 55, 62, 90, 99–101, 115–18, 120, 123, 140, 151, 176, 186, 195, 198, 200, 201, 203, 204, 209. *See also* History, comparative
Condorcet, Marquis de, 72, 124
Confucianism, 38, 45, 47, 53, 58, 61 n., 199; Neo-, 44 n. *See also* Confucius
Confucius, 37, 40
Conservatism, 71–73
Constituted bodies, 69–71
Copernicus, 154
Corbett, Sergeant Boston, 193
Corcyra, 26
Cornford, F. M., 27, 32
Coulborn, Rushton, 43 n.
Craven, Avery, 137, 179 n.
Culture, 66–67, 87–90, 95, 185, 187–88, 189, 191, 199, 200, 203. *See also* Anthropology
Cumberland, Duke of, 38
Cyert, R. M., 108 n.

Darwin, Charles, 122, 155 n., 164
Davis, Jefferson, 131
Delolme, Jean Louis, 70
Democracy, 21, 69, 71, 138, 140, 152 n., 158, 179; totalitarian, 68; Western, 68
Demography, 138
Denney, Reuel, 92 n.
Determinisms, 7, 12–13, 34, 124, 126, 136–37, 154, 188, 190, 206. *See also* Marx; Marxism
Deutsch, Karl W., 97 n., 191, 192 n.
Dewey, John, 46
Dickens, Charles, 81, 82
Diocletian, 26
Dodd, William E., 135
Dodds, E. R., 32, 33
Douglas, Stephen A., 131
Dray, William, 148
Dubs, Homer H., 37 n.
Duncan, David, 164 n.
Durkheim, Émile, 62
Duverger, Maurice, 170
Dynastic cycle, 41–42, 49–51, 59, 124, 199, 201

Index

Eberhard, Wolfram, 50 n.
Economic interpretation, 9–10, 17, 30–32, 191, 196. *See also* Marx; Marxism
Economics, 126, 137, 165 n.
Egypt, 6
Eliot, Sir Charles, 46
Emerson, Ralph W., 81
England, 9 n., 72, 98
Enlightenment, 64
Ennin, 51 n.
Epigraphy, 6
Evaluation, vi, 11, 12, 15, 32, 51–52, 60–61, 125, 183–84, 186, 189–90, 194, 196, 208, 209
Explanation. *See* Cause
Extrapolation (of historical events), 29–30, 113, 117–18, 123, 198. *See also* Imagination

Fairbank, John K., 50 n.
Fan Wen-lan, 47
Farber, Maurice, 95 n.
Faÿ, Bernard, 121 n.
Feidler, Fred E., 8 n.
Feigl, Herbert, 157 n.
Feng Chia-sheng, 50 n.
Feudalism, 43, 54, 62–64, 124, 153, 200–201
Feuerwerker, Albert, 54 n.
Fine, John V. A., 33 n.
Finley, M. I., 21 n., 23 n.
Fisher, H. A. L., 171
Fitzgerald, C. P., 52, 53 n.
France, 67, 69, 72, 74, 95, 127 n.
Francis, John de, 50 n.
Frank, Tenney, 20
Franklin, Benjamin, 115
Freud, Sigmund, 79, 84–87, 88, 89 n., 103, 122, 203
Freudianism, 84, 85, 88, 203. *See also* Freud; Psychology
Fromm, Erich, 87–89, 93

Galileo, 154
Gay, Edwin F., 165
Genealogy (of generalizations), xii, 6, 6 n., 120, 126, 128 n., 130–44, 195, 206–7, 209
Generalizations: evaluative, 189, 190 (*see also* Evaluation); hidden, 116, 187; implicit, 186, 192, 197; labeling, 9, 21 n., 26 n., 35–36, 39, 43–45, 49–50, 52–56, 62, 63,

69 n., 107, 113, 124, 125, 129 n., 196–203 (*see also* Classification); latent, 28–29, 117 n., 190–91, 208; limited, 27–28, 35, 75, 113–14, 117–20, 147, 152, 162–63, 173, 174, 191, 197, 200, 205, 206, 207; regularity, 35–36, 41–43, 49–51, 56–58, 74 n., 113, 123–28, 140, 199, 200, 202, 206
Geneva, 68, 72, 74
Geography, 116, 138
George, Alexander, 188
George, Juliette L., 188 n.
George III, 71
Germany, 67, 69, 139, 165
Geyl, Pieter, 19, 155, 159, 168
Gibbon, Edward, 38
Giddings, Joshua, 132
Ginsberg, M., 95 n.
Glazer, Nathan, 92 n., 173 n.
Glotz, Gustave, 20
Gobineau, Count Arthur de, 154
Godechot, Jacques, 67
Goffman, Erving, 90
Goldman, I., 90 n.
Goldsen, Rose K., 163 n.
Gomme, A. W., 9 n., 30, 31
Gooch, R. K., 127 n.
Gorer, Geoffrey, 90 n.
Granet, Marcel, 44 n., 62
Gray, J., 46 n.
Great Britain, 67, 69, 74
Greco-Roman world. *See* Antiquity
Greece, 6, 8, 9, 9 n., 10, 11, 12, 13, 14, 17, 21, 23, 24, 26 n., 31 n., 32, 33 n., 79, 80, 126, 195
Greeks, xii n., 23, 27, 31, 32, 78, 196
Greeley, Horace, 132
Gresham, Sir Thomas, 119
Griffin, James B., 16 n.
Gross, Neal, 103 n., 105 n.
Groups, 80, 87, 103–10, 138, 181, 184, 191–92, 203, 205, 208. *See also* Aggregates; Types
Grousset, René, 55

Haas, Arthur G., 127 n.
Hadrian, 25
Hajime, Nakamura, 44 n.
Halperin, William, 121 n.
Hamilton, Alexander, 115
Han Kuo-ch'ing, 52 n.
Hasebroek, Johannes, 30, 31
Hegedus, Adam de, 78

251

Index

Hegel, G.W. F., 36, 45, 124, 137, 155
Heichelheim, Fritz M., 8 n., 9 n.
Hellenism, 23, 33, 197
Herder, Johann Gottfried von, 34, 155
Herodotus, 34, 80
Heuss, Alfred, 8 n., 24 n.
Hexter, J. H., 56, 180, 182
Hippocrates, 80
Historical relativism, 157 n., 160 n., 179
Historiography: American, 167; Chinese, 36, 45, 46 n., 48, 49, 54 n., 58, 60, 200; German, 7; Greek, 27, 28; legal, 24, 25; Marxist, 54 n.; Roman, 27, 28; Western, 28
History: American 62, 133; Ancient, 4, 5–8, 11, 14–19, 21, 24, 27, 29–31, 33, 35, 197, 198; Chinese, 36, 48–49, 50–57, 59, 60, 62–64, 199–201; Classical, 201; comparative, 30, 35, 46, 55–56, 113–14, 116, 120, 121–23, 128, 129 n., 139, 176, 198, 202, 204, 206 (*see also* Comparison); descriptive, v, 113–20, 206; Eastern, 29; English, 96; Far Eastern, 31; French, 70; German, 96; Medieval, xii n., 24, 29; Middle Eastern, 31; Modern, 24, 29, 195; Russian, 90 n.; scientific, 134, 135, 150, 155, 164, 178–81, 196; theory in, v, vi, 49, 56, 61–62, 64–65, 77, 83, 103, 105, 106, 107, 114, 117–29, 140, 147, 149, 150, 161, 163–72, 175, 178–88, 193, 197, 198, 199, 200, 206, 208; Western, xii n., 27, 29, 31, 53, 55, 199, 202
Ho-shen, 61
Hobbes, Thomas, 154
Hofstadter, Richard, 173, 175, 176 n.
Holland, 67, 69, 72, 74, 139
Homer, 10, 11, 14, 21, 196
Hook, Sidney, v n., 150, 152 n., 169
Howland, R. H., 16, 17
Hu Shih, 53
Hughes, H. Stuart, 155 n., 162 n., 170
Hummel, Arthur W., 46 n.
Hungary, 69, 72
Hypothesis, vii n., ix, 5, 9–10, 12, 42, 50, 57–58, 101, 114, 119, 121, 122, 124, 148, 150, 151, 160 n., 164, 166, 169, 174, 175, 176, 192, 199, 200. *See also* History, theory in

Ibn Khaldun, 45
Iliad, 10, 14. *See also* Homer
Imagination (in writing history), v–vi, 17, 118, 163, 166, 168–69, 172, 173, 198. *See also* Extrapolation
Indonesia, 98
Inkeles, Alex, 94 n.
Ireland, 67, 69, 72
Italy, 67, 69, 124, 139

Jackson, Andrew, 6
Japan, 96
Jefferson, Thomas, 98, 100, 115
Jenks, Leland H., 104
Joachim of Floris, 124
Jolowicz, H. F., 24, 25, 26
Jones, A. H. M., 13 n.
Joseph II, 68
Justinian, 25, 125

Kai Yu Hsü, 47 n.
Kardiner, Abram, 87–89
Kluckhohn, Clyde, 83 n.
Kretschmer, Ernst, 79
Ku Chieh-kang, 46 n.
Kublai Khan, 55

Lafayette, Marquis de, 114, 117, 118, 119, 121, 122 n.
La Rochefoucauld, Duc de, 75, 76, 120, 160, 164, 171, 202
Larsen, J. A. O., 8 n.
Latin America, 67
Latourette, K. S., 51 n.
Lattimore, Owen, 50 n.
Lauffer, S., 22, 23
Law, 24, 25, 26
Lazarsfeld, Paul F., 33 n., 120 n., 163, 165, 166 n.
Legge, James, 37 n.
Lerner, Daniel, 150 n.
Levin, Harry, 92
Levinson, Daniel J., 94 n.
Lincoln, Abraham, 131, 135, 141 n., 184, 186
Lipset, Seymour Martin, 93 n.
Literary: influences, ix, 7–8, 31–33, 48, 62, 171, 198, 200; style, 3, 16, 18, 42, 77, 79, 81, 115, 116, 140, 143, 172
Livy, 6
Loewenberg, Bert J., 157
Logan, John A., 132

Index

Logic, 18, 158, 167, 174, 209
Louis XV, 6, 71
Louis XVI, 71, 118
Low, D. M., 38 n.
Lowell, E. L., 9 n.
Lowenthal, Leo, 93 n.

Ma Luan-lin, 42 n.
Macartney, Lord, 61
McClelland, D. C., 8, 9 n., 12 n.
Maccoby, Eleanor E., 92, 92 n.
McDougall, William, 79 n.
McEadwin, Alexander W., 103, 105
Machiavelli, Niccolò, 123
McMaster, John Bach, 134, 135
Madison, James, 115
Mahan, A. T., 121, 122
Maier, F. G., 5 n.
Mandate of Heaven, 60
Mao Tse-tung, 47, 54
March, J. G., 108 n.
Marryat, Frederick, 82 n.
Martineau, Harriet, 82
Marx, Karl, 46, 124, 155
Marxism, 12 n., 34, 47, 54, 68. *See also* Determinism; Economic interpretation
Mason, Ward S., 103 n., 105
Mathematics, 9, 12, 14, 75, 174, 196
Mead, George Herbert, 90, 92
Megarian decrees, 26
Merton, Robert K., 103, 105, 108 n., 162, 175
Mesick, Jane Louise, 82 n.
Mesopotamia, 6
Messinger, Sheldon L., 92 n.
Metaphysical problems, 3
Metternich, Prince von, 127 n.
Meyer, Eduard, 19
Meyerhoff, Hans, vi, vii n., xi n., 21 n., 125, 129 n., 148 n., 160 n., 183
Michael, Franz, 50 n.
Michell, Humfrey, 9 n.
Michels, Robert, 152 n., 170
Middle Ages, 7. *See also* Feudalism; History, Medieval
Millhauser, Milton, 155 n.
Mills, C. Wright, 173
Momigliano, Arnaldo, 20 n., 27, 28
Mommsen, Theodor, 7, 19
Mongols, 60
Montesquieu, Baron de, 46, 70, 71, 124
Mornet, Daniel, 121

Mote, Frederick W., 57 n.
Motivation, 9 n., 125, 178–81, 184, 186, 187–89, 192, 193, 205, 208. *See also* Psychology; Social role
Mowrer, O., 83 n.
Mowry, George, 103 n.

n Achievement 8–10, 12–14, 125–26, 196
Nagel, Ernest, 160
Namier, Sir Lewis B., 152 n., 158
Napoleon I, 182
National character, viii, x, 77–103, 116, 124, 126, 148 n., 202, 203–6. *See also* Self-image
Nationalism, 78, 96, 136, 139, 140, 192 n.; Southern, 179 n.
Nef, J. U., 127 n.
Nevins, Allan, 141
New Jersey, 188
Newton, Sir Isaac, 119
Nicolson, Harold, 92 n.
Nivison, David S., xi n., 40 n., 48, 56, 61 n., 213
Nomothetic historians. *See* Generalizations, regularity; Prediction and control
Northrop, F. S. C., 62
Norway, 139
Notestein, Wallace, 152 n.

Orange, Prince of, 71
Oriental Despotism, 56
Oriental Society, 56, 57, 62
Ottoman Empire, 45, 139

Particular. *See* Unique
Peisistratus, 30
Peloponnesian War, 5, 11, 26, 27, 30, 32
Pericles, 26
Periodization, 9, 9 n., 11, 13, 23–26, 62, 125, 181, 184, 196, 197, 198, 201, 208
Personality, ix, x, 78, 79 n., 83 n., 87, 88, 89, 94 n., 109, 138, 188 n., 189, 203, 204. *See also* Character
Peru, 9 n.
Phillips, Ulrich, 137
Philology, 116
Philosophy, v, vii, 20, 71, 74, 80, 113–14, 116, 121, 123, 124, 126, 129, 139, 148, 156, 159, 160, 163, 164, 168,

253

Index

178, 180, 189, 191, 195, 206; Chinese, 62; Western, 62, 63
Physics, 34, 119, 157 n., 176 n. *See also* Science
Piaget, Jean, 90
Pierson, George W., 82 n.
Pirenne, Henri, 121, 122
Pitt, William, 74
Plato, 14, 84
Poland, 67, 68, 69, 72, 74
Political science, 137, 138, 154, 165
Pollard, Edward A., 132
Popper, Karl, 34
Populism, 191
Portugal, 139
Postan, M. M., 165
Potidaea, 26
Prediction and control, 114, 119, 123, 127–28, 148, 206
Professionalism, 33–34, 122, 194, 195, 198
Protestant ethic, 121, 122
Proust, Marcel, 157, 176
Prussia, 67
Psychiatry, 138
Psychoanalysis, 85–87, 203
Psychology, vi, 8–10, 32, 74, 77, 79, 84–94, 103–10, 126, 137–38, 157, 167, 178–79, 188–89, 191, 203, 209; Gestalt, 101. *See also* Motivation; Social role
Pulleyblank, Edwin, 41 n., 44 n., 46 n.

Quantification, vi, 5, 8–10, 11, 12, 29, 30, 34–35, 126, 129 n., 138, 145, 146, 165–66, 168, 172–77, 195–96, 203, 207, 209

Reichenbach, Hans, 148 n.
Reischauer, E. O., 51 n.
Renaissance, 6, 7, 27
Revolution, viii, x, 21 n., 66, 75, 97, 107, 119, 120, 122, 125, 128, 129, 139, 202; American, 67, 68, 72–74, 121; French, 67, 68, 70, 71, 73, 74, 121 n.; Second American, 136
Rhodes, James Ford, 134, 135
Riesman, David, 93, 94, 148, 170
Role-set, 105, 106, 108, 205
Rome, 5, 6, 8 n., 11, 17, 23, 24, 28, 32, 33, 67, 75, 89, 125, 197
Roosevelt, Theodore, 103, 106
Rostovtzeff, M. I., 19

Rousseau, Jean Jacques, 70
Rowland, Benjamin, 127 n.
Rule, John C., 213
Russia, 67, 90, 139

Saint-Simon, Count de, 155
Sandys, J. E., 7 n.
Sansom, Sir George, 46 n.
Sargent, S. Stansfield, 88 n.
Schlesinger, Arthur M., Jr., 153 n., 157
Schlesinger, Arthur M., Sr., 92 n.
Schmoller, Gustav, 165
Schouler, James, 134
Schulz, Fritz, 26
Science(s), v, vii n., 5, 8, 12, 13, 15, 21 n., 31, 34, 75, 127, 129 n., 150, 151 n., 154, 156, 157, 157 n., 173 n., 175 n., 180, 181, 194; behavioral, vi, 102, 138, 140, 188, 191; social, v n., vi–viii, 27, 32, 52, 66–67, 75–76, 103, 119, 126, 129, 137–38, 140, 141, 148, 154, 157, 160, 162, 162 n., 164, 165 n., 167, 168, 170 n., 172, 174, 200, 202–5. *See also* Physics
Sears, Robert R., 92
Self-image, 39–40, 42, 43, 45, 48, 52, 57, 59–65, 199, 201. *See also* National character
Serf, 23
Severi, 25
Seward, William H., 136
Shafer, Boyd C., 78
Shih, Vincent Y. C., 50 n.
Sibree, J., 36 n.
Sieyès, Abbé, 70
Sinocentrism, 43
Sinology, 48, 62, 65, 200
Slavery, 10, 12, 13, 21–23, 28, 29, 33, 125, 126, 132, 133, 135–36, 137, 141, 184, 190–91, 197
Smith, Adam, 31
Smith, Marian W., 88 n.
Social norm, 103
Social organization, 178, 179
Social role, x, 84, 90–94, 103 and n., 104–10, 119, 125, 126, 138, 202, 203–5. *See also* Motivation; Psychology
Social sciences. *See* Science(s), social
Sociology, 90, 92, 99, 103, 126, 137, 152 n., 157, 163, 179, 173 n.
Solon, 30
Sorokin, Pitirim A., 9 n., 155, 156 n.

254

Index

Spain, 9 n., 139
Sparta, 14, 23
Spencer, Herbert, 46, 164
Spengler, Oswald, 155
Ssu-ma Kuang, 41
Statements: factual, 3, 20, 29, 149, 150, 151, 183, 185, 186, 195; general, 3, 4, 5, 8, 12, 146, 147, 149, 167, 171, 175, 176, 195, 199, 205, 206
Statistics. *See* Quantification
Stein, Ernst, 7 n.
Stephens, Alexander H., 132
Stern, Fritz, 174 n.
Stier, Hans E., 8 n., 24 n.
Stouffer, Samuel, 99, 100, 204
Stowe, Harriet Beecher, 133
Strasburger, Hermann, 10–11, 13, 14, 17
Sun, E-tu Zen, 50 n.
Sweden, 67, 69, 139
Switzerland, 67, 69, 72
Syme, Ronald, 5 n.

Tacitus, 6
Technology, 39, 153
Textual criticism, 19, 29, 46
Theory. *See* History, theory in; Hypothesis
Thompson, J. P., 82 n.
Thucydides, 4, 26, 27, 32, 34
Tocqueville, Alexis de, 70, 81, 82
Totalitarianism, 88, 97
Toynbee, Arnold, 8, 36, 62, 154, 155, 156, 158, 168
Training of historians, 16–17, 143–44, 161, 181, 184, 192–94, 207, 208, 209
Trends, 113–14, 121, 123, 148, 174, 175, 206
Trollope, Frances, 81, 82
Truman, Harry S., 4
Turgot, Jacques, 70
Turner, Frederick Jackson, 121, 122, 136, 140, 166 n., 188
Twain, Mark, 5
Twichett, Denis, 57 n.
Types, 23, 107, 164. *See also* Aggregates; Groups

Unique, the, in history, vii, 8, 27–29, 34, 62, 66, 113–18, 121, 139, 140, 195, 206
United States, 72, 83, 97, 98, 99, 107, 115, 132, 138, 181, 204. *See also* America

Van Buren, Martin, 183, 184, 186
Vico, Giovanni Battista, 34
Victor, Orville J., 131
Voltaire, 174 n.

Wallace, Sir William, 108
Walpole, Horace, 115
Wang Tung-ling, 52 n.
Wang Yü-ch'üan, 50 n.
Wang Yüan-liang, 39 n.
War, 27, 198
Ward, Barbara, 127 n.
Washington, George, 114, 119
Webb, Walter P., 137
Weber, Max, 19, 30, 62, 121, 122, 170
Wedgwood, C. V., 162
Wellington, Duke of, 182
Wells, Carolyn, 120
Wen T'ien-hsiang, 37 n.
Westermann, W. L., 33
White, Leonard D., 116 n., 148 n., 154 n.
White, William Allen, 188
Whitehead, Alfred North, 166
Wilder, Marshall P., 120 n.
Wilson, Henry, 132
Wilson, Woodrow, 107, 135, 188, 189 n.
Wittfogel, K. A., 50 n., 56, 57
Wood, Leonard, 103

Xenophon, 31

Yang, Lien-sheng, 41 n., 43
Yang of the Sui, 55
Yao Shan-yu, 50
Young, J. Z., 151

Zagorin, Perez, 156
Zborowski, Mark, 92 n.
Zilsel, Edgar, 157 n.

255